WAT/LO

THE NORFOLK RAILWAY

THE NORFOLK RAILWAY

Railway Mania in East Anglia,
1834–1862

John Barney

Mintaka Books

First published in 2007 by

Mintaka Books
7 Church Farm,
Colney,
Norwich,
Norfolk, NR4 7TX
Tel 01603 505129

Email john.barney@btinternet.com

British Library Cataloguing in Publication Data
A catalogue record for this book is available from the British Library

ISBN 978–0–9537809–3–8

Typesetting and origination by Carnegie Publishing, Lancaster
Printing and binding by Cromwell Press, Trowbridge

CONTENTS

List of Maps

Maps in the text

PREFACE

I FIRST BECAME INTERESTED in the history of the Norfolk Railway by attending a lecture given by Adrian Vaughan whose knowledge and enthusiasm for the subject is unrivalled. Since then my growing obsession has been largely a solitary affair over several years but I would like to thank the invariably helpful staff at all of the following libraries and archives; Guildhall Library; House of Lords; London Library; National Archives; Norfolk Local Studies, Norwich; Norfolk Record Office; Suffolk Record Office, Lowestoft; University of East Anglia; and York Railway Museum Library together with all those anonymous reporters for local and national newspapers and railway magazines without whose efforts long ago no work of this nature could be written.

Philip Judge redrew the maps from my incoherent sketches. My cousin Ian O'Brien, a mine of information concerning railways of the past, read and commented on the text. My thanks are due to both and to my wife Sarah who has not only accompanied me on expeditions to view the lines as they are now and persuaded me to extend the search for material to Danish libraries and booksellers but has insisted that the project was worth the pursuit and that a book should result.

John Barney   April 2007

CHAPTER I

INTRODUCTION

Railways, promoters, engineers and contractors

This is the story of a railway that was never more than ninety miles long, had just four years of independent operations, had great ambitions but few prospects, made more enemies than friends, and in 1848 had to give up the struggle to run trains and endure a shotgun marriage when its creditors allowed it no other option. Yet for fourteen years thereafter its ghost proved decidedly undead. During the 1850s, through the enterprise of its builder and sometime chairman Sir Samuel Morton Peto, it participated indirectly in an extension of its territory across the North Sea and to the shores of the Baltic. Finally in 1862, after years of frustration, it successfully held its own in the financial chess contest ending in the multiple merger which created the Great Eastern Railway. The company itself, the Norfolk Railway, was not formed until July 1845 following a merger between the Yarmouth & Norwich company, which had opened in May 1844, with the Norwich & Brandon, completed in July 1845. No continuous main line existed until some months later with the connection of the two railways by a swingbridge over the River Wensum at Norwich.

Before beginning the story of the Norfolk Railway itself something must be said to introduce the principal characters behind it and sketch the turbulent history of the companies whose future was entwined with it during its short lifetime. The Norfolk, with its main line running from Great Yarmouth westwards to Brandon in Suffolk, was the child of the remarkable engineering pair, George Stephenson and his son Robert. George was a largely self-educated colliery engineer in early life. Experiments with steam engines led him to locomotive construction and a leading part in the building of the Stockton and Darlington line that opened in 1825. There followed the building of the Liverpool and Manchester railway under his supervision and the construction of the famous locomotive, *The Rocket*, victorious at the Rainhill trials of 1829, which demonstrated the practicality of a railway reliant solely on locomotive power. Rejoicing in the unofficial (and perhaps self-applied) title of 'the father of the railways' George Stephenson acted both as engineer in chief and promoter of some of the more important lines in the north of England through the 1830s and became famous throughout Britain and indeed much of the world as a railway authority. Through his successful record, for the earliest railways were profitable, he built up a fortune for himself from railway investment and built up too a following of investors, particularly from Liverpool and elsewhere in Lancashire where accumulating profits from the cotton industry provided a readily available source of investment funds. It would appear that the Norfolk was primarily his brainchild as the first part of a line ultimately intended to connect the Midlands with the ports of the east coast.

Robert Stephenson was arguably the most successful of the better educated generation of engineers that followed the pioneers such as his father. His first achievements were in locomotive design and manufacture, but after a spell as a mining engineer in South America and subsequent involvement with the building of *The Rocket*, he landed, while still under thirty, perhaps the most important civil engineering assignment of the 1830s, the post of engineer in chief for the London to Birmingham line, a five year task involving unprecedented difficulties successfully overcome. Thereafter he practised as a consultant engineer for numerous lines and projected lines, both at home and abroad, greatly in demand at all times as much as an arbitrator as a designer, but respected in both spheres. His most famous works, all still visible today, are the Newcastle high level bridge, the tubular bridge over the Menai Straits, and the Victoria Bridge over the St Lawrence at Montreal.

George Parker Bidder was a child mathematical prodigy capable of lightning calculations. Enabled through a sponsor to receive an education at Edinburgh University, he met there Robert Stephenson, but it was not until ten years later, after training as an engineer mainly on survey and dock construction work, that he was recruited by Stephenson to work as his assistant, initially on the London and Birmingham project. Soon after he became Stephenson's partner taking on the main responsibility for many of the latter's assignments. In the 1840s he was principally engaged on railway work, especially in East Anglia, and achieved some fame as an unshakeable witness before Parliamentary committees where it was rare that even the most assiduous of opposing barristers could fault his presentations. He remained close to Stephenson both as partner and personal friend, the two making several trips abroad together (both were keen yachtsmen in the days when that implied a small ship with a professional crew) and later he acted as Stephenson's executor. Involved heavily in the early years of the Norfolk Railway, he reappears as its chairman in its final days.

The genesis of the Eastern Counties Railway will be described in Chapter 2. A stupendous overspend on its construction, necessitating a vast fund of capital that the limited earning power from its restricted mileage could not adequately service, meant disappointed shareholders and extreme dissatisfaction with its management. Ten years after its formation in 1835 its shareholders vented their unassuaged anger on the directors and elected George Hudson, 'the Railway King', to the board. Several books have been devoted to Hudson, York draper turned railway financial impresario, effective creator of the Midland Railway and other lines, who at that time was engaged in a battle with rival promoters to secure the rights to build the first direct line from London to York and the north. While Hudson still had many supporters, his fast and loose methods of financial management were by 1845 gaining him an increasing army of detractors. Nevertheless he at once became chairman, allied himself with a forceful colleague, David Waddington who became traffic manager and deputy chairman, and brought in others accustomed to his methods. The Eastern Counties shareholders were wildly excited at what they had achieved but Hudson was mainly concerned to use their company as a weapon in his war with what became the Great Northern Railway. While shareholders were pacified with dividends declared without the benefit of accounts, let alone profits, Hudson campaigned against the Great Northern by promoting an Eastern Counties line from Ely to Lincoln and York.

The Parliamentary battle for his northern route was lost in the summer of 1846 and thereafter Hudson was on the defensive in all his many concerns. The Eastern Counties network seemed incapable of profitable operation and suffered from an appalling safety record. Financial trickery concealed the true position and propped up an increasingly dishonest dividend policy. The railway mania of 1845 and 1846 and the consequent hunger for railway shares, coupled with numerous proposals for new branches, kept the share price to a reasonable level but when the market crashed in the following year the Eastern Counties' shares fell with the rest. By January 1849 rumours were circulating to the effect that Hudson would resign from the board and when he failed to attend the regular half-year meeting of shareholders in February a committee of investigation was appointed to examine the company's accounts. The committee's report proved fatal for all the financial irregularities were laid bare and Hudson resigned. The significance of his chairmanship to this account is that he was still at the head of the Eastern Counties and directly responsible for that company's actions in May 1848 when it assumed control of the operations of the Norfolk Railway.

Waddington also departed from the company for a period while Hudson's place as chairman was taken first by contractor Edward Betts and then by engineer Joseph Glynn. But when Glynn's policy of merging the company with both the Ipswich based Eastern Union Railway and the Norfolk was rejected by angry and suspicious shareholders in March 1851 Waddington was recalled and made chairman, thereafter exercising control in much the same dictatorial fashion as had Hudson. He was in office when the Eastern Counties acquired the bankrupt East Anglian lines of west Norfolk in 1852 and when it took over the operation of the Eastern Union from the beginning of 1854. However in time his seigniorial approach and negligent financial control, coupled with results but little improved, made him sufficient enemies to ensure his dismissal in 1856. Thereafter the Eastern Counties was managed in a more sober fashion but without any greater degree of success.

The Eastern Union Railway company was formed in 1844 to connect Ipswich to London by building a line south from Ipswich to the terminus of the Eastern Counties' original line at Colchester. The dominant person in its formation and subsequent direction was John Chevallier Cobbold, a solicitor, a member of a prominent Ipswich brewing and banking family, MP for Ipswich 1847–68 and an investor in the Eastern Counties, who had been frustrated by that company's failure to advance further. Also prominent in the direction was Samuel Bignold of Norwich, arch Conservative and influential secretary of the Norwich Union Life Assurance Society. 1845 saw the formation of the Ipswich & Bury, a close ally of the Eastern Union with which it later merged and the promotion of an extension north from Ipswich to Norwich so offering a formidable rival line to the Norfolk whose longer connection to London via the Eastern Counties' second main line through Cambridge and Ely had only just opened. The consultant engineer of the original line was the eminent Joseph Locke but virtually the whole of the Eastern Union system was designed and overseen by its resident engineer Peter Bruff.

The Eastern Union had on the whole a more successful and certainly a rather longer period of independent operation than the Norfolk. Apart from what became its main line from Colchester to Norwich, it promoted and fostered other lines in Essex and Suffolk, including an important branch to Harwich, and even attempted developments in Norfolk and in Lincolnshire although few of these reached fruition during its own active life. Had it succeeded in amalgamating with the Norfolk, as at one time was proposed, the two together might have served as an adequate counter-weight to the Eastern Counties but the latter, however inefficient, held the trump cards, two routes into London that could not easily have been bypassed. Merger of all three companies was the only sensible outcome in the public interest, but many years passed before this was achieved.

The contractor responsible for building most of the Eastern Union system was Thomas Brassey, originally a surveyor but ultimately the most successful of all the major railway contractors of the mid-nineteenth century. His greatest rival, but at a later stage also his partner in many enterprises both in Britain and abroad, was Samuel Morton Peto. Peto was by trade a builder, serving an apprenticeship in London under an uncle. As a young man he, together with a cousin, Thomas Grissell, inherited that uncle's business. After overcoming serious difficulties caused by the aftermath of a lawsuit and by another suit challenging his uncle's Will, the partnership of Grissell and Peto prospered in the 1830s.

The firm had only moderate experience in railway building before

Samuel Morton Peto

1842 although that included a difficult section of the South Eastern Railway at Folkestone and the Hanwell viaduct in West London, but it had a long and honourable history as building contractors including London housing, theatres, prisons, work at Windsor Castle, railway stations, the construction of substantial parts of the rebuilt Houses of Parliament and the erection of Nelson's Column in Trafalgar Square. From 1842 the firm became involved as contractors to first the Yarmouth & Norwich and then both the Norwich & Brandon and the Eastern Counties in the combined efforts of those companies to complete the first railway from Norwich to London. They built also the important Eastern Counties branch from Ely to Peterborough so connecting to existing and proposed routes to the Midlands and the North. Peto was at all times the leader on the railway and civil engineering side of the business, successful in maintaining close relations with influential railway personalities such as Hudson, Waddington and the Stephensons.

In 1846 the Grissell & Peto partnership was amicably dissolved with Grissell, whose aversion to risk was greater than Peto's, taking over the building side and Peto specialising in railways. Having moved his base to East Anglia in 1845 when he purchased an estate at Somerleyton near Lowestoft, Peto played thereafter a vital role in the Norfolk company, especially in relation to its finances and relations with other railway companies and also with the development of Lowestoft and its harbour. But the Norfolk was far from his only interest for he was involved with other railways in Britain and also in Canada, Scandinavia, Russia, Austria and Australia. However this is in no way a biography, being concerned only with Peto's activities between the years 1844 and 1862 and limited to those in East Anglia, in Denmark and in connection with North Sea shipping.

Railway formation, finance and accounting

Building a railway in the nineteenth century involved a complex preliminary period the object of which was to obtain an Act of Parliament which would create an appropriate company. A company incorporated by its own special Act of Parliament was necessary as only such a creature could be invested with powers of compulsory purchase of land. At an early stage an engineer was required to make at least an outline survey of the route and to prepare a report. Then local support had to be obtained, usually at public meetings, from the inhabitants of the towns and cities to be linked as well as from the landowners along the route. Parliament, which commonly sat from the end of January until mid or late summer, would not even start the legislative procedure until there were deposited with it detailed plans, estimates of cost and information concerning the attitudes of landowners. So whatever the standard of the original outline survey the engineer must next employ surveying parties to map and take levels along the route so that precise drawings accompanied by registers of all property owners affected could be prepared and duplicated by lithograph.

These plans and registers had to be deposited with the Board of Trade and with the clerk of the peace of each county along the route (and at a later stage with every parish affected by the line) by 30 November in the year preceding the session of Parliament in which a Bill was to be presented. Yet at this time the proposed company did not exist, the operation was in the hands of provisional committees only and nobody had power to enter land to survey so that hostile landowners might well cause modifications to or completely frustrate the preparation of the detailed plans. Once the plans had been deposited a prospectus would customarily be issued with the object of obtaining subscribers for all or as much as possible of the capital which was to be raised. Local subscribers were to be preferred since the degree of local support for the railway was often influential in persuading Parliament to assent to the scheme. A formal subscription agreement covering not less than seventy five per cent of the estimated cost of the project was one of the parliamentary requirements and a deposit of ten per cent of the capital promised under that agreement had to be paid into Chancery via the Bank of England before a Bill could be considered. To provide these funds subscribers were asked themselves to lodge a deposit with the promoters proportionate to their subscription. When a subscriber paid in his deposit he would be issued with a receipt known as scrip.

Once all the deposits of maps and money had been made in the correct manner and by the specified dates a Bill could be lodged with the Private Bill Office at Westminster. For this purpose specialist parliamentary agents were required as well as friendly MPs to steer the Bill through the several stages of progress. Before the Bill could reach the floor of the House of Commons it had to pass the scrutiny of the Standing Orders

1845: last minute rush to file railway plans at the Board of Trade

Select Committee at which point it could easily fail altogether on a technicality, sometimes a minor flaw in the plans, as many did. The Bill then proceeded to first and second readings. Unless it was rejected out of hand at this stage, which sometimes happened, it would be referred to a committee where it might be examined in great detail and where objections would be heard.

It was usually necessary to support the Bill by petitions and objectors might produce counter petitions. Witnesses to the desirability of the line were required and other witnesses might be heard on behalf of any objectors. All witnesses and especially the engineer were normally questioned and cross-questioned by counsel for promoters and objectors. If it survived this process the Bill returned to the House for a third reading but must then undergo a similar procedure in the House of Lords. Only when it had passed over all these hurdles was an Act granted, and only then did the company truly exist. At this point its provisional committee could be consolidated into a smaller board of directors that could proceed to the all-important task of acquiring the necessary land and placing contracts for construction. Once through Parliament (whether the Bill had passed or failed) the deposit was returned to the company which gave the directors funds enough at least to pay the bills of the various lawyers, agents and lithographers and the engineer himself.

The Act of Parliament that authorised the formation of the company also defined the precise amount of capital it was entitled to raise whether in shares or by loan. Usually loans were not to exceed one third of the share capital and none could be raised until half the share capital had been paid up. At this stage the company would allot shares to its subscribers in exchange for their scrip. The timetable under which it could then make further calls for cash from the shareholders would also have been defined in the Act as also its powers should shareholders default in payment of those calls. Shareholders could sell their shares at any time, could even sell scrip before formal allotment of any shares, but the company had the power to refuse to register their sale unless all deposits and calls had been paid.

If the company was to pay interest to shareholders while the line was under construction it had to take power in its Act to do so. Later this practice, initially almost universal but dangerous because it distributed resources originally acquired to pay for construction, was forbidden. If any significant variation of the course of the line was required after the Act was obtained or if branches were to be built or more capital required then a further Act would be needed. For such causes most companies needed a series of Acts, sometimes one every year until their system was finally complete, giving rise to large charges for legal costs that had seldom been allowed for in initial estimates. Mergers, leases of other railways and indeed any variation in the powers granted by the original Act required further legislation.

Because, in an effort to minimise the capital to be raised, railway projectors seldom allowed sufficient for parliamentary costs or interest on capital in their estimates, it was rare that enough capital was raised initially. Critics maintained that such costs should be charged against revenue before any dividends were paid but had such a purist line been maintained the deferral of dividends might have proved perpetual. Coupled with the fact that promoters seldom budgeted for anything more than the bare cost of engineering and laying the line and so frequently failed to allow for such essentials as stations, sidings, signalling systems and even rolling stock, it is hardly surprising that most railways staggered throughout their early lives in a state of financial crisis. Yet had adequate allowance been made initially for all the eventual costs the size of the capital subscription required might have been such as to deter the public from putting up any money at all.

An important reason for the success of Grissell & Peto in obtaining vital contracts was the partners' willingness to take a substantial portion of their remuneration in shares in the company whose line they were building. This practice, new at the time that they obtained the contract for the Yarmouth & Norwich, eventually became widespread to the extent that some railway companies were owned to a significant extent by the contractors who had built their lines. The greatest of these contractors, at least to the 1860s, had as large an organisation as any railway company, and to hold that organisation intact had perforce to build new railways. While many of these lines were abroad, others, such as Peto's later East Suffolk line, were largely created primarily by this need, being unlikely to pay in operation. And although three quarters at least of the initial capital of railway companies normally consisted of ordinary shares, risk capital that the shareholders must be prepared to lose if things went wrong, all too frequently many of those shares were held by contractors who had borrowed their subscription moneys from banks or finance houses. Thus the larger part of the whole edifice might be built on a foundation of loans, not only direct borrowings by the company (that were usually secured on its undertaking) but also short term loans to contractor shareholders never intended by the lenders to be risk capital.

In the 1850s a further development of this dubious form of finance occurred when contractors, and notably the partnerships of Peto & Betts and Peto, Brassey & Betts, actually undertook to lease and become the operators of the lines they were to construct at a guaranteed rental sufficient to pay satisfactory dividends to the shareholders who had put up the money for the line's construction. By this means they were promising that the railways they built would be sufficiently profitable to finance their construction. However, apart in some cases from an initial deposit with trustees, the backing to that promise was no more than their own reputation. If all went well the profits from running the railway paid the rental to the company that owned it and the shareholders received dividends on the capital they had provided. If there were insufficient profits to pay the rental and if the operators' assets comprised little more than railway shares already pledged to lenders, disaster would follow.

Railway accounting was necessarily complex due to the numerous transactions at multiple locations during both construction and operation but was usually confined to the recording of cash received and paid out. That is to say liabilities were not recorded and receipts not anticipated until settled by a remittance. So the books would show the cash balances in banks and in hand at any date but would not, for example, make any provision for contractors' bills for work done but not paid for. This was no serious problem for those running the business since they would necessarily have supplementary records and estimates to use when raising finance but it presented a major difficulty when reporting to shareholders.

Although there were few statutory accounting requirements, railway companies, building on the experience and custom of canal companies, by the 1840s invariably presented to shareholders at their half yearly meetings just two accounts. The first, the 'capital' account, recorded receipts from calls on shares and from loans raised on one side and payments made toward the costs of building the line on the other. The second, the 'revenue' account, only required once the railway was in operation, showed receipts from fares on one side and on the other payments made toward the costs of working the line and running the organisation. It was out of the balance on this account that dividends could be declared.

It was the capital account which caused the principal difficulties, partly because until everything had been paid for it was impossible to tell from the account what the line was actually going to cost or how much more capital would have to be raised; partly due to the temptation, sometimes the necessity, to charge payments there which, in a sterner view of reality, truly related to operations. The latter practice had the effect of presenting in the revenue account a rosier view of profitability than could be justified and so encouraged the declaration of dividends greater than was safe. Critics would call for a railway's capital account to be closed, made final, to crystallise the full cost of the line. Railway directors would seek to find ways to avoid such finality by pointing to extensions and branches yet to be completed even when all the costs of the main line had indeed been paid for in cash. As a result the balance on capital account tended to keep creeping, even leaping, upward even when a line was in full operation. Aware that their positions and investments depended on a buoyant share price and that the share price in turn depended on satisfactory actual and prospective dividends, directors were inclined in managing the company and in drawing up accounts to do everything possible to maximise profits. Maximum fares were governed by Parliament or the Board of Trade but the fairly loose regulations concerning safety could allow excessive cost cutting by unscrupulous management. And if the nature of a cost was debatable there would be every temptation to charge it to capital account rather than to revenue.

No allowance was customarily charged against operations for the depreciation of plant such as locomotives and rolling stock let alone for the long term maintenance of such items as the track bed itself or bridges. Ideally a fund should have been established, preferably invested outside the business, to provide cash to renew or replace such items at the end of their working lives. In the 1840s and 50s this was practically never done for, had it been, probably no dividends at all would have been paid from the majority of companies. And without the promise of dividends investors would not have been forthcoming and so few railways would have been built. Luckily renewals of rolling stock could often be justified as improvements so in turn justifying raising additional capital while most railways were sufficiently over-engineered that renewals of major works such as bridges or tunnels could be passed on to future generations without troubling too greatly the consciences of the initial builders.

Although audit of accounts had taken place since medieval times the process as late as 1860 was normally delegated to one or two share-holders who were prepared to volunteer and who would usually confine their work to ensuring that the books added up to the totals disclosed to shareholders and that there were valid receipts for all payments. There were few generally accepted accounting principles and little in the way of statutory guidance for the presentation of accounts. It was well established that dividends could be paid only from profits but there were no clear rules as to what was meant by profits. There was no professional institute providing a system of qualification for accountants but there were professional accountants to be found, especially in London, who specialised in audit of the largest companies, in investigations and above all in the liquidation of failed enterprises.

CHAPTER 2

Genesis of the trunk lines:
1834 to 1840

NEITHER NORWICH NOR NORFOLK was prominent in the early development of railways, although money from the Gurneys of Norwich, Quaker bankers, helped to finance the Quaker backed Stockton & Darlington. When the Liverpool & Manchester in the late 1820s proved the practicability of an entirely locomotive powered line and during the heroic struggles in the next decade to build the first true trunk line from London to Birmingham, Norfolk stayed quiescent. But as the country's financial situation eased in the mid 1830s and as both speculators and local men saw the advance of railways elsewhere, prospects for lines in East Anglia improved.

Norfolk at this time was, as it still is, a largely agricultural county, the several small inland market towns such as Diss, Dereham, Fakenham, Wymondham and Swaffham having little industry apart from activities connected to the produce of the land. Agriculture was emerging from the depression that had followed the Napoleonic wars and from the period of riots and rick burnings of the early 1830s but there was still much rural unemployment. The new Poor Law of 1834 had set up a countywide system of local parish unions with their impressive though forbidding workhouses and the Poor Law Guardians had much to do. A reasonably adequate system of main roads had been created through the preceding century by the several turnpike trusts but minor roads remained the responsibility of individual parishes. County councils did not yet exist and the other aspects of the administration of the county were primarily in the hands of the magistrates, to a large extent the major landowners, whether gathered in Quarter Sessions or sitting locally in twos and threes or even alone. Major cases, both criminal and civil, were heard by judges from the royal courts at the half yearly Assizes. The first Reform Act had only slightly increased the county electorate but had increased the number of county MPs from two to four, two in each of the new western and eastern divisions.

Norwich was by far the largest town and the only city. In the previous century it had risen to its highest degree of prosperity on the back of its woollen industry but this was now in serious decline, long overtaken by Yorkshire, while replacement industries such as shoemaking and food processing had yet to gather full way. Once the second largest city in England it was now much smaller than many rapidly growing cities in the north and Midlands. It still returned two MPs and despite reforms its municipal politics were vicious and parliamentary elections notoriously corrupt. There was however, despite serious poverty and unemployment, much accumulated wealth and some ambition. Of particular relevance, and despite an earlier failure to establish an alternative port at Lowestoft, there was a desire to take advantage of the river connection to the sea and re-establish Norwich as a port for seagoing ships. In this the city was in conflict with the port of Great Yarmouth. In 1835, and until and even after the first railways, transport to and from Norwich of heavy goods that came to or left Yarmouth by sea, especially imported coal, was by wherry on the River Yare. Norwich merchants maintained that they lost up to five per cent of the value of goods by pilferage or by breaking bulk at Yarmouth. They believed that the Haven Commissioners there and the merchants of that town, despite or perhaps because of a large income from port dues, deliberately obstructed any improvement to the navigation that would allow seagoing ships to pass through Yarmouth and sail up the river to the quays at Norwich itself.

Yarmouth and King's Lynn were the two main ports of the county although Wells on the north coast had local importance, especially in the export of malt. Yarmouth was at that time the largest exporter of grain in the country although by export is meant not shipment abroad but coastal transport to London and the industrial north. It was also a substantial importer of coal from the north that was distributed inland by the river system of the Bure, Yare and Waveney which converged on the town. Although its own harbour was merely the mouth of these rivers and somewhat difficult of entrance the roads outside the harbour were sheltered by offlying sands and formed a valuable anchorage and refuge for the hundreds of ships that plied coastwise between London and the north. Servicing these ships with supplies and mail was a commercial opportunity for the several companies of beachmen who operated fast yawls from the beach. But the main basis of the town's economy was its large fishing fleet, some vessels plying for flat fish and turbot but more for mackerel and more yet for herring on whose catch a large processing industry was dependant. Impatient of Norwich whose maritime ambitions it resented, the town harboured intense suspicion of Lowestoft, close by in Suffolk, which it had long attempted to dominate but which, though far smaller, maintained a rival fishing fleet. Yarmouth returned two MPs and, like Norwich, had a reputation for corrupt elections.

The ancient port of King's Lynn had but a modest harbour on a difficult river but still maintained a busy trade in exported grain and imported coal. The town had only slight connection to the rest of Norfolk for its main river connections were inland via the River Ouse to Ely, Huntingdon, St Ives, Bedford and generally to the villages of the southern

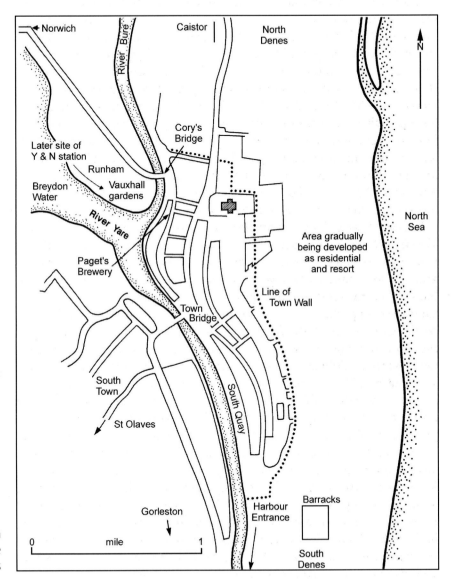

Great Yarmouth
prior to the
railways

Fens. Via tributaries of the Ouse barges reached also to Thetford, Bury
and Cambridge itself. By the 1830s the town was experiencing severe
competition from Wisbech where the river connection to the sea had
been enhanced and which, via the much improved main channel of the
River Nene, had taken over Lynn's former trade with Peterborough and
Northamptonshire. Only the minor navigations of the Wissey and Nar
connected Lynn by water with any part of the interior of Norfolk. Lynn
was smaller than Yarmouth and much smaller than Norwich but the
Reform Act had nevertheless left it with two MPs. Elections were thought
to be less corrupt than in the other towns but closely managed by the
town's elite. From 1837, and throughout most of the period covered by this
work, affairs at Lynn were much concerned with prospects for the Norfolk
Estuary project which was a plan greatly to improve the river entrance
and drain a large tract of land in the Ouse estuary. Eventually carried
out in the early 1850s, though with but partial success, it is relevant in
that the contractors were Peto & Betts and the principal engineer Robert
Stephenson.

Thetford was the fourth corporate town within the county although
in many ways more associated with Suffolk. Important in Saxon times
it had stagnated for centuries and in the 1830s was little more than a
village of note chiefly for its position on the coaching road to London and
Cambridge. For many years it had returned two members to Parliament,
its tiny electorate being dominated by the earls of Grafton from their
nearby seat at Euston. The Reform Act had somewhat widened the
electorate but still left the town with its two members, now the smallest
pocket borough in England. For centuries the Assizes had alternated
between Norwich and Thetford but an Act of 1832 had deprived the latter

of even that annual excitement. For a brief period in the 1840s it became of some importance in the railway politics of the area but otherwise almost its sole, though not unimportant, contribution to the economy of the area was in the manufacture of agricultural machinery.

Despite still considerable local prejudice against the railways throughout the country, more especially by landowners whose parks and privacy were threatened, they were by the mid-1830s increasingly seen as a sign of invincible improvement, their existence opening new opportunities for primary producers, manufacturers and merchants alike. The arguments put forward in Norfolk in favour of a railway involved principally; the speedy transport of fish from Yarmouth to inland markets; the value to be saved by the elimination of driving animals one hundred miles to Smithfield; the ease of bringing coal inland from the ports; and the prospect of day visits to the metropolis by Norfolk businessmen. As yet it was hardly foreseen how much this cheap, swift means for carrying people would serve as a medium of social change. The full possibilities of commuter travel, of cheap excursions and seaside holidays, of a mass market in tourism and in the development of the seacoast resorts themselves, eventually to become the mainstay of passenger traffic in Norfolk, were appreciated by few.

By late 1835 three separate and competing lines from London to Norwich were being canvassed and discussed at public meetings in Great Yarmouth, Thetford and Norwich itself. All had their genesis in London and each obtained much the major part of its financial support from interests outside East Anglia, more especially from Liverpool and Manchester, prosperous cities with capital to spare and unbounded railway enthusiasm. Two of the routes were conceived primarily as lines from London to York via Cambridge, their proposed branches to Norwich being initially important as capable of generating revenue earlier than their main lines. That most favoured in Norfolk was known as the Northern & Eastern, whose engineer was the experienced James Walker.

Walker's East Anglian branch line was to leave the projected London to York main line at Trumpington outside Cambridge and proceed along the fen edge to Barton Mills and then through Thetford, Attleborough and Wymondham to Norwich. From there it was to take a direct route to Yarmouth via Acle. Plans were deposited in November 1835. This route was a revision of an earlier proposal surveyed by the canal engineer Nicholas Cundy that had been hawked around the City of London for some years previous without attracting significant support. At a later date a Norfolk man who had been connected with the survey said that Walker had been personally little concerned with the branch, which was essentially Cundy's, and indeed had not entirely approved it.

The direct rival was a route surveyed by engineer Joseph Gibbs entitled the Great Northern Railway (not related to the later railway of that name). This was intended to run from London via Dunmow and Cambridge to

York with a branch through Suffolk into Norfolk. The branch was to diverge from the main line near Saffron Walden running thence to Bury from where it would take a direct line to Norwich passing only through minor villages. Entering the City from the southwest, it required first a deep cutting and then a tunnel in order to reach a terminus between King Street and the Wensum with a wharf on the river. There was no extension to Yarmouth included in the plans, which, as with the Walker line, were deposited in November 1835.

The third contender with ambitions to serve Norfolk was the Eastern Counties Railway which planned to build from London to Norwich and Yarmouth via Chelmsford, Colchester and Ipswich, a route more commercially promising than the two lines via Cambridge since the towns and districts to be linked were far the more populous. The Eastern Counties had been in prospect for rather longer than the other two and its first prospectus was issued in 1834 but enthusiasm had been slow to build and a provisional committee was formed only in October 1835; thereafter promotional meetings were held all along the line. The intended route as shown on a plan deposited in November 1835 was also engraved on the very first Norfolk editions of the Ordnance Survey issued in 1837 and 1838.

The projectors of the Walker line, as the Northern & Eastern was commonly known, had worked hard to obtain their local support both in East Anglia and the North. By October 1835 they had formed provisional committees in London, Norwich and Yarmouth as well as in towns along the projected main line to the North. The London committee had seven prominent Norfolk names amongst its members including two county members of Parliament, Sir Jacob Astley (Whig) and Edmund Wodehouse (Conservative), and Norfolk baronets Sir William Browne Folkes of Hillington and Sir Thomas Beevor of Hargham Hall. The Norwich list was less aristocratic but contained a number of names well known in that city. The Yarmouth group contained several magistrates who were to be involved with railway promotion in the next decade. The London committee of the Gibbs line contained no recognisable Norfolk names while the Norfolk committee drew most of its support from Norwich rather than the county. The list included the mayor and deputy mayor, two aldermen, the chamberlain and the town clerk, Samuel Bignold, secretary of the Norwich Union, and Colonel (later Major-General) Sir Robert Harvey of a local banking family.

The several public meetings in Norfolk in the latter part of October all overwhelmingly supported the Walker line as being best for the county. Thetford might indeed have been expected to reach this conclusion since neither of the other lines was to come anywhere near to it. Major support came at Thetford from the earl of Euston, through whose large estate it did not pass, and the only dissent came from a landowner whose estate was affected but who withdrew his opposition after a site visit at which the company representative explained how well he would be compensated. The meeting in Great Yarmouth was reported in the press in some detail. It was stressed that a railway was essential to the town (though some shipowners were less sure) and consequently the Gibbs scheme, which did not come to Yarmouth at all, was rejected out of hand. The Eastern Counties, the shorter to London of the other two, was also given short shrift because it was held to be of even more benefit to Colchester, Ipswich and potentially Harwich, ports closer to London. What Yarmouth wanted at this stage, as expressed by one attendee, was a route 'to the heart of the Kingdom' although it also required fast transport for fish to London.

Over one thousand people came to a meeting at Cambridge in November. Representatives of both the Northern & Eastern and the Great Northern attended including both engineers Walker and Gibbs. Previously there had been an unseemly slanging match between the two companies conducted by newspaper advertisement and it appears that the Northern & Eastern had been quoting different figures to different audiences. The two engineers were a good deal politer to each other than were their respective promoters but Walker's argument proved the winner and the meeting overwhelmingly supported his line. One factor in the minds of those from Cambridge must have been that under the Gibbs scheme Norfolk traffic would avoid Cambridge altogether since his eastern branch line was to diverge further south at Saffron Walden. On the other hand an earlier meeting at Saffron Walden had greatly preferred the Gibbs line for the same reason. Moreover that line had the support of the influential local landowner Lord Braybrooke while the Walker line, by passing through his estate at Audley End did not, a fact that would cost its successors dear in extra works, including two short tunnels, to hide the trains from his mansion.

Even before a parliamentary battle could begin the Northern & Eastern published in February 1836 an apologetic advertisement. For the present they would limit their Bill and thus their line to the section London to Cambridge. Their surveys, they said, for the York line and for the Norfolk branch were not yet in sufficiently good form. So these would be left and a further Bill would be submitted to Parliament in 1837. It never was, and the omission of the Norfolk line at this stage seems odd as the plans had in fact been deposited. Perhaps the problem was finance. In any event their Bill for a line London to Cambridge went through Parliament with little reported opposition other than from the Gibbs supporters while the Great Northern Bill was defeated on the floor of the House before ever reaching a Committee stage. The motion for a second reading, introduced by a Norfolk MP, ran foul of the notorious Colonel Sibthorpe who opposed all railway bills and who on this occasion was supported not only by others of a like mind but also by a number of landowners along the line who protested that the plans were inadequate and misleading.

No sooner had the Northern & Eastern announced its self-imposed attenuation than the Eastern Counties responded with an advertisement of its own. It had, it said, been going to limit its Bill to a line ending at Ipswich due to opposition to the route further east and north. In consequence it had closed its subscription books. But in the new circumstances it could be not allowed that no line at all would go to Yarmouth and so the Eastern Counties would now apply for the full route originally planned and further subscriptions would be accepted. Although the company later said that the progress of its Bill through Parliament had been exceptionally swift and easy, and although it certainly had little trouble proving its commercial case with a cloud of favourable witnesses, its directors seem to have overcome numerous landowner objections, especially in rural, park infested, Essex, by the simple but expensive process of promising them very large sums of money for their land and inconvenience.

While the Bill was still in debate the Eastern Counties had been to the trouble of sending a deputation to Norfolk to interview prominent citizens, to smooth out possible objections, and to obtain a further petition in support of their project. That from Norwich was said to carry well over three thousand signatures but one MP (William Gladstone) commented that these had been obtained by giving all who signed a luxurious meal and plenty to drink. Given customary Norwich electoral processes at this time the accusation seems highly probable. At any rate the Act was obtained with Royal Assent on 4 July 1836, simultaneous with an Act for the cut down Northern & Eastern.

The first general meeting of the Eastern Counties in August 1836 was full of optimism with wild forecasts of generous profits. Most of the capital, said Mr Bosanquet the chairman, had come from outside the area and very little from Norfolk or Suffolk. Indeed it subsequently appeared that only £32,000 had been subscribed from Norfolk out of two millions eventually raised. Nevertheless Colonel Harvey and S. P. Edwards of Yarmouth, were amongst the twenty-one on the first board. There was plenty of enthusiasm nationally for railways in 1836, a brief time of commercial prosperity, and the chairman mentioned to shareholders that several feeder railways were already being planned in conjunction with their own including one connecting Ipswich with Bury St Edmunds, one running along the Waveney Valley to Harleston, Bungay and Beccles, and an ambitious route to connect Norwich with Leicester via Dereham and Stamford. As regards the latter, whose engineer John Braithwaite was also engineer to the Eastern Counties, it was reported that the survey was nearly complete and a prospectus would soon be issued. The line was to cross the Great Ouse at Denver. However by 1837 capital was in short supply and not one of these projects ever got so far as to go before Parliament.

It remained for both the Eastern Counties and the Northern & Eastern to build their railways, but little went according to plan. The Eastern Counties ran early into trouble. Much of Essex may be flat but by no means all, while built-up areas and gentlemen's parks were widespread.

There were expensive works required, especially the long viaduct needed in outer London and large outlays to acquire property or to compensate landlords for disturbance (and this despite statements at earlier public meetings that no parks and hardly any houses would lie on the route). In particular a dispute with Lord Petre over crossing his park at Ingatestone proved absurdly expensive both in compensation and legal costs. Much property had to be acquired and demolished on the outskirts of London itself and near the proposed terminus at Shoreditch.

Although the original estimate for construction of the whole Eastern Counties line had been no more than two years with construction beginning at both ends, there seems to have been little alarm at first that works began only in London and that progress was very slow. The *Norfolk Chronicle* carried a short report in July 1837 on a shareholder inspection of the works then completed over the Lea marshes near Stratford at which the directors had made various optimistic remarks prior to entertaining themselves to a dinner at Greenwich but otherwise that year passed without a single press report in Norfolk concerning the railway.

Progress in 1838 was slow and estimates of costs continued to rise. The directors commissioned Robert Stephenson, fresh from his labours on the London & Birmingham Railway, to report on revised estimates made by Braithwaite. The former confirmed the worst fears of the latter. In April 1839 the board announced that the capital available, including borrowings, would not permit the railway to be built further than Colchester and they proposed to stop there. Not surprisingly this produced protests from the towns and cities now to be left stranded. In particular J.C.Cobbold of Ipswich was prominent in backing a legal challenge. A writ was issued seeking to compel the company to complete its line to Yarmouth but this failed when tried in the Court of Queen's Bench and indeed it is hard to see how the company could have raised the capital to comply had the decision been otherwise.

Even though there was now no prospect of the Eastern Counties reaching Norwich in the foreseeable future the Norfolk press remained decidedly complacent. For example a report in February 1840 on the completion of the viaduct at Shoreditch leading to the company's temporary terminus referred to 'a great undertaking'. A bridge designed by Braithwaite was both 'a splendid work of art' and the 'admiration of the engineering world, foreign and domestic'. The new terminus was to be the 'grandest ornament in the metropolis' and all the better because its building had caused 'the annihilation of some hundreds of wretched dwellings'. Perhaps the report had been inserted by Mr Edmund Browne of Norwich whose son was mentioned as being resident engineer at the viaduct. In any case it was a Mr Browne of Norwich who was highly supportive of the company's management at the half-yearly meeting of shareholders just a few weeks later.

Map A1   East Anglia, Proposed Lines 1835

N&E: Northern & Eastern (and later proposed route of East Anglian Railway). 'The Walker line'. Approximately 115 miles London to Norwich. Main intermediate points Bishops Stortford and Cambridge.

GNR: The Great Northern Railway. 'The Gibbs line'. Approximately 112 miles. Main intermediate point Bury St Edmunds.

ECR: Eastern Counties Railway. Approximately 114 miles. Main intermediate points Chelmsford, Colchester and Ipswich.

Also shown is the shortest possible route of 105 miles which would pass through no major intermediate points at all.

None of the routes faced serious engineering problems. The central route would have met more severe gradients than the others but as a consquence had the advantage over more level routes of requiring fewer level crossings.

The boxed area is shown in more detail in Map B on Page 221.

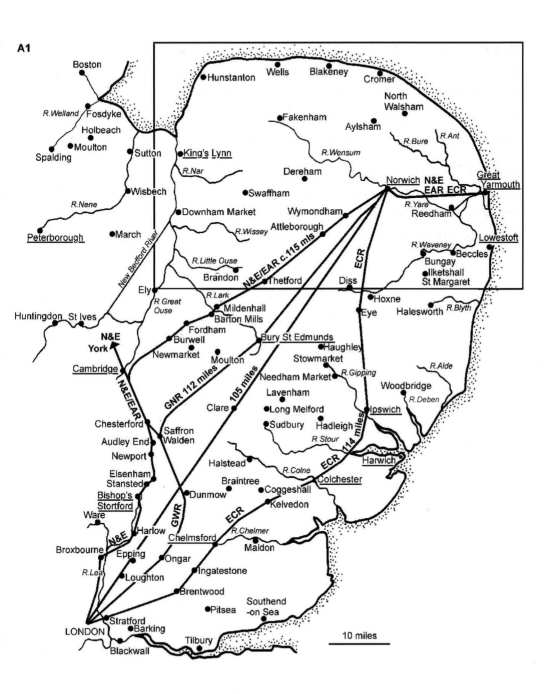

A1

Boston
R.Welland Fosdyke
Holbeach
Moulton
Spalding
Sutton
Wisbech
R.Nene
Peterborough
March
Huntingdon St Ives
N&E
York
Cambridge
Chesterford
Audley End
Newport
Elsenham
Stansted
Bishop's
Stortford
Ware
Broxbourne
R.Lea
Harlow
Epping
Loughton
LONDON Stratford
Barking
Blackwall
Tilbury

Hunstanton
Wells
Blakeney
Cromer
North
Walsham
Fakenham
Aylsham
R.Bure
R.Ant
King's Lynn
R.Nar
Dereham
R.Wensum
Swaffham
Downham Market
Wymondham
Attleborough
R.Wissey
New Bedford River
R.Little Ouse
Brandon
Thetford
Ely
R.Great
Ouse
R.Lark
Mildenhall
Barton Mills
Fordham
Burwell
Newmarket
Moulton
Saffron
Walden
GNR 112 miles
N&E/EAR
N&E/EAR c.115 mls
Bury St Edmunds
Haughley
Stowmarket
Needham Market
R.Gipping
Lavenham
Clare
105 miles
Long Melford
Sudbury
Hadleigh
R.Stour
Halstead
Braintree
Coggeshall
R.Colne
Colchester
Kelvedon
Dunmow
GWR
ECR
R.Chelmer
Chelmsford
Maldon
Ongar
Ingatestone
Brentwood
Pitsea
Southend
-on Sea

Norwich N&E
EAR ECR
Great
Yarmouth
R.Yare
Reedham
ECR
Lowestoft
R.Waveney
Beccles
Bungay
Ilketshall
St Margaret
Diss
Hoxne
Eye
Halesworth R.Blyth
R.Alde
Woodbridge
R.Deben
Ipswich
ECR 114 miles
Harwich

10 miles

At that meeting it was announced that the line would soon be open to Brentwood although, pressed for a date, Braithwaite had to admit that in the current rainy weather little progress at all was being made. If the rain stopped he thought three months should be enough. Asked how long it would take to get to Chelmsford he replied bleakly that two years might do. The cost of the line through to Colchester was estimated at £2,137,000 (as against an original figure for the whole line to Yarmouth of £2,500,000). The company's total share capital when fully called up plus existing and proposed borrowings was £2,100,000. For all that the chief and practically the only vocal critic was Cobbold who maintained that the land for the whole line should have been bought before any works were begun. Another shareholder objected that in such case the railway would never have been built at all.

Browne made a long speech praising the management and deploring the poor support they had received from Norwich in particular and especially Norfolk's poor record in subscribing capital. He announced that a new petition was to come from Norwich signed by one of the MPs for the town, the mayor, sheriff, town council and two hundred and seventy-two burgesses. Whether this in fact materialised is not reported but at a Norwich council meeting a week later the petition was adopted although not without some opposition and debate. The chairman welcomed the news of the petition and said that the company, whose Parliamentary powers were shortly to expire, was to apply for a new Act to enable it to extend its line further but did not explain how it was to raise further capital.

The Eastern Counties did in fact manage to open its line to Brentwood by the beginning of July 1840 and a press report stated that as a result houses around Stratford, now unfashionably close to town, were unsaleable whereas property further out was now so much in demand that there was nothing to be had. Only six weeks later there occurred the first of what was to be a long and notorious series of fatal accidents on the Eastern Counties. On this occasion an engine ran out of control down an incline at Brentwood, tore up a length of track and precipitated itself and its train in a heap beside the line. Two men, one the driver, were killed at the time and another died of injuries in time to have his death announced at the inquest. Braithwaite maintained the driver had failed to shut off steam before the descent – these trains had virtually no brakes – but the press called for more rigorous government inspection of railways and investigation of accidents in the light not only of this event but also other accidents that year both on the Eastern Counties and on other railways.

Progress in building the Northern & Eastern was even slower than on the Eastern Counties, hampered, the directors complained, by lack of finance. Shareholders, disappointed by progress, had been reluctant to pay calls for cash to pay up their shares. It was not before September 1840 that the line reached Broxbourne, still well short of Bishop's Stortford the first major objective of the railway, and hardly more than a quarter of the full distance to Cambridge. In that year the company obtained parliamentary approval to abandon the project beyond Stortford and its nominal capital was reduced from the original £1,200,000 to £720,000. Its plans for its own London terminus at Islington had also been abandoned when it obtained agreement with the Eastern Counties to join that company's line at Stratford and share the terminus at Shoreditch but an annual rent of £7,000 payable to its rival and an additional charge of fourpence for each passenger were severe burdens and its operations were thereafter to a considerable extent at the mercy of its none too friendly landlord.

The announcement that the Eastern Counties would not go beyond Colchester drew little press comment in Norfolk. Railways were still seen in this conservative part of the country as a feature of the industrialised north and only a minority of merchants, manufacturers and farmers yet appreciated the danger of isolation that the eastern counties faced should rail connections to London and the Midlands not soon be established. Norfolk had been content to have a railway provided some other parties put up the money. Now, in 1839, it seemed that those other parties were in a fair way to lose their investments. No skin was being lost from Norfolk noses while those of London speculators looked to become bloody.

Interest revives

By the middle of 1840 the mood was changing. The benefits of the railways to other parts of the country were becoming more evident now London was connected from the north to Birmingham, Manchester, Liverpool and York; with the lines southward to Brighton and Southampton also complete; and with construction on the Great Western to Bristol proceeding apace. Compared to this, the progress in the east was pathetic. Now money was somewhat more plentiful than it had been since the mid 1830s and now rail projects in all parts of the country began once again to interest promoters and investors convinced afresh that there were good returns to be made.

The first signs of any renewed interest in Norfolk came with two advertisements. The earliest of these, inserted in the *Norfolk Chronicle* in July by a Yarmouth solicitor, was a formal notice of intention to build a railway from Yarmouth to Norwich, a Bill to be presented to Parliament in its next session. It was not stated on whose behalf the insertion was made but the route given, although defined merely by a list of parishes as was conventional, is identical with that originally chosen by the Eastern Counties in 1836 and is a simplified version of that refiled on behalf of that company the following spring. A month after this advertisement a *Norfolk Chronicle* editorial item said what a good idea it would be to have this railway and hinted that it had aroused considerable interest amongst 'many highly influential individuals' but did not suggest the identity of the organisation proposing to build it.

The second advertisement dated 22 October was more ambitious. Although it is in a similar formal style, merely listing a wide selection of parishes and promising a Bill to go to Parliament in the next session, the route was for a railway from near Bishop's Stortford (although at this time the Northern & Eastern had not yet reached Harlow) via Cambridge, Mildenhall, Thetford and Norwich to Yarmouth. This was a clear revival of the Walker branch line of the previous decade and implied close co-operation with the Northern & Eastern. An editorial comment in the *Norfolk Chronicle* two weeks before, despite that paper's earlier support for a Yarmouth/Norwich link, had enthused that a line all the way from Cambridge to Yarmouth was a much better proposition. It was understood that a survey had already been made and that a prospectus was expected.

A few weeks later a news item in the *Norwich Mercury* reported that a list of gentlemen were proposing a meeting of landowners to consider railway promotions. Lords Sondes, Wodehouse and Stafford and Baronets Beauchamp Proctor, Astley, Folkes and Preston headed the list while of the numerous country gentry there were included a Bagge, a Lombe, a Pratt, a Bedingfield, a Bulwer and a Keppel, all names of the highest respectability. While by this date, influenced by Whig reforms and especially by threats to repeal the corn laws, the majority of the once Whig Norfolk landowners supported the Conservative party, some of those on the list, such as Astley and Folkes (which two gentlemen had both lost their seats in Parliament at the general election in 1837) remained professed Whigs.

A formal notice of a meeting to be held on the 7 January at the Swan Inn, Norwich was issued on 19 December. This was specifically to be a meeting of landowners in favour of the construction of a railway from Norwich to London to consider the best means of securing its construction. But before it took place there was another meeting, this time in London on the 30 December, apparently arranged by the promoters of what became known as the East Anglian Railway. Here, although W. L. Chute, Conservative MP for West Norfolk, was in the chair, the meeting was initially addressed by J. U. Rastrick the engineer who had but recently completed the line from London to Brighton.

His was a most optimistic presentation. His line would follow roughly the old Walker route starting at Stortford and serving Newmarket as well as Cambridge and Thetford on its way to Norwich. The section from Stortford to Cambridge would be the hardest and might take three years to build but in the only case where any difficulty might arise with a landlord (Lord Braybrooke) terms had already been negotiated by the Northern & Eastern. The line from Cambridge onwards would be cheap to build. Much of the land was 'of inferior quality' (and so cheap to purchase) yet composed of such excellent material that cuttings 'might be cut upright' (which sounds dangerously sanguine). There would be many opportunities for branches and connections, not only to the towns of west and central Norfolk but also to central Suffolk, the fen country, Huntingdon, and Lincolnshire.

Amongst those present and enthusiastic for the line were the two Norwich MPs, the Conservative Marquess of Douro and his Whig colleague Mr Benjamin Smith, while Mr J. Harman, chairman of the London & Brighton Railway, attended to support his engineer. Others present included Isaac Jermy, Recorder of Norwich, Thomas Hammond, a Yarmouth magistrate and chairman of its fish merchants' club, and Samuel Bignold. It was the latter who struck the only discordant note. Norwich men, he said, would have been more enthusiastic if work had been planned to start there rather than at the London end. There had been a similar project two years before from which Norwich investors had hung back as they feared it would dry up some forty miles from London, as had the Eastern Counties. The chairman emphasised how important it was if the line were to succeed that capital should be forthcoming from Norfolk. If Norfolk investors did not put up their hundreds there would be little hope of City men contributing their thousands. Resolutions were passed supporting the proposed railway.

In the same issue of the *Norwich Mercury* that reported the London meeting appeared a letter from William Gurdon (a barrister, younger son of a Norfolk landowner and later Recorder of Bury) in response to one of the previous week from Richard Hanbury Gurney of Thickthorn. The latter, a former Whig MP for Norwich, had objected to any railway and enjoined landowners to think carefully how their lands would be affected. Gurdon who had issued his own circular on the subject, was strong for a railway but warned that landowners must support it and not be greedy. Greed, he said, was what had caused the Eastern Counties to stop at Colchester and the Northern & Eastern at Stortford.

At the Norwich meeting of landowners some two hundred were present. The chair was taken by Lord Sondes, a Conservative peer who had inherited Norfolk property through his mother and, despite having a Kentish seat, was at this time chiefly resident at North Elmham and influential in the political and sporting life of Norfolk. There was some difficulty over the initial motion, put forward by Chute, to the effect that a railroad was essential to Norfolk. While most present were inclined to adopt this and to move on to appointing a committee to determine the best means of obtaining one, there was an objection by the Recorder of Yarmouth, Nathaniel Palmer, who felt that the job of any committee was first to determine whether a railway was indeed essential at all. Although supported by Captain Philip Money, a recent mayor of Norwich, Palmer was opposed in speeches from Isaac Jermy and William Gurdon. Between Jermy and Palmer there was overt personal animosity with the latter accusing the former of looking for a speculative outlet for the funds of his moneyed City friends and of being a committed advocate of Rastrick's line to the exclusion of any other. At length a compromise resolution was adopted substituting the word 'desirable' for 'essential'.

There was much hedging over whether any specific scheme should be favoured and whether any other scheme than Rastrick's was on offer. While Gurdon said he did not know of any other scheme it appeared that he and Sir Jacob Astley had had conversations with both the Eastern Counties and the Northern & Eastern. For Rastrick's line the co-operation of the latter was essential but there was believed to be an Eastern Counties proposition to build from Kelvedon in Essex to Bury. Gurdon spoke at such length and so obscurely (or the reporter had such difficulty in making him out) that it is difficult to follow exactly what he was advocating. He was sure that there was no point in investment if no adequate return was expected; any railway must be commercially viable. There had been an exchange of correspondence between Gurdon and J.E.Lacon, a Yarmouth banker, in which Gurdon had suggested that a railway to Norwich from London was all that was required and that Yarmouth capital should be reserved to build independently between Norwich and Yarmouth. Jermy was even prepared for a railway that was not in itself viable financially since it would be of such great general benefit to the county. If necessary putting money into it, he suggested, should be treated as a contribution to the common good (he did not say how much of his own would be forthcoming or how this argument would ever bring in out-of-county capital).

The mayor of Norwich said that although this was primarily a landowners' meeting he considered that from the city's point of view a railway was absolutely essential and argument on that point otiose. When someone asked how landlords would react to a railway crossing their property Lord Berners and Sir Thomas Beevor each said that it would be welcome on his. At length the meeting proceeded to appoint a committee that contained most of those who had spoken. The final membership was Lords Sondes and Berners, MPs Chute and Edmund Wodehouse, the mayors of Norwich, Yarmouth and Thetford, baronets Sir Jacob Astley and Sir Thomas Beevor, Gurdon and Jermy (after objections by Palmer and a vote), J.E.Lacon and a Mr Birch.

Jermy then proposed that the meeting should hear a presentation by Rastrick who was outside the room. This was controversial and it was apparent that while some present were enthusiastic for the Rastrick scheme, others were strongly opposed and presumably supported some rival although this was never openly admitted. Jermy thought Rastrick would require an hour or more; Gurdon hoped for no more than a ten-minute summary; while Palmer objected to hearing him at all. At length, after a vote, it was agreed to hear Rastrick but at this point many left the meeting. Rastrick's presentation was similar to those he had already given in London and a few days before at Thetford. He stressed that it was essential to deposit plans by 1 March that year if a Bill was to be considered by Parliament in the 1842 session and he was insistent that a new company should build not only from Cambridge but from Stortford as he was convinced the Northern & Eastern would never fill in that gap.

At this period the *Norwich Mercury* is the more rewarding paper to follow as the editor was clearly interested in railways and maintained that it was high time that Norfolk had one. Several editorials are devoted to the subject from January to early March. The paper in mid-January, despite a plea from a correspondent, could not initially bring itself to support any proposal by the Eastern Counties. The present directorate might be honest, as the correspondent had urged, but the company's history had begun with a 'dishonourable endeavour to bribe away a Parliamentary opposition' and had since shown a want of care and had allowed itself to be plundered by its servants and deluded by its architects and engineers.

However it was equally scornful of the tactics employed by the supporters of the Rastrick line. Despite what they had said at the Norwich meeting both Chute and Jermy were committed to that line as evidenced by the terms of the resolutions at the London meeting. That meeting had been 'huddled up' expressly to forestall the county and 'if possible impose its resolutions on the latter.' The language used by the line's supporters in articles in the London papers was inflated and differed from what was provided to the local press. The proceedings at the Thetford meeting were likewise suspect. Anyway the Rastrick line ran through countryside too barren to be productive of revenue while the original Eastern Counties line ran too close to the coast. Connections of either to Newmarket, whether from Cambridge or from Bury, were all too probably inserted to please the racing community. The editor's preference would be for a line to Bury and thence direct to Norwich with a branch from Bury to a terminus at Thetford to serve west Norfolk.

The new committee acted swiftly but, in the view of the *Norwich Mercury*, entirely inadequately. Having met just once, admittedly for six hours, and after hearing presentations by Rastrick, Braithwaite (for the Eastern Counties), Mr Drake, a Dereham solicitor (who presented some vague figures for the likely traffic on the Cambridge line) and solicitors for a line proposed by Robert Stephenson (first mention of this line found in the press) they reported their findings in advertisements published on 30 January. In this they recited the persons who had appeared before them and certain letters they had received and then summarised the schemes of which they had heard. These were:

1. Rastrick's line from Stortford to Yarmouth which he had surveyed and which he estimated would cost £572,000 for 22 miles Stortford

to Cambridge, £1,126,095 for 63 miles Cambridge to Norwich, and £291,512 for the final 18 miles from Norwich to Yarmouth. In total approximately two million pounds (to which it was later noted a further £200,000 needed to be added for engines and rolling stock). Gross annual revenue from this line when completed was estimated at £460,000 without any analysis of which section would contribute what.

2. A proposed extension by the Eastern Counties line to leave their main line at Kelvedon (between Chelmsford and Colchester at a point they had not then reached) running via Coggeshall, Halstead and Sudbury to Bury. Though not yet surveyed other than in outline this was estimated to cost some £600,000. Some major stockholders in the Eastern Counties might, it was said, be prepared to invest in this section. Braithwaite opined that a further line from Bury to Norwich might cost another £600,000 and an extension thence to Yarmouth a further £250,000.

3. A revised and improved line from Stortford to Cambridge now suggested by the Northern & Eastern deviating from the line originally approved in Parliament and later abandoned. Their engineer, the first appearance noted in the region of George Parker Bidder, estimated that this would not cost more than £18,000 per mile.

4. A single track line between Yarmouth and Norwich to cost only £200,000 proposed in a report by Robert Stephenson. A detailed survey had been made on his behalf by engineers Bidder (again) and James Routh.

5. A branch from a railway being considered once again to run from London via Cambridge and Lincoln to York proposed in a letter by Joseph Gibbs. The branch would run from Cambridge to near Ely and then eastward past Brandon, bypassing Thetford, and onward to Norwich and Yarmouth. There was no indication of cost.

Having set out these plans and proposals the Committee concluded that in their opinion a line by Cambridge to join the Northern & Eastern was the best option for Norfolk and that they would not support any company that did not propose to build the whole distance from Yarmouth to Stortford.

The next editorial in the *Norwich Mercury* was scornful of the report and found its conclusions extremely disappointing. They had earlier warned that it was important not to become entangled with existing companies, least of all the Eastern Counties. They had felt that 'all the engines of influence, interest and intrigue' would be employed to entangle any new company with one or other existing party. What had been hoped for was a mature examination of the several proposals taking advice from independent engineers and receiving detailed estimates of costs and profitability. What they had received was 'crude, vague and insufficient testimony' on a most important matter provided entirely by interested parties. Moreover the version of the conclusions in the *Norfolk Chronicle*, after the recommendation of the Cambridge line, had added the words 'and the Committee will strenuously oppose any other plan.' 'Friends' of the *Mercury* had asked that similar words be inserted there but the editor had refused to tamper with the text as submitted. Nevertheless he concluded that the committee was not corrupt, just insufficiently diligent. The editorial pointed out that the suggested cost of some £600,000 for the section Stortford to Cambridge was the same as Braithwaite's figure for the much longer line Kelvedon to Bury. How was even this to be found, let alone the entire sum of over two million for the whole line?

There were a number of letters to the editor of the *Mercury* in the weeks following the Norwich meeting. Jermy wrote to counter criticism that the paper had made of his conduct at the meeting. He had merely responded to an attack by Palmer. He objected to the contention in the paper to the effect that he was committed to the Rastrick scheme. He defended the committee's proceedings but implied obliquely that some members were not disposed to spend much time on the affair and that it was a pity that several had left before the end of the one day of business. What was needed was a much smaller committee supplied with some funds to conduct its own investigations.

Gurdon, who had apparently drafted the report, nevertheless seems to have agreed with the editorial criticisms and maintained that he had 'positively dissented' when the conclusions were drafted. His unctuous letter affirmed that he still greatly respected the other members whose rank, station and property he could not aspire to. They would surely have done more if they could have foreseen how the matter would descend into bitter competition. However he then went on to put arguments in favour of the Rastrick line. Braithwaite's might be cheaper but Rastrick's was better placed to serve the whole of the county, including Lynn, especially if it went via Brandon. He also repeated his argument that there was no need to build on to Yarmouth which town ought to be grateful if Norwich capital should bring a railway within twenty miles distance.

An anonymous correspondent quoted revenue figures for existing lines in more promising situations and suggested that there could never be enough revenue from a Norfolk/London line to justify the cost of construction. A correspondent signing himself Norvicensis wrote a series of letters critical in particular of the Northern & Eastern and of any line that proposed to depend on it whether to get to Stortford or indeed anywhere. It had never had enough cash to build half its projected line and had positively declined to go any further than Stortford yet could now find resources to build a branch to Hertford and Ware. Rastrick's line would be at its mercy as it, in turn, was at that of the Eastern Counties in view of its shared London terminal and use of Eastern Counties tracks from Stratford. Yet early circulars supporting the Cambridge line had assumed as a matter of fact that the Northern & Eastern would not only get to Cambridge but would go on as once planned to York. If it did not, and it was unlikely in the extreme, what price the Norfolk connection with Midlands and North?

He wrote again pointing out divisions in the group supporting the Cambridge line as evidenced in correspondence. While Jermy was content if the Norfolk contribution was small and the returns negligible, Gurdon insisted it must pay. He believed the Stortford/Cambridge gap was too expensive for the new company to build but Rastrick emphasised that the Northern & Eastern would never close it on their own. Anyway freight arrangements at present, whether by sea or by coach were quite adequate. The Norwich MP Smith wrote to disassociate himself from the proceedings at the London meeting. He had merely gone as an observer and had emphasised there that there should be no party disputes over the choice of line. While he refrained from saying so there is a strong implication that some of the disagreements were because the Rastrick line was seen as more convenient for the Conservative landowners and their supporters such as Jermy while the more commonly Whig or Radical Norwich merchants and manufacturers and the *Mercury*, their paper, wanted something more direct. However neither party were prepared to put up the money.

In the papers for 20 February appeared four advertisements in formal style giving notices of intention to lodge Bills empowering the building of railways and listing in each case the parishes, that would or might be affected. The railways and plans were to be the Rastrick line referred to as the East Anglian Railway, Stortford to Yarmouth; the Eastern Counties extension, Kelvedon to Bury; an untitled railway, in fact Robert Stephenson's route otherwise known as the Valley Line; and the Norwich & Yarmouth railway, being the refiled Eastern Counties route with plan attributed to Braithwaite.

From the plans for Rastrick's line it can be seen that Newmarket was to be bypassed, contrary to statements at the London and Thetford meetings. Now the route ran along the Fen edge from near Cambridge via Burwell and Fordham to Mildenhall and thence to Thetford. In Norwich a short branch left the main line in Trowse to cross the Wensum twice, the second time close downstream of the Foundry Bridge to run towards a terminus somewhere at the lower end of Rose Lane. The main line carried on south of the Yare crossing it at Postwick and then taking a route via Acle to alternative Yarmouth termini, one west of the Bure and one on the North Denes.

As regards the two Eastern Counties proposals the company's half-yearly report issued in February had contained the following:

It is the intention of the Company, to lodge the plans ... of an extension … from Kelvedon … to Bury … and likewise to lodge afresh, the plans … of the line originally chosen by this Company, between Norwich and Yarmouth, so as to get a renewal from Parliament, of the powers to take land between these towns, in aid of the powers the Company already has, … to construct a Railway between them; and this latter step will be taken more particularly for the purpose of providing an independent Company with the means of speedily making a Railway between Norwich and Yarmouth, without a Parliamentary contest, and without deposits …

However whatever the true intention of this action, it was of no benefit to the promoters of the Stephenson line who did not plan to build on the same route and did not escape the need for a deposit or a Parliamentary contest.

There was a meeting of importance held on 21 February in Yarmouth mainly to discuss the Rastrick line. No discussion took place concerning the Stephenson line since at that time all Yarmouth thoughts were concentrated on a line to London. Anything less was of little interest, especially not to the fish merchants whose produce easily reached Norwich by road, nor to the shipping interests as a line just to Norwich would compete with the river navigation. Rastrick was expected to address the meeting but arrived late after J. E. Lacon had made a detailed presentation favouring his line.

Lacon's argument was that despite its length the line would be comparatively cheap to build and there would be much traffic for it from Yarmouth formerly sent by sea. Moreover, although the Northern & Eastern could hardly be held up as a good example it had opened nearly twenty miles out of London for an expenditure of little more than one million whereas the Eastern Counties had raised share and loan capital of well over two million and had opened as yet even less mileage. It was highly unlikely that it would ever get to Bury, let alone Norwich, and Yarmouth did not want to be dependent on a line that would probably open a branch to the competing port of Harwich. The Eastern Counties had in any case 'never yet been exceeded in extravagance or accidents'. When Rastrick turned up after eighteen hours travel his main point was again the importance of the new company building all the way through to Stortford. This might be the most expensive section but would accordingly yield the greatest revenue. The meeting duly tended to favour the Rastrick line but its predictable action was to appoint a local committee to watch over progress. The main caveat entered was that Yarmouth would support no railway that did not begin construction at the Yarmouth end.

Gurdon wrote again to the *Mercury* in early March. He now threw doubt on Rastrick's costings that he felt were too high, especially in view of Bidder's estimate for a revised Stortford/Cambridge link at £8,000 per mile less than Rastrick. But he much doubted Braithwaite's costings too.

His record was not good and he had not actually surveyed the line. Surely the county should have everything recosted and then put to a government engineer such as Mr Frederick Smith or Professor Barlow? He then threw in a suggestion for a new route coming to Norwich via Lavenham. Finally he indulged in some arcane estimates of traffic designed to show that the Rastrick route would pay, though no more than moderately, or at any rate better than the alternative.

The last *Mercury* editorial on the subject that spring published on 6 March was polite to Gurdon as 'a public benefactor' but deprecated his idea that Yarmouth should look after itself. Yarmouth was a coming town with new developments and could not possibly be ignored. Contrary to its previously expressed opinion the paper then made out some case for trusting the Eastern Counties. True their cost so far had been excessive, with £700,000 spent on land to buy off opposition and £500,000 to construct their London entrance, but those items apart their record on estimation had not been so bad and they did not believe that the chairman had entirely abandoned any plan to go further. After all they had actually bought the site of their proposed Norwich terminus at Carrow. The writer thought the figures quoted at Yarmouth by Lacon for Yarmouth traffic were reasonable but could not see the point of a railway starting both there and at the other end. This could only result in more completed but disconnected fragments. Nor did they think Yarmouth right in fearing competition from Harwich. Competition had to be faced. In sum the paper was sure the money for the Rastrick line could never be raised. The Eastern Counties would probably get to Bury eventually. But Norfolk would never raise the money to connect Bury to Norwich and Yarmouth, so the parsimonious inhabitants of the county would have to learn to live with their isolation and take the stagecoach to Bury!

After this outburst the local press was silent on railways until the following November apart from one letter from the dogged Norvicensis in June criticising yet again the record of the Northern & Eastern (one imagines that he must have had shares). That railway was expecting to reach Harlow by later that summer and in fact did so, arriving just two miles short of Stortford by November. However although Bidder was holding out the prospect of just another £500,000 to go on to Cambridge (at £20,000 per mile rather than the £18,000 quoted in January), the shareholders obviously felt no desire to find more capital beyond a final call on their reduced shares for the last leg to Stortford. A report on the August half year meeting of the Eastern Counties recorded that contracts had been let for the rest of the distance to Colchester and a review of the estimates by Joseph Locke had confirmed Braithwaite's latest figures and assured the directors that there was capital enough to complete. But there was no further mention of any leap on to Bury.

CHAPTER 3

The Yarmouth & Norwich Railway: 1842 to 1844

ALTHOUGH THE STEPHENSON PROPOSAL for a line limited to Yarmouth/Norwich and running close to the north bank of the River Yare had been put forward by lawyers no later than the time of the Norfolk committee report in January 1841 it had been swiftly dismissed by such as the *Norwich Mercury* and scarcely even discussed at the Yarmouth meeting despite being the only project that looked reasonably likely to pay. And although the formal plan was duly filed on 1 March 1841 in anticipation of a Parliamentary Act in the following year little further appears to have been heard of it until November. The first press report is of another meeting held in Yarmouth on the nineteenth of that month with the mayor of the town taking the chair. Even then the only persons recorded as being present on behalf of the putative company were its lawyers but a report on the line by Robert Stephenson was read.

Stephenson's report was detailed and precise. He had first planned the route simply by reference to the Ordnance Survey from which it seemed obvious to him that the extra two miles of line required to follow the river valley via Reedham was more than justified by the flatness of the route in comparison with the competing projects that went via the higher land direct from Norwich to Acle. He compared the different gradients in some detail. Further he emphasised that while Braithwaite and Rastrick planned to cross navigable rivers once and three times respectively his line did without any such crossing by the expedient of moving the river out of the way! Thus he planned to cut off a bend in the Yare at Thorpe St Andrew by diverting the river to the south through a short canal and so allow his railway to stay on the newly formed north bank. He was certain that a railway competing with a navigable river must avoid crossing it if at all possible to obviate the need for swing or lift bridges at a time when most river craft carried tall masts.

He also compared the proposed position of the termini on the three competing lines. Rastrick's, on the west side of Rose Lane, was nearer the centre of the city but would be expensive as it involved an extra river crossing to get there. Braithwaite's, south of Carrow Bridge, was too far away. His own at Thorpe must be, he said, the best and cheapest compromise. Similarly in Yarmouth it might be well to carry the line over the Bure and to the seashore, as Rastrick proposed, but cheaper by far to stop at Runham on the western bank. All the time, whether in his positioning of the termini, in choosing a longer but flatter line with fewer earthworks, or in taking less valuable land, he sought for the cheapest capital cost. He had employed Bidder and Routh to carry out the detailed survey and had subsequently walked over much of the ground himself. Finally he produced an estimated cost of just less than two hundred thousand pounds including land purchase and rolling stock.

After Stephenson's report had been read the presenting lawyer spoke to the meeting stressing again many of the advantages of the line. Especially he pointed out that the sum of money required was certainly within the capacity of Yarmouth and Norwich to provide and if they managed to do so the line would not only pay but would remain under local control. He greatly doubted whether anyone was going to provide the more than two millions that Rastrick's line would require. So surely it would be best to build Stephenson's line as far as Norwich and then see who, Eastern Counties or anyone else, would be prepared to build to meet them. A representative of Rastrick's line was present and assured the meeting that his party too would be putting forward a Bill. However it emerged in the debate that while Stephenson's lawyers were already treating with landowners and canvassing their support for the Bill as required by Parliamentary Standing Orders, Rastrick's lawyers had not as then even started to do so.

A week later a series of short advertisements began to appear for the Valley Line. These merely stated the capital at £150,000 in shares of £20 each with two pounds deposit being required, named the engineer and solicitors, gave an estimate of the annual revenue £60,000 as originally estimated by the Eastern Counties but anyway 'upwards of £40,000' and said that plans and a prospectus could be obtained from the solicitors. Early in December the *Mercury* published in an editorial a paper, for which the *Mercury* itself disclaimed responsibility, comparing the three lines. The unnamed author queried why the Eastern Counties, having laid plans for a Yarmouth/Norwich line in 1836 and having gained then the power to build it were only now proposing to do so. Their attitude was that of the dog in the manger and it must be that they were merely concerned to block any competition. As to Rastrick's promoters, they had surely abandoned any hope of raising money for the whole line and were now (the first news of this) proposing merely a Yarmouth/Norwich line. The gist of the short paper was backing for Stephenson's line, chiefly on his reputation, but also on the obvious grounds of cheapness of construction.

A rather fuller advertisement for the Valley Line appeared in early January, the principal additional information being a list of what was

Yarmouth & Norwich
RAILWAY.
Mr. Robt. Stephenson's, or Valley Line.
Capital £150,000.

PRELIMINARY LOCAL COMMITTEE.
William Baynes, Esq.
Charles James Beart, Esq.
John Ives Cooke Fowler, Esq.
Francis Riddell Reynolds, Esq.
John Caporn Smith, Esq.
Thomas Fowler Steward, Esq.

ENGINEER IN CHIEF.
Robert Stephenson, Esq.

SOLICITORS.
Messrs. White & Borrett, 35, Lincoln's Inn Fields.
Messrs. Rackham and Cooke, } Norwich.
John Oddin Taylor, Esq. }
Charles John Palmer, Esq. Great Yarmouth.

ACCORDING to the Estimates of Mr. Robert Stephenson, the above Line from Yarmouth to Norwich may be constructed for the unusually small sum of £150,000 ; and the Traffic between the two towns having been taken by the Eastern Counties Railway Company at upwards of £60,000 per annum, and being certainly at a low estimate calculated to produce a revenue of upwards of £40,000, the Shareholders may rely with confidence upon receiving a high rate of Interest upon their Capital.
The Shares are £20 each, on which a deposit of £2 per Share will be required ; *which will, however, be returned in case the proposed Bill be not introduced into Parliament in the next Session.*

referred to as a Provisional Local Committee. This contained just six names without any indication of their residence or status although one, Francis Reynolds, has been traced as a solicitor in Yarmouth. None were prominent in Norfolk and their names were hardly such as to cause a flood of subscribers. At the same time advertisements appeared in the press calling a meeting of landowners opposed to the line, naming amongst the requisitioners Sir William Beauchamp Proctor of Langley Hall, John Francis Leathes of Herringfleet Hall and, by their agents, Lord Rosebery, Edward Walpole and the Dean and Chapter of Norwich cathedral.

There was a further Yarmouth meeting on 15 January, called by the mayor, to consider the findings of the committee set up the year before as regards the two lines now seriously in prospect. The committee believed that they were committed to Rastrick's line although there was doubt over this now that the promoters were proposing only the Yarmouth/Norwich section. Its principal advantage was the better position of its termini. Their chief objection to the Valley Line itself was that the diversion of the river might interfere with navigation but their main fear was that the promoters were in some way linked with the Eastern Counties which company was regarded with the greatest suspicion. It was admitted that the Rastrick line was more expensive but this was in part because it was double-track and partly because of its extension into the towns at either end.

Those arguing for the Valley Line had to admit that there had been much opposition by some landowners at a recent meeting but stood firm on the cheapness of the Stephenson route and the unassailable reputation of its engineer. They emphatically denied that they had any arrangement with the Eastern Counties, saying they thought rather that they were unpopular in that quarter. There was a move to call both engineers to a further public meeting and an attempt to get the respective promoters to merge their interests. But the latter course proving unacceptable after a brief discussion outside the main meeting, the former was not pursued. Instead the committee, with one opposer and one abstainer, voted to support the Rastrick line. The opposer, Mr Yetts, later joined the Valley Line committee; the abstainer was Mr Charles Cory, a Yarmouth solicitor, of whom the railway was to hear much more.

An editorial a week later in the *Chronicle* reviewed the history of the two proposals and said the Yarmouth meeting result was a dreadful surprise to the Valley promoters but suggested that the Rastrick line at this stage was now only 'a cloak for opposition to the Valley Line' with hopes of being bought off. The editor felt that there was now a serious risk that

Yarmouth & Norwich
RAILWAY.
STEPHENSON'S LINE.

THE Directors beg to give Notice, that on and after the 1st of February next, no further applications for Shares will be received except from persons resident or connected with the Counties of Norfolk and Suffolk.

Those parties to whom Shares may have been allotted prior to that period, may pay their Deposits on such Shares to the credit of the Yarmouth and Norwich Railway Company at Messrs. Gurneys and Birkbeck, Norwich, or Messrs. Glyn, Halifax, Mills, and Co. London, when receipts for the sums so paid will be given them.

Applications for Shares may be addressed in the meanwhile to Messrs. Rackham and Cooke, Norwich, I. O. Taylor, Esq. Norwich; C. J. Palmer, Esq. Great Yarmouth; Messrs. White and Borrett, 35, Lincoln's Inn Fields, London; and to the Secretary, 6, Warnford Court, Throgmorton Street, with whom Copies of the Parliamentary Contract and Subscribers' Agreement lie for Signature.

HENRY PATTESON, Secretary.

N. B.—The Norwich Provisional Committee will meet every Tuesday, Thursday, and Saturday, at the Office of Messrs. Rackham and Cooke, Saint Giles' Street, Norwich, where all communications are to be sent addressed to John Longe, Esq. their Chairman.

neither would be built. However an advertisement of 26 February announced that opposition had been withdrawn and that the Bill for the Valley Line would be supported by the principal promoters of both lines. In fact the Valley promoters had indeed bought off the opposition at a price of fifteen hundred pounds, discharged by the allotment of fully paid shares, enough perhaps when sold to pay their legal and other expenses.

The advertisement listed an almost entirely new provisional committee. Just one survived from the earlier list, Reynolds, the Yarmouth solicitor. In addition there were now Norfolk worthies, Sir Edmund Lacon of Yarmouth, banker, brewer and elder brother of J. E. Lacon, and John Longe of Spixworth, a major landowner; the mayor of Yarmouth, William Hurry Palmer, draper and shipowner; from Norwich Horatio Bolingbroke, merchant and insurance company director, William Herring and Thomas Read; and from London Adam Duff (of 62 Moorgate and residing at Blackheath), Captain Tyndale (of Alexander Square, Brompton, holder of the Waterloo medal and apparently in command of large sums of capital), Captain Lawrence RN, and (although otherwise resident at Tapton House, Chesterfield) the famous George Stephenson himself.

A great deal can be learnt from the record of the progress of the company's Bill through Parliament. Although there were forever to be complaints of a lack of local support there were eventually over 100 local subscribers promising to contribute a total of £34,608 though more of these came from Yarmouth than from Norwich. The heavy money, 43 subscribers promising £80,900, came from outside, mainly London, brought in, he later boasted, through the influence of George Stephenson. Twenty-two persons were listed as having subscribed in sums of £2,000 and over including from the committee Stephenson, £5,000, Reynolds, £2,000, Duff, £6,700 and Tyndale, £6,600. Other major subscribers, not committee members, were C.J.Palmer, who acted as local solicitor for the company, £7,000, and Charles Cory, £2,000, both of Yarmouth, Francis Mills of Glynn Mills bank, £5,000 and, highly significantly in view of later events, Samuel Peto and Thomas Grissell, £5,000 each. Smaller but substantial subscriptions were made by others whose names will recur such as Norwich banker Robert Harvey Harvey

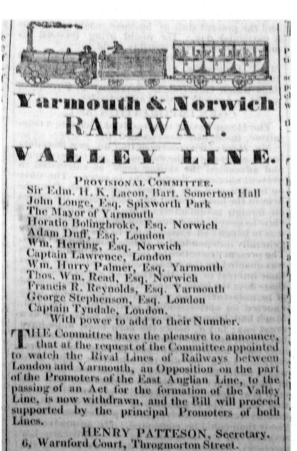

(Harvey & Hudson Bank), John Norgate (Norwich wine merchant) and William Yetts of Yarmouth. All subscriptions together brought the total to £115,580, in excess of three quarters of the target of £150,000 and hence enough to allow the Bill to proceed but some way short of the full requirement. Eleven persons were nominated as the first directors, most of whom had been on the provisional committee but including also J. E. Lacon and a new name, William Johnson, draper and shipowner, of Yarmouth.

Opposition came from the Eastern Counties which petitioned against the Bill as did several landowners and the commissioners of the River Wensum and of the Norwich bridges. Witnesses called in favour of the line included Robert Hammond, fish merchant from Yarmouth, Edward Willett, Norwich cloth manufacturer, and William Hurry Palmer. Hammond, who assumed that the line under discussion would eventually reach London, spoke of the need for fish, which currently travelled in vans by road, to reach Billingsgate by six in the morning for immediate sale. Delay to eight meant no sale before the afternoon and lower prices. Willett said cloth too went from Norwich by road to London but would go there by sea via Yarmouth once the railway was built. Without a railway the only practicable route for goods to Yarmouth was along the river by wherry which suffered from uncertainty of timing and thus the chance of missing a sailing at the seaport. Better still would be a completed line to the metropolis.

A Norwich wharfinger looked forward to the railway even though it might obviate wherry traffic but was concerned that there was no rail connection planned to the Yarmouth quays. Fast steamers had been tried along the Yare but had been withdrawn having caused excessive damage to the banks. Road traffic including the mail coaches, it appeared, used the old road via Caister since the newer road across the marshes from Acle was narrow and sometimes flooded. When counsel for the Eastern Counties pressed Palmer to say that he would prefer a continuous railway to London he admitted he would but said that Yarmouth was disappointed in the Eastern Counties management and had supported their proposals in 1835 only because they had undertaken to start building at Yarmouth as well as London. For the first time emphasis was put on the current growth of Yarmouth as a resort and on the extensive building then taking place on the Denes. Much detail was given of comparative costs and likely fares.

Surprising support for the line came from Thomas Trench Berney of Morton Hall, a landowner of marshland through which the railway would pass. He was of the opinion that all the marshland owners would benefit from the railway since the proprietors would be bound in their own interests to make extensive improvements to the drainage of the whole area including the provision of steam drainage to relieve the existing windmills. Sadly for him the evidence from the engineer disabused him on several points: the railway would certainly involve drainage but could look after itself while any major scheme for the area would require a separate Act and no doubt contributions from landowners.

The entire engineering evidence was presented by Bidder who withstood an entire day of cross examination, chiefly by counsel for the Eastern Counties who took him through the detail of the line virtually yard by yard. Counsel was acute but Bidder was entirely a match for him and apparently held the entire project in his head. Every point was answered courteously even when on occasion he permitted himself a pointed correction on the lines of 'Learned counsel may have failed to appreciate ... etc.' He had first looked over the country for Stephenson in 1840 and had then returned in 1841 for a full survey with Routh. He gave the following statement of the estimated costs:

	£
Land and compensation	28,000
Excavations and embankments	28,144
Rails, chains and spikes	30,059
Sleepers and wedges	12,954
Ballasting and laying road	12,144
Bridges and piling	18,443
Fencing	4,911
Road diversions and crossings	1,331
Carrying establishment (rolling stock, five engines and the cost of the electric telegraph etc.)	36,450
Parliamentary expenses and superintendance	13,550
Contingencies	14,014
Total	£200,000

This was detail the like of which was seldom available at such an early stage and was supported by Bidder's statement that the firm of Grissell & Peto had agreed to undertake the work at that price. It was also unusual in including an allowance for parliamentary expenses. Moreover, in the event the only item to prove inadequate was the cost of the land. However Bidder's evidence concerning estimates of likely traffic and running costs was sadly optimistic predicting a surplus sufficient to fund an eleven per cent annual dividend, something never remotely achieved.

At the time that this evidence was taken before a Commons committee, mid-April, the company had agreed terms for land with the earl of Rosebery, one of the main objectors, and had the assents of most others but no agreement as to price. When evidence was given before a committee of the House of Lords in early June 'all objections had been withdrawn' and it seems that this had been achieved through promising more satisfactory prices than in the estimate. Very little evidence was required of the company on this occasion and only Sir Edmund Lacon and Bidder were called. The company's Act received the Royal Assent on 18 June 1842.

The first general meeting of the company was held on 5 August in the Victoria Hotel at Great Yarmouth. The atmosphere seems to have been one of mild exhaustion after the parliamentary fight. George Stephenson was in the chair. Robert Stephenson was absent but George Bidder was there as was James Routh, now the designated site engineer. J. E. Lacon was elected treasurer (which required him to stand down as director) and a Mr Patteson of London was elected secretary, his appointment being justified on the grounds that the directors' main business would be in London until the completion of the line. A simple cash account was presented that showed that 1,521 of the 7,500 shares as yet remained unissued (or, if issued, then no deposits had been paid). £11,958 had been received as deposits at £2 per share and some £5,565 had been paid out, mainly in legal and Parliamentary expenses although about £1,000 related to land purchase.

One shareholder complained that the accounts were inadequate and there would be no update for a further six months but the chairman pointed out that any shareholder could inspect the books of account and promised that the maximum to be laid out for preliminary expenses would be £10,000. Director's fees of £625 were voted to be divided amongst the board. Not for the last time George Stephenson pointed out how poor had been local support in the form of capital subscribed and how much the company owed to him for bringing in such a large part of the capital. The Act allowed the company to pay interest of five per cent per annum on paid up capital which should be an incentive for calls to be paid as due or even in advance. Bidder reiterated the £200,000 estimate that had been made in the prospectus and before Parliament.

By the next meeting in February 1843 held at the Royal Hotel in Norwich some important progress had been made. Contracts had been agreed for only about half the land required but now, at last, the subscription list was full and this would enable the company to purchase compulsorily and have the purchase consideration determined, if necessary, by a jury. George Stephenson, continuing as chairman, inveighed against those landowners whose livelihood came from ownership of the land yet who opposed a railway that would shorten the journey to London markets taken by their tenants' cattle from ten days to one. Once more the poor local support in the form of capital was to be regretted; this after all was to be the first step in connecting the East Coast to 'the interior and to the manufacturing districts'. In contrast to the chairman's views on landowners and local capitalists he and Lacon were lavish with praise for the contractors who were to build the line, emphasising in particular their respectability.

The contractor partners Grissell and Peto could indeed claim respectability. But the most cogent factor in their tender gaining the approval of the directors was probably that they had been prepared to take £30,000 of the contract price in shares, an arrangement that at once solved the problem of the subscription list and eased any difficulty over initial cash flow. So structured it was unthinkable that the building contract could be given to anyone else. Moreover, as hinted before Parliament, the contract was itself unusual at that time in that the contractors undertook to provide within a fixed price not only the line itself but the necessary locomotives and rolling stock, in fact a railway in working order complete with an electric telegraph signalling system. In this state, assuming that the company did not wish to work the line itself, it could, said the chairman, easily be leased out for a term of five or seven years. The contract required the line to be open by the spring of 1844 but there was an important let-out clause if, due to failure of land purchase in time, work could not begin by April 1843.

Not all shareholders were happy and it is clear that they had been influenced by rumours that the company was facing a cash shortage. In fact by the end of December 1842 little more cash had been collected than had been the case four months earlier and of course the new contractor shareholders were not going to pay any deposit on their shares. However the chairman was able to tell the meeting that since December the majority of a first call of three pounds a share had been paid up notwithstanding that it was not strictly due until the following October. There was a complaint too that no report had been circulated prior to the meeting and that even there it had merely been read aloud. This was excused on the grounds of time shortage and the split of the board between London and Norfolk. But nine months after the company had obtained its Act there was still no sign of work on the ground.

A week after the meeting the indefatigable Norvicensis wrote again to the *Norwich Mercury*. He took great exception to George Stephenson's attack on the objecting landowners. They had their rights under the law. Until the company had filled up its subscription list it could not have gone before a jury. So just how had this been done? He made snide remarks also about the company's engineer being the son of the chairman. In any event, he wrote, an engineer was not a land valuer and should not pretend to act as one. Of course by this time Robert Stephenson was probably the leading civil engineer in the country, had triumphantly completed the London & Birmingham line, was inundated with new projects from all parts of the kingdom and had, as his father mentioned at the meeting, some 1,000 miles of railway under construction on the Continent. It would be remarkable had he had much time to spare for the tiny Yarmouth & Norwich and in fact he seldom attended meetings, leaving the line under the general supervision of Bidder. Nepotism hardly came into it.

Work did begin on the line in late March with the first sods being cut close east of Norwich at Postwick Hall Farm near Thorpe Asylum. From then onwards railway news, often from points far beyond East Anglia, became more frequent in the newspapers as the first signs of what was to become the railway mania of 1845/46 began to appear. In March the Eastern Counties had at last reached Colchester, freight service beginning at once and a passenger service following shortly after. The coaching trade immediately adapted to the new terminus, splashing quarter page advertisements in the newspapers boasting of the shortened time to London from Norfolk. London & Birmingham shareholders approved the construction of a branch line from Blisworth in Northamptonshire to Peterborough, a clear encouragement for an East Anglian line to join them there.

Even before any work had begun on the line the company had taken further thought on the question of the Yarmouth terminus. There was a problem in that the only access to the planned site from the town was by way of a privately owned suspension bridge over the river Bure on which tolls were chargeable. This bridge had been erected in 1829 by a Mr Robert Cory to replace an ancient ferry that had been his property since 1810 when he had bought the farm on the west bank to which it ran. Before building the bridge he had obtained an Act that confirmed his rights to the crossing and made it clear that no other crossing was to be permitted. The bridge had become of importance when the Acle turnpike over the marshes had been completed in 1831 cutting four miles from the previous route to Yarmouth from Norwich.

There was no question of running the railway over Cory's bridge for which purpose it was unsuitable, the deck being flexible and having an excessive gradient. It was also narrow so that two carriages or even carts could not pass and it was clear that traffic to and from the station would be inhibited. Nevertheless solicitor Charles Cory, son of Robert and trustee for himself and his numerous siblings who now owned the bridge, had agreed to improve the roadway to accommodate the increased traffic by adding footways on either side. Meanwhile the railway had bought the land for the station, originally part of Robert Cory's farm, which lay under a covenant forbidding any owner to effect any other river crossing. Cory had also been persuaded to take up a substantial shareholding in the railway. The whole arrangement was unpopular in the town and in early 1843 the company put forward a Bill to obtain powers to build their own bridge on a site of their choosing, such bridge to be of a type that would carry the line itself into the town and allow at least a horse tramway on the quays. Not surprisingly Cory took objection to the proposal and succeeded in having it rejected in Parliament.

In May 1843 the *Mercury* carried a flowery piece on the works proceeding apace at Thorpe and Reedham including the new canal at Thorpe St Andrew on which work had begun that month. The reporter enthused over the fine, brawny, muscular workmen, so skilled at their tasks, but queried why they were sometimes to be found lounging on the highway to the alarm of respectable females. Three months later the magistrates in Norwich were hearing complaints about such behaviour by 'railway excavators' who, having been paid on a Thursday, at once drunk their earnings and lay about in groups on the Thorpe Road. One Mr Dunham, a subcontractor, and a Rachel Ashead, described as 'his shopkeeper', brought a complaint against three workmen who had used abuse against the latter. The labourers had brought a counter summons against her for using the truck system, but as they did not appear this could not be heard. Dunham paid his men fortnightly in cash but issued tickets in the interim for use only in his shop. He denied he made payment in a pub. The magistrates slated him severely but could make no order.

In the end only one landowner appealed to a jury over the terms offered by the railway for crossing and taking his land. This was Mr T.G.Tuck of Strumpshaw who called several witnesses, estate agents, lawyers and Daniel Gurney, a banker and antiquary and a cousin of Richard Gurney of Thickthorn. The case was heard in May at the Shirehall before the Sheriff and a special jury (that is to say a jury composed of substantial property owners who had inspected the land in question). The value of the land over which the railway was to run was not a major issue. The worth of fourteen acres of farmland was readily agreed at £667 being thirty years purchase of a rental of £22 per acre. Tuck's far more contentious claim was for severance as the railway would divide his property and cut off, subject to accommodation crossings, his house and farm from the riverside staithes. Moreover it would interfere with his game preserves and spoil his view. It was admitted by his witnesses that some railways increased the value of property through which they passed but this could hardly be the case here when the nearest station was to be a mile away. He claimed anything up to £10,000 but certainly not less than £5,000, chiefly calculated by putative loss of rental value of his house that had recently been extended.

His tactics in calling so many and varied witnesses told against him and opposing counsel (Sir William Follett, the Solicitor General), who called no witnesses himself, had a fine time pointing out the contradictions in their evidence and their lack of experience in dealing with railways. Daniel Gurney, who had dedicated much time to opposing all railways and had even set up a will trust to ensure that his campaign endured beyond his death, made a poor showing, and indeed had nothing to offer beyond prejudice. Tuck had greatly damaged his case by attempting late in the day to clear land in an apparent attempt to make a park and so enhance the value of what he was about to lose. In fact the railway was not going to come particularly close to his house from which it would be scarcely if at all visible. The jury awarded just £850 for disturbance, and with that the last property obstruction to the line was removed.

In early August the *Chronicle* carried an astonishing 'puff' for the Yarmouth & Norwich attributed to a Leeds stockbroker, R.B.Watson & Co, anticipating the company's own half year report and evidently inspired by talking to an enthusiastic director. A dividend of seven per cent was confidently forecast once the line was in operation which the contractors had undertaken to procure by June 1844. Extension to Cambridge was predicted and an eventual connection to the Midlands. The contractors were said to hold one third of the shares with one of them alone holding one-eighth of the capital.

A cloud appeared on the horizon in August when, after a public meeting in Ipswich, a committee including J.C.Cobbold was formed to promote a line in co-operation with the Eastern Counties from Colchester to Ipswich with branches to Harwich and Bury St Edmunds and, ominously, an extension to Norwich. Plans for parts of these lines had already been prepared by engineer Peter Bruff. Significantly the meeting had been attended by the mayor of Norwich and others from that city. The railway that they agreed to form became the Eastern Union. Now if the object of the promoters of the Yarmouth & Norwich had been to secure the shortest route to London co-operation with this new enterprise should have been welcomed. That it was not, but for some time largely ignored, confirms the view that their main objects at that time were still the Midlands and the north and that plans for extension westward were already well advanced.

At the half-year meeting of the Yarmouth & Norwich, held in early September 1843 at Yarmouth, the chairman was in an ecstatic mood. Nearly £50,000 had now been raised from shares and another call was shortly due. Due to the speed at which works had gone forward it would be essential to make all calls at the earliest possible date. The meeting agreed to a proposition to borrow £50,000 at five per cent which funds had already been offered to the company. Work had proceeded according to the best expectations and should be complete by the following June unless the winter was unusually wet. The only bad news, although not by now unexpected, was that the total land cost would be some £15,000 in excess of the original estimate. Cory queried certain payments in the accounts including one of £1,500 made in paid-up shares. While this was explained only as a debt of honour it was in fact the sweetener paid to the East Anglian projectors to withdraw opposition.

Cory was predictably a critic of the company at this time since, while he had won the first round of the bridge battle earlier in the year, the company was already preparing revised bridge plans to go before Parliament in 1844. Later in September a new Bill was prepared, virtually identical to its predecessor. The plans which accompany it, though issued from Robert Stephenson's own office, do not carry conviction. The crossing was to be close to the site of the station but the tramway, once across the bridge, appears to make such a tight turn towards the Yarmouth quays that no truck, however short its wheelbase, could be imagined to round the corner. When this Bill was examined in Parliament in the following March evidence for the company stressed the unsuitability of Cory's bridge for railway traffic while two Yarmouth magistrates gave evidence in favour of the new bridge. However Cory, as the principal objector, won his case, and the Bill was rejected.

Much of the September meeting was taken up with discussion over the prospects of extending the line westwards to Brandon. Peto said that if that line were built it would terminate forty miles from Newport (to which Hertfordshire town, north of Stortford, the Northern & Eastern had recently extended), forty from Peterborough, and forty from the Eastern Counties at Colchester. Rather than chose one partner and face competition from the others the company should invite them all to come to Brandon. He would undertake to build the line at £10,000 per mile. The secretary said that the line had been surveyed and the plans lodged and if the money was forthcoming they could go to Parliament next session. Bidder said that a line had indeed been surveyed (in fact by him on behalf of the London & Birmingham) all the way from Weedon on the London & Birmingham to Norwich and if they built to Brandon there would be a race by the other lines to meet them. The chairman challenged Cory and other Norfolk shareholders to put down £500 each to start off a new subscription list.

There must have been many negotiations behind the scenes for otherwise Brandon, no more than a village in north Suffolk, would never have been seriously proposed as a terminus for the main line of a railway. As early as November 1842 plans had been deposited on behalf of an unnamed engineer for a railway from Stortford via Cambridge and Brandon to join the Yarmouth & Norwich at Trowse, thus roughly following the line later taken by the Norwich & Brandon. But no prospectus or Bill has been found to suggest on whose behalf this was surveyed. An advertisement of early November 1843 in formal style of an intention to build the Norwich & Brandon, with a branch to Thetford, gave no hint of a proposed junction with any other line. But on the same day that advertisement appeared a special meeting of the Yarmouth & Norwich shareholders was held and there it was announced that the new company was to be formed 'to connect with the extension or extensions of the united companies Eastern Counties and Northern & Eastern'.

In fact the companies were not to merge; instead the legal form of the union, effective from 1 January 1844, was a lease granted by the Northern & Eastern to the Eastern Counties of its whole undertaking at a rental sufficient to service the capital of the former company. But whatever the legalities the Eastern Counties was to take control of the line to Stortford and, having raised nearly one million pounds of new capital for the purpose, intended to build further to Cambridge, Ely and Brandon and also from Ely to Peterborough while shareholders were beguiled by plans for a future extension to Lincoln. Despite the apparent accord between the companies which were to operate in concert, simultaneously with the deposit of the Norwich & Brandon plans there were deposited in the name of Robert Stephenson plans for a line from Stortford via Cambridge and Ely to meet the Norwich & Brandon not at Brandon but well to the north-east of Thetford, this line rather than the latter to continue in a large curve into Thetford itself. One has to assume a subsequent major revision of the plans in the Thetford area before full agreement was reached. Another indication that competition preceded union was that, also in November 1843, Braithwaite, presumably on behalf of the Eastern Counties, deposited plans for a direct competitor with the Cambridge route, a line from Colchester to Thetford (via Bury) where it was to join the Norwich & Brandon.

At a special meeting of the Yarmouth & Norwich in November 1843 it was announced that the company's share capital would be increased

YARMOUTH & NORWICH RAILWAY.

The Yarmouth and Norwich Railway will be opened to the Public

ON WEDNESDAY, FIRST OF MAY NEXT.

Trains will leave **Norwich** at Nine and Eleven o'clock in the Morning, and at Four and Seven o'clock in the Afternoon.

And from **Yarmouth** at Eight and Ten o'clock in the Morning, and at Three and Eight o'clock in the Afternoon.

Fares:--First Class 3s. 6d.--Second Class 2s. 6d. Third Class 1s. 3d.

Tickets to and from NORWICH and YARMOUTH on the SAME DAY :

First Class 5s.--Second Class 4s.--Third Class 2s.

By Order, G. N. TOOTAL, Secretary.

Norwich, 18th April, 1844. (1525

by £50,000. An equal sum would be subscribed for shares in the Norwich & Brandon but of this £15,000 would return to the Yarmouth & Norwich as a contribution to the use of the Thorpe terminus. The new company would also pay the cost of the connecting link via a swing bridge at Carrow. The sum returned would cover the previously reported overspend on land. The capital eventually authorised was £37,500 in shares and £12,500 in mortgage loans but in the event no part of this was used to subscribe for Norwich & Brandon shares. Rather part covered the previous overspending but the rest was retained to fund the proposed Yarmouth bridge notwithstanding the company's continued failure to obtain permission to build.

April 1844 saw much reporting of railway activity. There was the prospectus for the Lynn & Ely, nothing to do with the Yarmouth/Norwich and Norwich/Brandon companies, but their first Norfolk rival which took advantage of the rising enthusiasm for railways and the projected advance to Ely of the Eastern Counties to connect Lynn to the growing national system. The committee was composed chiefly of well known west Norfolk names, landowners and merchants, while the engineer was to be J.U. Rastrick who, it was said, was confident that the work, once started, could be completed within nine months. What the ancient port of Lynn probably needed even more than the direct London connection this project promised was a connection to the west and thus to the Midlands. A proposed branch of the Lynn & Ely from Magdalen Road near Downham to Wisbech was a first step in this vital direction but it was to be many years before a westward link was established north of Ely. Meanwhile the

Board of Trade inspector of railways, General Pasley, had been conducted over the Yarmouth/Norwich line on 12 April and pronounced himself satisfied. The grand opening was set for 30 April with regular passenger traffic to begin the following day.

Ceremonial openings were a standard feature of new railways in those years and Norwich, Yarmouth and the railway company combined to give the public and more particularly the principal citizens a memorable day out. A twelve carriage train left Norwich at eleven a.m. taking a large invited party and a brass band to Yarmouth. Stations at both ends and along the way were decorated with flowers and banners and another band met the train in Yarmouth at the end of the fifty minute journey. A cold collation was served at the station and carriages were laid on to take those who wished to the seaside. Meanwhile several hundred from Yarmouth travelled (paying fares) to Norwich for the day to visit the sights and particularly a flower show and the waterside meadows at Thorpe. The invited party, augmented with guests from Yarmouth, returned to Norwich at two p.m., the journey time cut to forty-two minutes. At four o'clock 150 guests were entertained to a grand dinner at the Assembly Rooms given by the contractors and presided over by Peto with numerous toasts but apparently few speeches. This was made up for the next day when a dinner was given for the directors by the shareholders and friends of the railway at the Victoria Hotel in Yarmouth.

All these events were reported at length in the local papers on the Saturday following. The *Mercury*'s article, a full front page including an

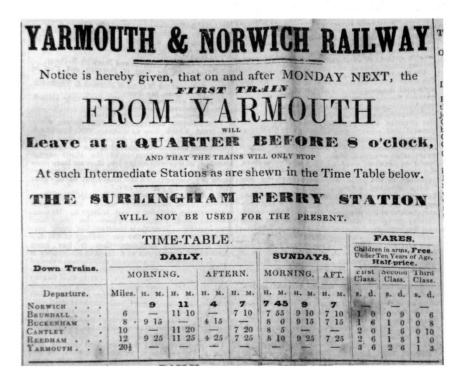

YARMOUTH & NORWICH RAILWAY

Notice is hereby given, that on and after MONDAY NEXT, the

FIRST TRAIN

FROM YARMOUTH

WILL

Leave at a QUARTER BEFORE 8 o'clock,

AND THAT THE TRAINS WILL ONLY STOP

At such Intermediate Stations as are shewn in the Time Table below.

THE SURLINGHAM FERRY STATION

WILL NOT BE USED FOR THE PRESENT.

Down Trains.		TIME-TABLE.								FARES. Children in arms, Free. Under Ten Years of Age, Half-price.		
		DAILY.				SUNDAYS.				First Class.	Second Class.	Third Class.
		MORNING.		AFTERN.		MORNING.		AFT.				
Departure.	Miles.	H. M.	H. M.	H. M.	H. M.	H. M.	H. M.	H. M.		s. d.	s. d.	s. d.
NORWICH . .		9	11	4	7	7 45	9	7		—	—	—
BRUNDALL . .	6	—	11 10	—	7 10	7 55	9 10	7 10		1 0	0 9	0 6
BUCKENHAM . .	8	9 15	—	4 15	—	8 0	9 15	7 15		1 6	1 0	0 8
CANTLEY .	10	—	11 20	—	7 20	8 5	—	—		2 0	1 6	0 10
REEDHAM . .	12	9 25	11 25	4 25	7 25	8 10	9 25	7 25		2 6	1 8	1 0
YARMOUTH . .	20½	—	—	—	—	—	—	—		3 6	2 6	1 3

illustration of Thorpe Station with Chalk Hill appearing like an Alp behind, was the more flowery, the reporters pulling out all their rhetorical stops as indeed did the various speakers at the Yarmouth dinner. The *Chronicle* was rather more sober and factual yet devoted even more space, giving a useful if incomplete history of the formation of the company and an extensive description of the line and stations. Both papers gave a detailed description of the electric telegraph system that was the pride and joy of the engineers.

The two towns had a new toy but without further connections it was only a toy. While there were four trains a day in each direction there was little point in encouraging goods traffic until there were better onward connections while a shortage of rolling stock and engines made for time-keeping failures. Moreover, though normal for the time, the third class accommodation was initially entirely open to the weather, which might be acceptable on a fine summer's day but hardly at other times. The shine soon wore off, but already, in April even before the opening, the Norwich & Brandon had obtained its Act of Parliament. That same session saw also an Act authorising the formation of the Eastern Union and its line from Ipswich to Colchester.

CHAPTER 4

The Norwich & Brandon Railway
and its rivals:
1844 and 1845

THE NORWICH & BRANDON RAILWAY seems to have had rather
less trouble than did the Yarmouth & Norwich in raising the initial
subscription on its projected capital of £380,000. Nationally railway
shares were becoming ever more desirable at this time although Norfolk
was as yet still reluctant to subscribe. The company's Act names only
twelve subscribers who were also the initial directors but judging from
those who subscribed the next year to a share issue for proposed branches
it would seem that northern and especially London interests were again
predominant while many shares were again taken up by the contractors.
Landowners were realising the many benefits a railway could bring and
there seems to have been no serious opposition to the Brandon line. Peto
later boasted that he personally had negotiated all the land purchase
contracts and that not once had it been necessary to go before a jury. The
engineering pair Stephenson and Bidder and the contractors Grissell &
Peto were again employed as they were on the Eastern Counties extension
coming north from Newport to join the Norfolk line at Brandon and on
their link from Ely to Peterborough.

Of the first directors four (Duff, Bolingbroke, Tyndale and Sir Edmund
Lacon) were on the board of the Yarmouth and Norwich while a
further two, J. E. Lacon and Edward Tootal were respectively treasurer
and secretary of that company. There were six new men, Samuel
Anderson, Robert Crosbie, R. W. Kennard, E. F. Maitland, Henry Wilson
and Captain Charles Wardell. Samuel Anderson, describing himself
as a merchant of 55 Upper Brook Street, was later a major subscriber
to the Lowestoft Railway; Robert Crosbie was from Liverpool and an
associate of George Stephenson; Robert William Kennard, ironfounder
and banker, was a director of the Northern & Eastern Railway; and
Captain Wardell was involved with and a substantial subscriber to a
number of Peto's projects. Nothing at all has been discovered concerning
Henry Wilson and of Maitland only his forenames, Ebenezer Fuller, and
his address at Park Place, Henley. Significantly Crosbie was at that time
a director (and deputy chairman) of the Eastern Counties as was Kennard

by virtue of his position on the board of the Northern & Eastern, while Samuel Anderson was later to be a director of the same company.

It may seem odd that the two Norfolk companies had not been amalgamated from the start but that was not how things were then done. Each company and line needed its own Act as did each extension or branch line built by an existing company. At this time it was thought easier to deal with lines piecemeal in their passage through Parliament and also easier to raise capital from differing interests if matters could be divided between separate organisations each apparently financially viable on its own. Only when the lines had been completed did all the problems of joint operation by competing or even by co-operative companies become evident. Even then it was more common at first to solve these problems by one company taking a lease over the lines of another and paying a rental, leaving the capital structures undisturbed, than by a full scale merger, although either required the authority of an Act.

Nevertheless, it must always have been the intention of the promoters to operate the Yarmouth & Norwich and the Norwich & Brandon as a single entity as the arrangements for the Carrow bridge and a shared station at Thorpe make clear. At the first shareholders' general meeting of the latter company in August 1844 amalgamation was already being discussed notwithstanding that it was only some weeks since the company had received its parliamentary sanction. The proposition was to form a new company that would issue one of its shares in exchange for each share in either of the old companies thus placing no premium on either. Bidder, though the engineer and not a director, presented the argument in favour.

Not all the shareholders present agreed. In particular Mr Yetts of Yarmouth, now a shareholder in both companies, was anxious that each should operate for a year independently to demonstrate its financial potential before merger terms were set. He was doubtful of the profitability of the Yarmouth & Norwich, especially as regards goods traffic, as he thought that coal traffic would continue to move by river. Bidder's counter argument was that without merger the position of the Norwich & Brandon was dangerous. Suppose the Yarmouth & Norwich were to merge with Ipswich's Eastern Union which had also received its Act in the recent session, was already building from Ipswich to Colchester, and was now proposing to build to Bury and Norwich? Another shareholder, Mr Joseph Lawrence, a London stockbroker whose name will recur, was strongly in favour of early merger. Yetts eventually divided the meeting on the resolution but found no support.

The meeting considered and approved plans to build branch lines from Dereham and Diss to join the main line at or near Attleborough. The latter point of junction was chosen, said Bidder, because Dereham would be brought that much closer to London than if connected via Norwich, while due to the easier topography the line Diss/Attleborough could be built and operated at half the cost of Diss/Norwich. He predicted that the branches could be built at £9,000 per mile and talked down the proposed Norwich branch of the Eastern Union. He felt the latter would do best to come as far only as Diss and there join the Norwich & Brandon's branch rather than run a line in direct competition. All experience showed, he said, 'that whenever traffic was subject to competition, it was not worth competing for.' Of course additional capital would be required and a figure of £190,000 was mentioned although in the following year a sum of £220,000 was authorised to cover just the Dereham branch and a late change of plan to divert the main line through Thetford.

In contrast to the delay that had occurred between formation of the company and the start of construction on the Yarmouth & Norwich, the land for the Norwich & Brandon had been provisionally contracted for even before the company's Act and construction began at once. According to a *Chronicle* report one thousand men were already at work near Ketteringham and in Norwich itself at the end of August 1844 while the labour force was expected to build swiftly to three thousand. With so many engaged on such a comparatively level line it is not surprising that it was completed and opened in less than one year. The main agent acting for Grissell & Peto was George Merrett who had occupied a similar position on the Yarmouth & Norwich and was later to take on maintenance of the completed lines.

When the Yarmouth & Norwich had opened in the previous April the affair of the Yarmouth bridge remained entirely unsettled. Unwilling to submit their passengers to tolls the railway company had opened their own ferry service between a basin dug next to their station and the town. Not surprisingly Cory lodged a Bill in Chancery hoping for an injunction but the case was referred to the Assizes in Norwich that August. There counsel for Cory argued successfully that Cory had not only the rights to his toll bridge but also sufficient rights to block any resuscitated ferry or competing bridge. The only case for the railway was that its ferry route was possibly outside the Bure itself and thus outside the area in which Cory's rights were exclusive.

A special jury had been empanelled but the judge, who was upset that the Court of Chancery had brought him into the matter at all, opined that whatever the decision reached the dissatisfied party would merely go back to Chancery and the whole procedure would be repeated. He therefore persuaded counsel for both sides to adjourn and reach a settlement, which they did, the jury being discharged with a guinea each for their trouble. What was agreed was that a new bridge would be built at the company's expense at a site to be agreed with a government surveyor. The necessary Bill would be promoted by Cory but his expenses would be paid by the company. The new bridge, which the company would maintain, and its approaches would be owned by Cory who would continue to collect the toll on one halfpenny per foot passenger. Goods, carriages and their drivers would cross free but the company would guarantee minimum tolls of £600 per annum. Passenger trains would not cross the bridge.

By the autumn the country's and more particularly stockjobbers' enthusiasm for new railways, probable and improbable, had gathered strength. Several were conceived in Norfolk and Suffolk although the majority of the 1844/45 crop never achieved birth or, if built later, followed a varied route. Apart from the proposals for branches of the Norwich & Brandon already referred to, those for which parliamentary approval was sought in the spring and summer of 1845 were:

Lines toward London and the south

The Eastern Union Railway

A line from Ipswich via the valley of the Gipping, Stowmarket and Diss to Norwich. Strong support was being given to this by a Norwich committee already dissatisfied with the performance of the Yarmouth & Norwich and the prospects for a London route via Brandon and Ely. This committee included Samuel Bignold, now a director of the Eastern Union, outgoing mayor William Freeman, T.O. Springfield, manufacturer and the leading Liberal politician, John Norgate, the wine merchant who had invested in the Yarmouth & Norwich, and Edward Willett who had previously given evidence in its favour. The majority of subscribers to this line, to the Ipswich & Bury railway and to a further branch proposed to Harwich were from the Ipswich area but there were a several from Norfolk too. However the majority of the money was promised from Yorkshire where there must have been most active brokers while the contractor Thomas Brassey was promising some ten per cent of all the money to be raised.

The Ipswich & Bury Railway

A route between those two towns in connection with the Eastern Union branch as above. The Eastern Union and the Ipswich & Bury were jointly administered and later merged. From Ipswich to Haughley, close north of Stowmarket, the routes of the two proposals were identical.

The Norwich Direct

The initial proposal was a line leaving the Northern & Eastern at Elsenham near Stortford and running cross-country via Bury St Edmunds to join the Norwich & Brandon at Thetford. The possibility that this line would be built may have been the original cause of the late diversion of the Norwich & Brandon to run through Thetford rather than, as originally planned, to bypass it to the north.

The engineer was to be the famous Sir John Rennie, the secretary and chief promoter was Bury solicitor Francis Eagle, and the capital to be raised was £760,000. The subscription list was packed with the names of residents of Bury and the surrounding area promising relatively modest sums but little money was to come from elsewhere and clearly the project had not attracted support from substantial financiers. However there were two surprising individual subscriptions, £100,820 from Yarmouth solicitor C.J.Palmer and £98,840 from Norwich barrister, Whig politician and incoming mayor Sir William Foster Bt. It is hard to believe that such vast sums could have been promised from the individual fortunes of either gentleman and one must presume that both were acting as front men for clients or for some syndicate.

The Diss & Colchester

This was to run from the Eastern Counties near Colchester via Hadleigh, Needham Market, Stowmarket and Eye to Diss where it would join the proposed Norwich & Brandon branch. It avoided Ipswich and was later justified as an act of self defence to stop or cripple the Eastern Union's Norwich extension. In addition the company projected and filed plans for a branch from Diss via Harleston, Bungay and Beccles to Reedham, reaching the latter by a junction with the Lowestoft Railway (see Chapter 7) at Haddiscoe. Also mentioned was a possible branch to Bury. This was a joint proposition backed by the Eastern Counties and the Norfolk. George Stephenson, Adam Duff, Robert Crosbie, Samuel Anderson, Charles Tyndale, Charles Wardell and Robert Kennard were all on the provisional committee as was a new name John Bagshaw, a former East India merchant (director of the Eastern Counties and later MP for Harwich). Robert Stephenson and George Bidder were to be engineers while the bankers were Denison, Hayward & Kennard of London and Liverpool. The company, when formed, hoped to raise £850,000 capital. The subscription list suggests that the promoters had canvassed their business friends looking for individual subscriptions of £2,000 or more of which there were over fifty. Peto and Grissell had offered £40,000 each as had Francis Mills, already a shareholder in the two Norfolk lines. Other significant but lesser subscribers were George Merrett, Edward Ladd Betts, engineer and later Peto's partner (and brother-in-law), George Carr Glynn, banker and director of the London & Birmingham, and the committee members already named.

Eastern Counties extension to Bury

This was a formalisation of the earlier Braithwaite proposal to build from Colchester to Bury. From Colchester to Hadleigh its route was identical to that of the Diss & Colchester with which it was presumably in alliance. Thereafter it turned westward to Lavenham. Simultaneously the Eastern Counties filed a proposal for a line from Cambridge to Bury to form a complete route Cambridge to Colchester, thus to forestall any similar cross country route by the Ipswich & Bury.

The Diss, Beccles & Yarmouth

This was a scheme got up by a consortium of London financiers led by a lawyer Wilkinson looking to take advantage of the dissatisfaction by many Yarmouth merchants with the route being constructed via Norwich and Ely. At the Diss end it looked forward to the Eastern Union scheme to advance from Ipswich via Diss to Norwich and was at this time definitely unfriendly to the Norfolk lines although not connected financially with the Eastern Union. The engineer was Captain Moorsom who had worked under Stephenson on the London & Birmingham. Much of the proposed route was similar to though not identical with that planned for the Reedham branch of the Diss & Colchester except that at its eastern end it crossed the Waveney near Haddiscoe and then terminated in Yarmouth South Town on the west side of the Yare near the town bridge. The subscription list looks thin with the larger subscriptions, none vast, from London but some local interest, mainly from Beccles, a few from Norwich and just one from Yarmouth.

Lines to the north and west

The East Dereham & Norwich (otherwise the 'Dereham Direct')

A proposal for a line to run from near St Stephen's Gate in Norwich through Earlham and Bowthorpe and thence roughly along the line of the Tud valley to Dereham. Some detail of the support and subscriptions is given below.

The Lynn & Ely

The prospectus for this project, to connect Lynn to London via the Eastern Counties at Ely, was referred to in the previous chapter. The initial capital requirement was £200,000. Substantial financial support for this and the next, associated, line came from west Norfolk, and especially from Lynn itself, with numerous smaller subscriptions, some as low as £50. However total subscriptions from outside the area, largely from Lancashire and the north west, were even greater including £13,750 from H.C. Lacy of Manchester who became chairman.

The Lynn & Dereham

Closely related to the Lynn & Ely with which it was to share a terminus at Lynn and with which it eventually merged, this line was to run via Narford and Swaffham and hoped to effect an end-on junction with the Dereham Direct with which however it had no financial connection although originally a common chairman of the provisional committees in Lord Sondes. The capital requirement advertised was £330,000.

The Lynn & Hunstanton

While advertised in October 1844 and sharing committee members with the Lynn & Dereham, it was nearly twenty years before this railway came into being. This may be because the initial capital requested was £500,000 which, if not a misprint, came to about £40,000 per mile for a line to a place that then was no more than a village.

The Wells & Thetford

This rather unlikely route was originally a landowners' project by north Norfolk landowners to develop that area and capitalise on the dubious prospect of Wells as a major port. The line was to run south from the Wells quayside via Fakenham and Dereham. A connection to London via the Norwich Direct was looked for by the extension to Thetford. The provisional committee included lords Leicester, Hastings (the former Sir Jacob Astley) and Sondes and also a Keppel, a Lee Warner and a Fitzroy from the local gentry. The engineer was one James Green with the better known James Rendel as consultant. The capital looked for was £400,000.

The foregoing list omits a Yarmouth & Norwich Bill to authorise an extension from Thorpe across the Wensum into Norwich to a station near the junction of Rose Lane and King Street in order to satisfy critics who objected to the considerable distance that goods and livestock must be moved in order to reach the existing terminus. The economy of keeping its termini outside Yarmouth and Norwich had been the principal reason why the Yarmouth & Norwich had been cheaper to build than the failed East Anglian proposals; now the virtues of termini in the towns themselves were becoming appreciated. The Bill also proposed a capital increase of £40,000 to pay for the extension notwithstanding that shareholders had earlier been given a figure of £12,000 as the likely cost. Perhaps because it was thought that the generality of shareholders would be taken aback at the scale of capital now required the subscription list was made up of Peto, George Stephenson, Kennard, Duff, Tyndale and Wardell plus just two other investors, each promising £5,000. However this project, while approved in Parliament, was later expanded in connection with developments for further lines to the west and north dealt with in the next chapter. When these were cancelled and the Norwich Paving Committee declined to authorise and find funds for an associated widening of London Lane the extension and station were cancelled too and the associated capital never raised.

The list also excludes the Lowestoft Harbour & Railway Company, a creation of Peto who had purchased the Somerleyton estate close to the town in October 1844 and also the rights to Lowestoft harbour and the river navigation between Reedham and Lowestoft. The railway, from Lowestoft to join the Norfolk line by a bridge at Reedham, was always intended, at least by Peto, to be leased to the Norfolk Railway by which it was ultimately acquired. Important as an adjunct to the Norfolk system yet thought by some to be a millstone around its neck, the early history of this considerable enterprise will be treated in detail in Chapter 7. There was also a proposal for a short branch to Loddon from Reedham put forward originally in the name of the Yarmouth & Norwich but dependent on the bridge to be built at Reedham by the Lowestoft.

Throughout late 1844 and into the spring of 1845, while the only railways actually building in East Anglia were the Norwich & Brandon and the Eastern Union's main line south from Ipswich, arguments raged over which of the new proposals should be supported, which opposed. First there were local meetings, editorials and correspondence in the press, then arguments before the Board of Trade, and then hearings before parliamentary committees. If all else failed it was possible to petition the House of Lords. And there were no doubt the unreported discussions and deals within and between boardrooms.

Looking at matters from the probable point of view of the combined boards of the companies soon to become the Norfolk Railway, it was clear that their own propositions, the branches to Dereham and to Diss, must have first priority for support. But the first board minutes of the Norfolk Railway the following summer show that almost as much attention had been paid to promoting the Diss & Colchester and to its extension from Diss to Reedham, proposals that had been submitted for approval to the shareholders of both Norfolk companies (in February 1845) as had been the proposition that the Norfolk should lease or buy the Lowestoft line once it was completed. Substantial sums it later appeared had been paid out in respect of the Diss & Colchester proposals which it was hoped would be partially met by the Eastern Counties.

Most likely the directors would originally have taken a neutral stance as regards the Norwich Direct. If it succeeded it would be a useful brake on the ambitions of the Eastern Counties although they must of necessity co-operate with the latter to achieve their route to both London and the Midlands. The line itself, though creating the shortest route London/ Norwich yet proposed, looked expensive to build and, passing mainly through empty and far from level countryside, unlikely to pay. However by the spring of 1845 Peto had contracted (provisionally one must suppose) to build the Thetford to Bury section and the Norfolk had agreed to lease and operate it. The Lynn & Ely can have been of little concern to them but the Lynn & Dereham pre-empted a route they might have liked for their own extension at a later date.

The Wells & Thetford, if taken seriously, might have seemed a threat. The Norfolk's own branch to Dereham was planned to extend later to Fakenham, Wells & Blakeney on more or less the same route as the Wells & Thetford. There must have been negotiations between the companies which persuaded the Wells company to cut short its proposed line at Dereham and some Norfolk shareholders to promise substantial subscriptions. It rather appears from the subscription lists that the more aristocratic members of the committee were reluctant to put up any money at all. Instead what might be called the Peto connection, including Peto himself, Grissell, Robert Stephenson, Betts, Wardell, Tyndale and Duff together were promising some £35,000 of about £120,000 subscribed. The rest was to come from numerous merchants, shipowners, small tradesmen and farmers of Wells and its surrounding area.

The real threats came from the Eastern Union with its proposed extension to Diss and Norwich, and the two lines whose promoters hoped to join that extension, the Yarmouth/Diss and the Dereham Direct. The latter was to start close to the proposed Eastern Union terminus in Norwich at Victoria Gardens by St Stephen's Gate. If it was built the Norfolk's own Dereham branch would lose much of its purpose. The Waveney valley proposal largely duplicated the Diss & Colchester's Waveney valley route but allowed Yarmouth a route south that would run entirely outside the Norfolk system. The main line from Ipswich to Norwich, a substantially shorter route to London than via Brandon, seemed likely seriously to damage the Norfolk whose best hope, should the Diss & Colchester venture fail, was that the Eastern Counties, controlling both routes at the London end, would favour the Brandon route as providing a greater proportion of Eastern Counties mileage.

The Norfolk papers that autumn and winter are thick with references to railway projects, advertisements, letters to the editors, editorials and accounts of meetings. Every possible combination of railways was canvassed while all the major Norwich traders joined in a petition to the mayor in support of a direct line south from Norwich to Ipswich and thence to London. The main controversy in Norwich concerned the Dereham branch of the Norfolk system versus the Dereham Direct. In contrast to the Norfolk line, the Dereham Direct was very much a local product although closely linked by common committee members to the Eastern Union. Six of the provisional committee listed on the prospectus were well known Norfolk or Norwich men, county magnates Lords Sondes and Bayning, banker Major General Sir Robert Harvey, Samuel Bignold and manufacturers Edward Willett and T. O. Springfield. Their engineer was William Gravatt whose initial plan was simply for a line from St Stephen's Gate past Chapelfield in Norwich along the higher ground south of the Tud valley through the parishes of Earlham, Bowthorpe, Colton, and Mattishall to a terminus on the west side of Dereham. At some later time it was hoped to go on to Fakenham and Lynn. The capital required was £150,000 on which a return of nine per cent was confidently predicted.

The subscription list is impressive and demonstrates that middle class Norwich had found a cause to support. One hundred and twenty-three individual subscriptions have been traced of which only four are from outside East Anglia and only

PROSPECTUS
OF THE DIRECT
East Dereham and Norwich Railway,
With a view to its immediate extension from Dereham to Lynn Regis, with a branch to Fakenham.
CAPITAL £150,000,
Divided into 7,500 Shares of £20 each.
Deposit £1 per Share.
Provisional Committee.

Rt. Hon. the Lord Sondes
Rt. Hon. and Revd. the Lord Bayning
R. W. Collett, Esq. M.P.
The Mayor of Norwich
The Sheriff of Norwich
J. Hopkinson, Esq. London
Rev T. Paddon, Mattishall
J. F. Bacon, Esq. London
T. Utton, Esq. Broome
Wm. Grounds, Esq. Hoe, near Dereham.

Major-Gen. Sir R. J. Harvey, C.B. K.T.S.
T. T. Berney, Esq. Morton Hall
S. Bignold, Esq. Norwich
T. O. Springfield, Esq.
J. Wright, Esq.
Edwd. Willett, Esq.
Thos. Browne Evans, Esq. Enstone Hall, Oxfordshire

with power to add to their number.
Bankers.
The Commercial Bank of London.
Messrs. Harveys and Hudsons, Norwich.
Engineer.
Wm. Gravatt, Esq. F.R.S.

seven from outside Norwich and its immediate surrounds. Two of the latter are from J. C. Cobbold and George Josselyn of Ipswich, directors of the Eastern Union which was looking to connect its Norwich branch end on to the Dereham line. Harvey (£4,000), Bignold (£1,500) and Willett (£4,000) of the committee (the two latter also Eastern Union directors) came through with subscriptions. Neither peer thought it necessary to do so. Other large subscribers were A. A. H. Beckwith, Norwich solicitor (£5,000) John Norgate, wine merchant, (£4,500) and John Wright, manufacturer (£4,000). The average subscription promised was just under £1,000; the range was from £6,000 (William Stitt Wilson, a Norwich banker and yet another Eastern Union director) down to £100. Apart from twenty-three persons describing themselves as gentlemen, there were from the Norwich area nineteen solicitors, ten merchants, nine grocers, six manufacturers, four bankers, four ironmongers, three each of drapers, druggists, surveyors, brewers, surgeons, booksellers and accountants, two each of wine merchants, jewellers, builders and yarn agents, and twelve others, the sole representatives of their trade or profession.

A public meeting in Norwich in early October 1844 had debated the respective merits and demerits of the competing lines. One speaker was Nathaniel Palmer, the Yarmouth Recorder who had played such a prominent part four years before in the debate on the East Anglian proposal. Samuel Bignold suggested that Palmer had by his opposition prevented that line from being built but Palmer denied this. His understanding was that the solicitors had been bought off. In any event he was now a supporter of railways but warned the meeting to consider the public

An agggressive but abortive proposal by the Dereham Direct

good and not allow their pockets to be picked by engineers and solicitors. The solicitor for the promoters of the direct line, unabashed by Palmer's warning, spoke at length on its merits. It was, he said, the initiative of local landowners, the money market had been consulted, and one quarter of the shares were still available for local subscription (although the prospectus had asserted that subscription in full was 'already provided for').

The Norwich & Brandon line from Dereham was now to come to Wymondham rather than to Attleborough and to curve towards Norwich rather than towards London. Despite this alteration those opposing thought that if this were the only line built it would be detrimental to the Norwich cattle market by the castle. Either the animals would suffer because they must be driven up the steep hill from Thorpe or they would be sent to other markets altogether. Those against the direct line pointed out the failure to provide a connection to Yarmouth and the consequent necessity to haul coal up from the river by horse and cart. The general difficulty of having multiple stations around the city without rail connections was aired.

These objections may have been why, when the plans for the direct line were filed the following month, there had been added connections to the Norwich & Brandon and a branch to the River Wensum at New Mills. There were two plans for the former which may have been in the alternative or which may both have been intended to allow for connections to east and west. One ran in a large curve westward from Chapelfield through Eaton to head ultimately east, joining the Norfolk line in Lakenham opposite Trowse Newton. The other left the main line at Bowthorpe in an easterly direction, ran downhill rather steeply to cross the Yare into Colney, and then south to Cringleford, joining the Norfolk line after a westerly curve near Keswick Bridge. The New Mills branch ran almost precipitously downhill from near Chapelfield to the river.

Once the plans for all the railways going before Parliament in the coming year were available a flood of notices of objection and of meetings of objectors filled the papers. Typical was a notice of objection to the Lynn & Dereham in early January describing the project as unnecessary and uncalled for and without any prospect of return to which were appended nearly one hundred names of owners and occupiers of land on the proposed line. Naturally there was a counterblast soon after pointing out how much the price of coals in Swaffham would lower if the railway were to be built. A public meeting in Yarmouth later that month is of especial interest. This featured the findings of a committee to consider which of the routes now proposed would be best for the town. The three lines under consideration were the Norwich Direct, the Moorsom route along the Waveney to Diss, and the competing Stevenson route to Diss via Reedham. Each (assuming either the Eastern Union built to Diss or the Diss & Colchester gained approval) could provide Yarmouth with a shorter route to London than would the route via Brandon, Ely and Cambridge.

Map A2   East Anglia, Actual and Proposed Lines January 1845

Shows the position as at January 1845 after plans and Bills had been filed with Parliament prior to the forthcoming legislative season.

This, the beginning of the Railway Mania, shows the multiplicity of lines projected in East Anglia at a time when the only operational lines were the Eastern Counties to Colchester, the Northern & Eastern to near Newport and the Yarmouth & Norwich. Building were the Norwich & Brandon (shortly to be merged into the Norfolk Railway with the Yarmouth & Norwich and shown as such on the map), the extension of the Northern & Eastern by the Eastern Counties to Brandon and the Eastern Union line between Ipswich and Colchester.

Lines and proposals westward of Cambridge and King's Lynn are not shown except for the Peterborough/Ely branch of the Eastern Counties on which, though authorised, construction had barely begun. Lines and proposals southward of Suffolk are shown only so far as they were or might have been relevant to developments in Norfolk and Suffolk. The boxed area is shown in more detail in Map B on Page 221.

Key

———————	Completed lines	/ Jointly
— —	Lines under construction	// In competition
- - - - - -	Proposed lines	

Abbreviations of railway names

D&C	Diss & Colchester	L&D	Lynn & Dereham
DB&Y	Diss Beccles & Yarmouth	L&E	Lynn & Ely
ECR	Eastern Counties	LR&H	Lowestoft Railway & Harbour
ED&N	East Dereham & Norwich	N&E	Northern & Eastern
	(Dereham Direct)	ND	Norwich Direct
EUR	Eastern Union	NR	Norfolk Railway
I&B	Ipswich & Bury	W&T	Wells & Thetford

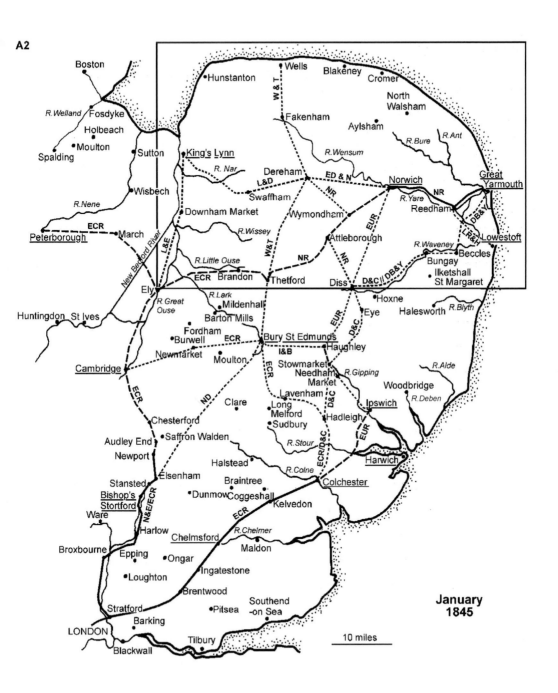

January
1845

10 miles

There were strong feelings evident and the report of the meeting is studded with interjections of 'hear, noise, confusion', 'yes, yes', 'no, no' and even 'no, no, immense confusion, uproar'. Recorder Nathaniel Palmer, yet again a protagonist although he protested that he held no shares, was the main supporter of the Norwich Direct notwithstanding this meant Yarmouth reliance on the Norfolk system as far as Thetford. He believed this route would pay much better than the other two. He contradicted opinions that it passed through barren countryside and would suffer from severe gradients. There was no water carriage to compete with since the line left the last navigable river at Norwich. The Marquis of Bristol himself had subscribed £2,000, which showed, he said, that the line was of benefit to Bury. He made no reference to the huge subscriptions in the name of Charles Palmer and Sir William Foster but warned, correctly, that most railway projects were undercapitalised, did not allow for working capital requirements, and so were unlikely to provide the returns originally hoped for.

The supporters of the Moorsom line protested that they had not had time to bring either Wilkinson or Moorsom to the meeting. One speaker asserted that no railway that ended on the west bank could be of benefit to Yarmouth's harbour, being away from the main quays and in any case outside the town limits. The Mayor, presiding, said that he had originally supported Moorsom but did no longer since Yarmouth should not favour a route that was mainly for the benefit of Ipswich. A supporter of Moorsom contrasted his route with Stevenson's equivalent since Stevenson and Peto would always favour Lowestoft. At this Peto himself spoke, to say that he would ensure that Lowestoft harbour tolls were never less than those of Yarmouth. It is difficult to say from the report of the meeting what was the conclusion but dislike of Stevenson, Peto, Lowestoft and the Brandon route to anywhere appears to have predominated and the majority were prepared to support both the Norwich Direct and the Moorsom Waveney line. However there were others present who merely advocated delay in choice or a course of leaving it to the railway promoters themselves.

The Board of Trade had created a special department to vet railway schemes even before they were submitted to Parliamentary scrutiny with the intention of weeding out projects not apparently in the immediate public interest or creating too great a strain on the capital markets. The results of their deliberations were published late in January 1845. The Board gave its unqualified approval to only three of the schemes, the Ipswich & Bury (at this stage and for a further two years still a separate company) line to Bury, the Eastern Union line to Norwich, and the Lynn & Ely. They had 'no objection' to the Lowestoft line or the Loddon branch or to the diversion of the Norwich & Brandon to take in Thetford. They advised a postponement of five lines, the Diss, Beccles & Yarmouth, the Dereham Direct, the Reedham branch of the Diss & Colchester, the Lynn & East Dereham and the Dereham branch of the Norwich & Brandon.

Five were rejected as unnecessary altogether, the Diss & Colchester main line, the Eastern Counties branches from Colchester and from Cambridge to Bury, the Norwich Direct, the Diss branch of the Norwich & Brandon and the Wells & Thetford.

The Board's report favoured the Eastern Union route to Norwich as it ran via Ipswich which none of the others did. Ipswich had the advantage that London could be reached by sea as well as by land and this factor should serve to limit the fares that the Eastern Union could charge between Colchester and the metropolis. At 113 miles the line was not the shortest from Norwich to London: the Norwich Direct would be only 110 miles but served virtually nowhere en route except Bury which needed no lines other than that proposed from Ipswich. But Norwich certainly needed an alternative route to the roundabout line to London via Brandon and Cambridge. None of the three lines proposed to reach East Dereham was objectionable in itself but the Board doubted the traffic estimates that had been submitted and advised that it would be best to wait until the trunk lines had been completed before building any of them. It seemed unlikely that there would ever be enough traffic to justify both the Dereham Direct and the Dereham branch of the Norwich & Brandon. The Board considered there to be no real need for a Waveney Valley route at the present time. Yarmouth now had one railway and, being itself a port, was already in sea communication with all other ports.

This was a considerable victory for the Eastern Union/Ipswich & Bury as all the possible rival routes to Bury and to Norwich were refused and a defeat for the Norfolk Railway in that all its proposed branches or associated lines were either turned down or to be postponed. The *Mercury*, which now strongly favoured the Eastern Union route (the proprietors and those of the *Chronicle* had subscribed for shares) was triumphant. It advised those potential companies whose projects had not met with approval to wind up and return the capital so far subscribed while, where a project was merely to be postponed, the capital receipts should perhaps be deposited with trustees. Nobody took this advice. Even where a project was indeed pursued no further and its deposits returned the subscriptions received were often little more than enough to pay lawyers and engineers for work already performed. If there was more another railway would be only too glad to accept the money as a deposit on its own shares. In any case the Board of Trade's rulings were advisory only. They did not prevent any promoters from proceeding with a Parliamentary application and nearly all did so. Their first step was normally to get up a substantial local petition explaining the great necessity for their particular railway.

At about this time three other potential railways in East Anglia began to advertise in the hope that knowledge of their projects would influence the Parliamentary decision makers notwithstanding that they had no prospect of appearing themselves before Parliament until the following year. These were the Essex & Suffolk (capital required originally £750,000, later upped to £1,000,000: engineer J.W. Bazalgette – later the chief engineer for the London sewers), the Chelmsford & Bury (capital required £750,000: engineer originally R.W. Thompson, later Robert Stephenson, although he afterwards withdrew) and the Ipswich & Yarmouth (capital required £700,000: no engineer advertised but later James Rendel, better known for harbour works, and N. Beardmore). Each of these was anxious not to be lost sight of as they were in some degree potential competitors of the Eastern Union.

The Essex & Suffolk was a line proposed from Thetford via Bury, Lavenham and Long Melford to the small Essex port of Maldon with branches to Chelmsford and to Clare and with two connections to the Eastern Counties mainline south and west of Colchester. Its advertisement suggested that the ultimate destination northwards was not merely Thetford but the port of Lynn. It assumed, accurately but somewhat presumptuously, that the Norwich Direct would never be built and proposed to reserve a proportion of the shares for Norwich Direct subscribers. The Chelmsford & Bury proposal was for a direct link between the named towns with connections to the Eastern Counties but hinted at wider ambitions for extensions to Maldon in the south and Thetford in the north. A curiosity is that neither of these railways, covering virtually the same ground, deigned to mention the other. The Board of Trade report had mentioned the Chelmsford & Bury and, without expressing any opinion on its merits, had observed that, in contrast to the Norwich Direct, it at least would provide rail communication for Sudbury, Halsted and Braintree.

The Ipswich & Yarmouth was to run close to the Suffolk coast via Woodbridge and Halesworth. Its first advertisement made much of the strategic military value of a coastal line to rush troops to any threatened point. Less stress was placed on the vulnerability of such a line to being cut by an invading army. More relevant to the impending Parliamentary campaign was its admission that if the Eastern Union line to Norwich were approved then their own would most probably never be built. Meanwhile the Diss, Beccles & Yarmouth advertised to announce an arrangement

Norwich and Dereham
RAILWAY.

THE Provisional Committee have the pleasure to announce to the Shareholders and the Public, that they have directed the necessary proceedings to be adopted for an early application to Parliament, in the next Session, for the making of this important Line of Railway.

Having received, from nearly all the influential Landowners, and from the Occupiers on the Line, and also from the Inhabitants and Traders of the Ports of Yarmouth and Lynn, as well as of the City of Norwich, the strongest assurances of support—and the Norfolk Railway Company having, in order to give every facility to the obtaining the sanction of the Legislature to the project, agreed with the Committee to petition Parliament in favour thereof, and to use their influence in support of such application, the Committee entertain no doubt whatever of ultimate success. (3956

EDWARD WILLETT,
Chairman.
Railway Offices, Market-place, Norwich,
August 9th, 1845.

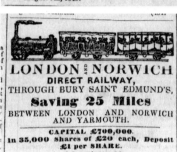

LONDON and NORWICH
DIRECT RAILWAY,
THROUGH BURY SAINT EDMUND'S,
Saving 25 Miles
BETWEEN LONDON AND NORWICH AND YARMOUTH.

CAPITAL £700,000.
In 35,000 shares of £20 each, Deposit £1 per SHARE.

Wells and Thetford
RAILWAY.
Capital £400,000, in Shares of £25 each.
DEPOSIT £1. 10s. 0d. PER SHARE.

Provisional Committee.
The Right Hon. the Earl of Leicester, Holkham
The Right Hon. the Lord Hastings, Melton Constable
The Right Hon. the Lord Sondes, North Elmham
The Hon. and Rev. Thomas Keppel, Warham
Sir Roger Martin, Bart. Burnham Hall
The Rev. Daniel Henry Lee Warner, Walsingham Abbey
Colonel Fitzroy, Sennowe Lodge
Thomas Truesdale Clarke, Esq. Swakeleys, Middlesex
[With power to add to their number.
Acting Engineer.—James Green, Esq.
Consulting Engineer.
James Meadows Rendel, Esq. F.R.S.

WELLS & THETFORD RAILWAY.

Having made a careful and minute examination of the country through which this Railway is intended to pass, I am enabled with confidence to report that it is particularly favourable for such a work; there are consequently no engineering difficulties; the land throughout the line will be obtained at a much lower rate than the average cost on similar works; the earth in excavation is uniformly favourable, and the buildings will be of a moderate and comparatively inexpensive character; in short there is no part in the whole Line which can be considered as heavy.

THE
WAVENEY VALLEY,
OR
Thetford, Bungay, and Yarmouth
RAILWAY,
With a Branch to Halesworth.

(Provisionally Registered pursuant to the 7th and 8th Victoria, cap. 110.)
Capital £450,000 in 18,000 Shares of £25 each.

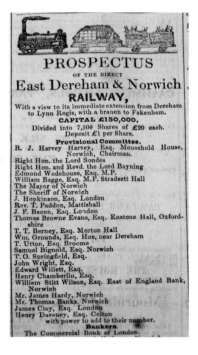

A selection of advertisement headings from 1844 and 1845

reached with the Eastern Union whereby the latter company would lease their line once completed at four per cent on the cost of construction plus half any surplus profits, a fairly standard arrangement at that period. The committee of the Lynn & Dereham advertised their scorn for the Board of Trade's view of their line. They intended to petition Parliament. Their traffic estimates had been prepared by a 'well-known traffic statist' and the opposition to their line was solely from a competing navigation (the Nar).

At the half year meeting of the Eastern Counties in February 1845 the chairman announced that progress towards Brandon was good and declared a modest dividend. There was heavy criticism from members of the company's poor record of profitability. Comparisons with the London & Brighton Railway were made with shareholders objecting to what seemed to them excessive costs of working on the Eastern Counties which came to nearly fifty per cent of receipts from fares compared with a much lower percentage on the Brighton line. Robert Stephenson, acting as consultant engineer, explained that the rate to consider was that of operating costs per mile of track; here the figures of the two railways were approximately the same. The London/Brighton route had the advantage of lucrative passenger traffic while East Anglia, with its economy based on agriculture and lacking heavy minerals to transport, was not good territory for a really profitable railway (something they might have thought about rather earlier). The Yarmouth & Norwich shareholders, meeting the same month, received a dividend at the rate of five per cent per annum for the half year. On the markets their shares stood at a large premium, as did those of the unfinished Norwich & Brandon, but then at this stage pretty well all railway shares, even the Eastern Counties, were quoted over par. At the Yarmouth & Norwich meeting it was explained that as yet freight traffic had not been pursued pending the opening of the connection to Brandon but had briefly been stimulated by a stoppage of river navigation for some days due to frost.

Once again shareholders heard that progress was being made toward building a bridge and extending their line onto the Yarmouth quays but following the compromise with Cory a new Act would be required. In fact an entirely new plan was being submitted and the meeting was declared special to approve the proposals. Bidder was now planning for the new line to diverge well before the river and cross north of Cory's bridge with

Norfolk Railway.

OPENING OF THE LINE.

THE Public are respectfully informed, that this Railway will be opened, in connexion with the Cambride Line,

ON WEDNESDAY,

July 30th,

FOR PASSENGER TRAFFIC

TO AND FROM

LONDON, NORWICH,

AND

YARMOUTH.

FISH will be conveyed to LONDON by the **6.30 p.m.** Up Train from Yarmouth, and arrive in London at **3.30 a.m.**

Trains for Heavy Goods will be put on shortly.

By Order, RICHARD TILL, Secretary.

one fork going to the beach and another curving in a wide sweep to run to the quays at their southern end. The cost would be some eight thousand pounds. A crossing near the station would have been preferred but the Yarmouth Harbour Commissioners had refused permission for a bridge there other than a swingbridge since the lower portion of the Bure was used at times as a refuge for wherries in bad weather. A swingbridge was deemed impractical on engineering grounds. In other respects it was as usual proving difficult to satisfy everyone in Yarmouth at once. Meetings there during 1845 rejected both of alternative proposals put forward by the railway for new stations, one close to the Bure on the east bank, the other half way along the proposed new line from the Bure to the sea.

By April Parliamentary committees were hearing evidence for and against proposals. The crucial Eastern Union Bill early ran into trouble when Bidder, for the Norfolk, was able to demonstrate certain serious errors in levels. The fact that the surveyors had been ordered off neighbouring ground by an indignant landlord, Mr Edwards of Old Newton, before it had been possible to complete their work was no excuse. Apparently Mr Edwards had admitted them until, as a lawyer asserted, 'they had brought poachers and other disreputable people with them'. No doubt these were just the staff holders of the survey party but the damage had been done.

The Wells & Thetford had now reduced itself realistically to the Wells & Dereham but this attenuation proved fatal as the hurriedly rehashed proposals failed to pass the rigorous detailed requirements of Parliamentary standing orders. The Dereham Direct also failed standing orders but advertised that as the failure was not on merit they would try again the following year.

Much attention was given to the Norwich Direct. Barrister Gurdon, so active in 1841, now acted for a number of companies including the Norwich Direct and on its behalf made an impassioned plea in which he bewailed the plight of maltings at Stortford that were closing due to a lack of connection to the farms of North Essex and Suffolk. Then the company, taking a hint from the committee, announced that they were contemplating a merger with the Chelmsford & Bury. However counsel for the latter denied that any such merger could take place. Much detail was given before the committee as to the likely costs of the twelve mile section Thetford to Bury that was to cost £179,000 exclusive of land. The land requirement was estimated at 150 acres that were expected to cost between ten and twelve shillings per acre, 12 acres per mile and 7 acres for stations. The Norfolk Railway was prepared to lease this section at the 'usual terms' of four per cent on cost and half the profits. The cost for the whole line, that could be built without either tunnels or level crossings, was given as £685,000.

There was a ding dong battle between advocates for the rival lines to Dereham. Even though the direct line had fallen at an earlier fence extensive evidence in its favour was called in support of its assault on the other line. Gravatt, giving evidence, estimated the cost of the main line as £140,937, the New Mills branch as £10,757 and a branch to Fakenham as £24,170. The route had been surveyed for double track but would initially be single. There would be ten bridges and sixteen culverts. Rail was allowed for at ten pounds per ton, a figure frequently quoted in railway costings at that time. The steepest gradient on the main line would be 1:55 for a distance of 5½ chains but 'by an arrangement with the Eastern Union this objectionable inclination will be avoided'. Peter Bruff, engineer for the Eastern Union, gave evidence in support of Gravatt. The New Mills branch, with a maximum gradient of 1:48, thought too steep for locomotives, would be worked by horse power.

The distance by the direct route was only fifteen miles to Dereham whereas the line by Wymondham would be twenty-two, nearly fifty per cent longer. Evidence in favour of the direct line was called from several tradesmen. One draper of Norwich said most of his stuff came from Huddersfield of which much arrived via London and then by sea to Yarmouth. Norwich, he said, strongly favoured the direct line for communication with the north but also because of their customer base in Dereham and the north east of the county whose business it was suggested would otherwise be diverted west and to London. Hardly more convincing was the Colney cattle dealer who maintained that 'the circuitous line from Dereham through Wymondham would not convey the slightest benefit on Norwich, but the direct rail was calculated to be very advantageous to that town'. Another witness explained that if animals came to Trowse they would have to be walked up the hill while passengers would have to walk through the cattle market to reach the centre.

The Wymondham route had its Dereham supporters who were concerned less about access to Norwich than with freight rates from London as for example a Shipdham ironmonger, a Hardingham miller and a Dereham woolmerchant, the latter's exports to France going via London. There were others from Swaffham and Fakenham. Lacking a railway, iron requirements in central Norfolk came from Birmingham to Hull and thence by sea to Lynn or Yarmouth. Lord Hastings maintained that communications from northern Norfolk to London were of more importance than with Norwich. Previously a supporter of the Wells & Thetford, he regretted its loss but said that the Dereham/Wymondham route would do nearly as well. Lord Wodehouse of Kimberley, through whose lands a section of the line would run, was said also to be in favour. Compared to all this the evidence concerning the Diss branch proposal was meagre. A Diss merchant said that locally most merchants and tradesman would much prefer the Attleborough connection to Yarmouth, the Midlands or London than any connection to Ipswich but would have no objection to having that as well. The main upshot of the Parliamentary procedures was that the Board of Trade advice was overturned in three cases. The Lynn & Dereham succeeded in its appeal and was allowed to proceed as was the Dereham branch of the Norwich & Brandon. On the other hand the Eastern Union branch to Norwich was turned down, not it seems because of errors in its plans, but on a technicality where it failed to comply with parliamentary standing orders. Nevertheless it was clear that it would be back in the following year. The only others successfully through Parliament were the Ipswich & Bury, the Lynn & Ely and the Lowestoft although the Loddon branch from the latter was, by decision of the promoters, not to be proceeded with.

Advertisements for the opening of the line through from Norwich to London via Brandon, Ely and Cambridge began to appear in June 1845 with the planned date of 1 July. There were to be seven trains a day from Norwich to Ely of which five would go on to London, the fastest scheduled to take no more than four hours. A note in the Lynn paper that month said that it was now quickest for passengers from Lynn to go to London by coach to Peterborough and thence by the recently opened rail link to Blisworth to join the London/Birmingham line but as soon as the new line opened to Brandon a journey through there would be quicker still. However there were delays in the opening, that eventually took place on 30 July. The cause was a slippage on the embankment near Ely that meant that the Eastern Counties section could not open and the Norfolk directors agreed it inexpedient to open their own line until there was a through route.

The grand opening ceremonies took place at Cambridge on a scale that put the festivities at Norwich the year before somewhat in the shade but although the newspaper prose was as purple as before the coverage in the Norwich papers was somewhat less, no doubt due to the distant location. Ceremonial trains ran to Cambridge from both London and Norwich, the band of the Coldstream Guards travelling on the former in open carriages and playing at the intermediate stops. There were cannon, flags and cheers at Ely and Cambridge to greet the train and at Cambridge a grand luncheon for eight hundred in a marquee serenaded again by the band. Present along with the directors of the two companies, local MPs, mayors and other worthies, the contractors, the engineers (but not Stephenson) and the masters of several Cambridge colleges were the bishops of Ely and Norwich and their retinues. And of course there were speeches. The clergy were especially complimentary to the spiritual care that Grissell and Peto had taken of their workforce. The Dean of

Cambridge Station

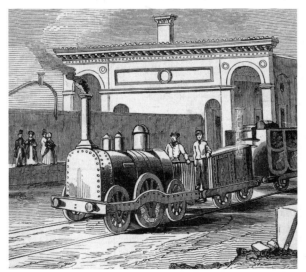

Ely referred to the 'judicious and liberal arrangements for their moral instruction and religious welfare' while worthy of all praise had been the 'peaceful and sober conduct of the labourers'. The Bishop of Norwich heaped praise on Peto for his care of his men with religious books distributed and schools for the men themselves and their children. He did not mind that Peto was a dissenter ... but hoped that he would die a churchman! (In Grissell's later reply to a toast he pointed out that he at least was a churchman and not all credit

should go to the dissenters.) There were many other speeches but the reporter was obliged to admit that due to heavy rain beating upon the tent not all could be heard. It was not just the worthies who were entertained. At Cambridge and elsewhere along the line the entire workforce was given lunch at the expense of the contractors.

So Norwich at last had its connection to London (which Ipswich did not have for another year) although Yarmouth awaited the bridge over the Wensum required at Carrow to connect the two Norfolk lines. This bridge was for that time a fairly major work of engineering as it was required to swing clear of the navigable channel. Designed by Bidder, the principal sections were cast at Grissell's Regent Ironworks in London and brought to Norwich by sea and river. Worked manually, it was over one hundred feet long, the opening section comprising two equal spans of forty four feet although only one of the passages beneath was navigable. Not complete until December it was declared safe after an inspection by General Pasley and two days later a crowd of city worthies were invited to observe the first train crossing, an occasion that brought forth a new effusive editorial in the *Mercury* on the virtues of progress. The bishop was of the party but the town council were in session and declined to attend.

CHAPTER 5

The Norfolk Railway, its ambitions, friends and competitors: 1845 to 1847

IN THE SPRING OF 1845 a merger bill had been put forward and duly passed through Parliament authorising the formation of a new company, the Norfolk Railway itself, on terms similar to those outlined at the Norwich & Brandon meeting a year before. The respective authorised share capitals of the two constituent companies when the Bill became an Act in July were Yarmouth & Norwich, £187,500 (£150,000 original and £37,500 authorised in 1844) and Norwich & Brandon £600,000 (£380,000 original and £220,000 extension capital authorised in 1845 in connection with the Dereham branch and Thetford diversion although only a deposit had so far been paid on the latter shares). The combined authorised capital of £787,500 was to form the initial share capital of the Norfolk which would also take upon itself the two companies' creditors and considerable loan obligations. With the authority of Parliament shares in the merging companies simply became shares of the Norfolk without the need for any share exchange.

From the formation of the new company so much was going on concerning railways in East Anglia that it will be less confusing to consider events from the summer of 1845 to the spring of 1847, the least financially troubled period in the life of the Norfolk Railway, in separate chapters. Thus the remainder of this chapter is concerned with the company's strategy and ambitions for further development and also, so far as they concerned the Norfolk, with those of its allies and rivals. Chapter 6 deals with the operation of the railway, with its actual expansion up to 1847 and the means whereby that was financed, while Chapter 7 is concerned with the related developments at Lowestoft.

The initial board consisted of Adam Duff, chairman, Sir Edmund Lacon, Horatio Bolingbroke, Captain Charles Tyndale, Samuel Anderson, R. W. Kennard, E. F. Maitland and Captain Charles Wardell, all of whom had been directors of the Norwich & Brandon while the first four named had been directors also of the Yarmouth & Norwich. Richard

Till, who had latterly been treasurer of the Yarmouth & Norwich, was appointed secretary and general manager. Shareholders at the company's first general meeting held in August 1845 urged the directors to strengthen the board and shortly after they co-opted George Stephenson (although he seldom attended meetings), Captain Lawrence, both formerly on the Yarmouth & Norwich board, and Sir William Foster, the Norwich barrister who had subscribed so handsomely to the Norwich Direct earlier in the year. Except that Captain Lawrence left after a year, having sold his shares, and was replaced by Mr Henry Newbery, a Lancashire silk manufacturer, there were no changes in this enlarged membership until 1848. Main board meetings were frequent but irregular, as were those of the traffic committee. Minutes for both these survive but unfortunately not those for the finance committee whose task it was to raise money, to meet the constant demand for loan repayments, and to pay the steady stream of bills. Nor are there any surviving annual reports, shareholders minutes or half-yearly accounts amongst the company's own records before 1852. However summaries of reports, accounts and proceedings at meetings can usually be found in one or other of directors' minutes, newspaper reports, specialist railway magazines (particularly the *Railway Times*) or *Bradshaw's Railway Shareholders' Guide*.

At their August meeting the shareholders endorsed the agreement by

NORFOLK RAILWAY.---OPENING OF THE LINE.

☞ The Public are respectfully informed, that this Railway will be opened, in connexion with the Cambridge Line, on **Wednesday, the 9th July,** for Passenger Traffic and Light Goods, to and from London, Norwich, and Yarmouth.

The Trains will run as follows :—

DOWN.	a. m.	a. m.	a. m.	a. m.	p. m.
	H. M.	H. M.	H. M.	H. M.	H. M.
FROM LONDON..............	—	—	8 . 0	11 . 30	5 . 0
" ELY	—	7 . 30	11 . 5	1 . 50	7 . 50
" NORWICH	8 . 30	10 . 45	2 . 15	4 . 30	11 . 0
ARRIVING AT YARMOUTH ..	9 . 15	11 . 30	3 . 0	5 . 15	11 . 45

UP.	a. m.	a. m.	p. m.	p. m.	p. m.
	H. M.	H. M.	H. M.	H. M.	H. M.
FROM YARMOUTH	5 . 30	9 . 30	3 . 15	6 . 30	8 . 30
" NORWICH	6 . 45	11 . 0	4 . 30	8 . 0	9 . 15
" ELY	9 . 0	12 . 50	6 . 45	11 . 30	—
ARRIVING AT LONDON	12 . 30	3 . 30	10 . 0	—	—

Fares for Stopping Trains.

LONDON.	1st Class.	2d Class.	3d Class.
TO NORWICH	£1 2 6	£0 16 0	£0 10 6
TO YARMOUTH	1 6 0	0 18 6	0 11 9

Fares for Quick Trains.

LONDON.	1st Class.	2d Class.	
TO NORWICH	£1 7 0	£0 18 0	
TO YARMOUTH	1 10 6	1 0 6	

the predecessor companies to lease or buy the Lowestoft Railway and application was to be made to Parliament in 1846 for permission to do so; it had proved impossible to gain parliamentary permission for this during the last session as insufficient notices had been given. Effusive compliments were given to Grissell & Peto for their speed and economy in building the line to Brandon but the costs of that extension were now being quoted as £12,000 per mile rather than the £10,000 at one time promised. A brief summary was heard concerning hostile lines and their success or failure in the legislative process. As to future developments the chairman explained to shareholders that Stephenson and Bidder had made an inspection of the whole region adjacent to the line. Definite proposals for branches would soon be put to the proprietors. All shareholders were to be paid five per cent interest on their capital for the preceding half year in lieu of a dividend.

By the end of September the board's plans for the coming legislative season comprised the following additional lines:

	Estimated cost £
Wymondham/Attleborough to Diss and thence to Eye and Stowmarket, there to join the Bury & Ipswich Railway. A replacement for and extension of the failed Norwich & Brandon branch of 1845.	160,000 (to Diss only)
Reedham via Beccles, Bungay, Harleston and Diss to Thetford. This was the Norfolk's plan to provide a shorter link to London for Yarmouth, bypassing Norwich. This replaced and extended the Diss & Colchester subsidiary proposal of 1845.	560,000
Dereham to Fakenham & Wells with extension to Blakeney, a bid to secure central and northern Norfolk traffic. Replacing the cut down Wells & Thetford project of 1845.	Not estimated

for all of which it was thought a further one million of capital might do. There was also the ongoing saga of the Yarmouth bridge.

Earlier the disappointed subscribers to rival railways in Norwich and Yarmouth had been holding meetings and debating whether they might not yet petition the House of Lords in favour of their rejected choices. At the Norwich meeting Willett and Harvey, both amongst the promoters of the direct line, repeated points made before. The Wymondham line was too long and hence slow, the Norfolk Railway directors were contemptuous of Norwich, and Norwich trade would be lost to other towns and centres. It was true that Norwich had been slow to invest in railways but now it was prepared to do so. Opening the Wymondham line would be disastrous for the city. The direct line would eventually provide better communication to the Midlands and north via Lynn than the roundabout way via Brandon, Ely and Peterborough that was all that the Norfolk could offer.

There was opposition. Mr Sultzer, (Norwich manufacturer and an investor in the Norfolk) could not understand in what way the Wymondham line would harm Norwich. He thought the reason so much play was made of the assertion was that the meeting was composed almost entirely of subscribers to the Dereham Direct. Mr Bolingbroke, now a Norfolk Railway director, said that it was all Norwich's fault. He had tried to persuade many now present (including Willett) to invest in the Norwich & Brandon but without success. The Norfolk was doing its best. For example arrangements had been made not to favour Yarmouth goods in preference to the water route if they were to be carried further inland. Now the Norfolk was proposing to bring its terminus into the city at a cost of £40,000. Norwich did petition in the form of an objection to the Wymondham & Dereham branch though to no avail as it was ruled out of order, the city having no standing in the matter. But something was achieved as the Norfolk's counsel said that his client would not oppose the direct line the following year. Indeed the Norwich & Brandon had agreed to support the Dereham Direct in the following Parliamentary season and proposed to lease the line if built.

The Yarmouth meeting was bitter as it was not understood why the Diss, Beccles & Yarmouth had withdrawn its proposals at a late stage. It appears that a landowner near Burgh Castle, Mr Ferrier, Yarmouth coroner and earlier a supporter, had raised a late objection. There was suspicion of treachery as the Norfolk had then persuaded the Diss & Yarmouth to join it at Reedham rather than seeing it cross the Waveney and run straight to Yarmouth. What was going on? Some said they had been humbugged by Wilkinson and his fellow promoters. As to the Norfolk's branch to Dereham, a handbill was being circulated saying that it would ruin the river trade and put all the boatmen out of work. However it had to be admitted that at a meeting the year before Yarmouth had declared itself against the Dereham Direct so should it be supporting a petition in its favour? In any case, said one speaker, the Wymondham line would be built and the direct line probably never, and in any case, if built, it was for the benefit of Norwich and what did that city care for Yarmouth?

From further speeches it is evident that the overriding feeling was hostility to the Norfolk line for supporting and developing Lowestoft plus disappointment that the Waveney route had been dropped (even though there had been virtually no Yarmouth subscribers). Many speakers accused others of conflicting interests and probably all were correct at least in this. When a vote was taken on a resolution to lodge a petition in favour of the Dereham Direct a show of hands was inconclusive and the room physically divided to ascertain where was the majority. This was in favour of a petition but then the mayor as chairman declared that such a resolution was ineffective as the question of such a petition was not on the agenda. When the mayor and others then left a rump remained and resolved to draw up a petition nevertheless that would be presented in the House of Lords by Lord Sondes on their behalf.

A day or so later Wilkinson of the Diss, Beccles & Yarmouth attended a further Yarmouth meeting to canvass support for a new try the following year. Ten thousand pounds had been spent on the 1845 failure and it must be worth while making a further effort although this time Beccles would be left out and Harleston included so obviating a double river crossing. He thought the Eastern Union would certainly be able to advance as far as Diss next year and would in all probability lease and operate the Waveney line if built. There was much discussion on freight rates for fish. The Yarmouth fish merchants were angry that the rates proposed by the Norfolk for fish were many times those they had scheduled for other goods such as sugar. Would Wilkinson pledge a maximum rate for fish? He would not and hedged, referring to Parliamentary control of rates, but still had support from some Yarmouth men who were so angry with the Norfolk that they were prepared, at least in the heat of the moment, to support the Waveney line even if its rates proved higher. Advertisements in August for this line suggested that it would now run additionally from Thetford to Diss and that there would be a branch from Bungay south to Halesworth but by October these further proposals had been dropped.

The ensuing year was the most manic period of the Railway Mania of the 1840s. From early in 1845 advertisements had been appearing in the Norfolk papers of railway projects to be submitted to Parliament in 1846. By the autumn the advertisements were in full flood. Not all related to lines that were planned to reach the area; some, ignored here, optimistically supposed that Norfolk investors might have money to spare for railways further afield. Three tables analyse the proposals affecting East Anglia other than those of the Norfolk itself:

A   Railways in which the Norfolk planned to take an interest or might have found it useful to do so;

B   competing lines in the Norfolk area; and

C   (contained in Appendix I) other lines that were designed to have some connection to the area from the west.

Omitted here and on the maps are any railways in Essex, Hertfordshire or Cambridgeshire planned by or in connection with the Eastern Counties or the Eastern Union but not affecting the Norfolk even indirectly. The former company, which elected George Hudson as its chairman in October, had numerous proposals nearer London in Essex (where it and the Eastern Union were engaged in a battle to decide which, if either, should be building a line to Harwich) Hertfordshire and Cambridgeshire. The Eastern Union was promoting lines along the Suffolk/Essex border.

Table A   Norfolk Railway allies and investments

Railway	Line	Comments
Dereham Direct Share capital £150,000	Norwich to Dereham (see Chapter 4)	The Norfolk now proposed to lease this re-engineered version if built.
North of Norfolk Share capital £170,000	Norwich to Cromer, later restricted to Norwich to Aylsham and North Walsham	The Norfolk proposed to lease this also and were to supply three directors.
Ipswich, Norwich & Yarmouth Share capital £1,200,000	Ipswich, Woodbridge and Halesworth, dividing at Ilketshall St Margaret, one branch via Beccles to join the Lowestoft near Reedham, the other via Bungay to join the Norfolk close south of Norwich.	Previously Ipswich & Yarmouth. The Norfolk expected to construct the northern sections of this jointly and to have joint running powers. It would also be taking a direct share interest. It may ultimately have planned to lease the whole line.
Thetford, Bury & Newmarket Share capital £400,000	Per title	The promoters advertised that the Norfolk was to lease the Thetford/Bury section and take a large share interest too.
Newmarket & Chesterford Share capital £350,000	From Newmarket to Chesterford on Northern & Eastern line (north of Stortford).	
Spalding & Brandon Share capital £500,000	Per title	In connection with the proposed Grand Union Railway from Nottingham to Spalding.

The figures for share capital here and elsewhere are taken from advertisements except in one case where the deposit paid into Chancery with the subscription agreement suggests a capital materially higher. In most cases the deposits suggest that the subscription lists on which the deposits were paid were incomplete or at least totalled less than the advertised capital requirement.

The strategy of the Norfolk directors at this stage was:

a) to obtain control over at least part of the route to the south via Stowmarket;

b) to construct a better route to London: for Yarmouth by building from Reedham, via Diss to Thetford and for both Yarmouth and Norwich thence over leased or allied lines to Bury and from there over other possible lines whether by Newmarket or by Lavenham and Sudbury to join the Eastern Counties nearer to London than at Brandon. Alternatively to achieve the same objective by co-operating with the coastal line, if necessary leasing it;

c) to own or control all branches north of their main line in Norfolk itself; and

d) to find if possible a better route to the west than via Ely/Peterborough

In the proceedings connected to the presentation of a petition by the city of Norwich to the House of Lords counsel for the Norfolk had stated that it would not oppose the Dereham Direct in the following year if it tried again. Now it appears the Norfolk had gone much further as the route had been largely resurveyed and re-engineered at their insistence by engineer A. A. Borthwick replacing Gravatt. The connection to the Eastern Union near St Stephen's Gate was now to be replaced by a terminus in the angle between King Street and Rose Lane to be shared with the already approved Norfolk extension from Thorpe station across the Wensum. The Colney/Keswick and New Mills branches had vanished. This adoption of the Dereham line by the Norfolk may have been what prompted the Eastern Union to promote a competing line to Dereham via the Wensum valley.

The route of the line from the Rose Lane terminal would run north (Prince of Wales Road had not then been built) through the lower Close, over what are now the Norwich School playing fields, close to the Great Hospital and then across the Wensum into Pockthorpe and to Heigham before climbing to higher ground through Earlham and Mattishall and along the south side of the Tud valley to Dereham where a junction with the Norfolk's new branch was now planned. An alternative connection to the Norfolk main line, perhaps to be built if the route through the Close was forbidden, was via a loop from Heigham inside the present outer ring road, crossing the Hingham, Newmarket and Ipswich roads and the Town Close to Lakenham, joining the Norfolk at Trowse Millgate. The North of Norfolk line was to share the new Rose Lane station and the Dereham line as far as Pockthorpe and then run via Catton, Spixworth and Crostwick to Coltishall and thence along the Bure valley to Buxton where it split into lines to Aylsham and to North Walsham. Its alternative connection to the Norfolk was a line from Thorpe station taking a tight curve to run along Riverside and then to Pockthorpe.

The Ipswich, Norwich & Yarmouth, was an updated version of the coastal line proposed earlier in the year by a group led by the Earl of Stradbroke (lord lieutenant of Suffolk). The western branch to Norwich, sometimes referred to as the Norwich & Halesworth, was a new feature of the proposal and was the subject of a separate Bill. By September 1845 Adam Duff and Captain Tyndale from the Norfolk board had joined the provisional committee and a capital contribution of £137,500 was to be subscribed by the Norfolk. In January 1846 a deposit on this investment of £19,000 had to be found and was borrowed temporarily from Gurneys Bank at a ruinous rate of interest.

The Thetford, Bury & Newmarket and the Newmarket & Chesterford together promised Norwich a line to London very nearly as short as the Norwich Direct. The former had a committee also headed by the Earl of Stradbroke and including one Right Honourable and four Honourables as well as the mayor of Yarmouth. Its principal engineer was to be Robert Stephenson. Preference was to be given to subscriptions from subscribers to the Norfolk, the Norwich Direct, the Ipswich, Norwich & Yarmouth and the North of Norfolk. Previous suggested routes skirting Newmarket had fallen foul of the racing lobby but these promoters maintained that their lines would be clear of all the training grounds and gallops. The Norfolk board minutes refer to 'an association' with this company and the intention to lease was later confirmed but there is no certainty that they had promised to subscribe.

The Grand Union Railway, intended to run from Nottingham to Spalding, was planning to extend further from there to meet the Norfolk. The Norfolk board was willing to meet half the capital cost of £500,000 for the Spalding/Brandon section but had first to consult the Eastern Counties under the terms of the agreement with them for the joint London line. Notwithstanding that it would compete with the Eastern Counties' Ely/Peterborough line that company seems not to have objected, perhaps because at the other end of its proposed system the Grand Union was to enter into arrangements to reach Lancashire with Hudson's other main interest, the Midland Railway. Adam Duff, Captain Wardell and Captain Tyndale of the Norfolk board joined the provisional committee. The engineers were to be Stephenson and Bidder plus Charles Vignolles for the Grand Union, but only the latter's name appears on the survey. The Grand Union was also projecting a line from Spalding via Sutton Bridge to King's Lynn there to join the Lynn & Ely.

Table B   Competition and other lines directly affecting East Anglia

Railway	Line	Comments
Ipswich & Bury	Extension, Haughley to Norwich	This proposal was the successor to the Eastern Union proposal of the previous year.
Essex & Suffolk Share capital £1,000,000	Maldon to Thetford, with hints of extension to Lynn	Apparent total duplication with Chelmsford & Bury.
Chelmsford & Bury Share capital £1,000,000	Maldon to Bury plus extension to Thetford	Apparent total duplication with Essex & Suffolk.
Norwich Direct Share capital £760,000	Now Walthamstow to Thetford via Dunmow and Bury, and with hints of extension to Lynn	Ceasing to be a serious proposition due to divisions amongst subscribers.
Waveney Valley Share capital £450,000	Yarmouth to Diss (now omitting Beccles). Branch Bungay to Halesworth	Revival of previous season's project. Possibly to be leased by the Eastern Union.

Railway	Line	Comments
Norwich & North West Norfolk Share capital £250,000	Norwich to Dereham via Wensum valley, with branch to Fakenham	Eastern Union backed alternative to the Dereham Direct. Being surveyed by Joseph Locke.
Lynn & Dereham	Dereham to Norwich extension	Duplication of Dereham Direct and North West Norfolk. Apparently never reached stage of survey.
Lynn & Fakenham Share capital £300,000	As title 'with extension to Holt' and hints at Cromer	Another project associated with Lynn & Ely and Lynn & Dereham.
Ely & Bury Share capital £300,000	As title	Closely associated with Lynn & Ely and Lynn & Dereham, with same chairman and several Lynn names on its committee.
North Coast Continuation Railway Share capital £100,000	Reedham, Acle and North Walsham	Advertised itself as 'in conjunction with North of Norfolk' but there appears to have been no connection.

The Ipswich & Bury line from close north of Stowmarket directly towards Norwich was of course the nemesis stalking the Norfolk. Their only hope of averting its approval was the promotion of their line to Diss and Stowmarket so replacing it with mileage of their own. To achieve that they would need to show that their indirect line would be substantially easier and quicker to build than would its more direct rival.

Neither the Essex & Suffolk nor the Chelmsford & Bury were any threat to the Norfolk which might have been happy to see either succeed. Indeed when the Norfolk's line Diss/Thetford was proposed it was the Essex & Suffolk with which they contemplated joining. However when that company first approached them they responded coolly, probably uncertain of the reaction of the Eastern Counties and later became more interested in a route via Newmarket. In August 1845 an announcement by the Essex & Suffolk reported that not only had they hoped to merge with their rival but also a joint negotiating committee, five a side, had actually been set up. However, although the talks had led to an agreement between the two parties, the Chelmsford team had agreed only by a majority and when the proposals were put to the Chelmsford subscribers they had been rejected. As a result three of the Chelmsford negotiating group had resigned as had their engineer and one of their firms of lawyers. The response from the Chelmsford a month later was an announcement of their intention to build, in addition to their main line to Thetford, a branch from Lavenham to Stowmarket. This, in conjunction with the Waveney Valley line and the Eastern Union, would make, they said, their line the shortest to London for both Norwich and

Yarmouth. Although the Norfolk eventually declined an interest in either by late October Adam Duff and Captain Tyndale had joined the Essex & Suffolk committee.

The Norwich Direct appears to have been dissolving in confusion. Mr Eagle, secretary and chief promoter, was putting forward an extensive revision of the former proposed route through Essex with a new route into London via Great Dunmow, Ongar and Walthamstow and a promise of a London terminal of its own in Tottenham. He had assembled a revised committee that included a few well known East Anglian names such as Lord Alfred Hervey MP, Captain the Hon E.T.Wodehouse, W.H.Windham of Felbrigg and Sir William Foster, now a Norfolk director. Eagle's advertisements spoke also of northward extensions through Thetford to Lynn, branches from Bury to Diss and from Thetford to Swaffham and even the use of the atmospheric system of propulsion shortly to be installed by Brunel so disastrously on the South Devon Railway. However simultaneously another provisional committee of subscribers was placing advertisements proposing a return of subscribers' money and warning the public to take no notice of advertisements issued by Mr Eagle. As an alternative to repayment the Thetford, Bury & Newmarket had agreed to issue their scrip in exchange for scrip in the Norfolk Direct.

There was much support in Yarmouth for the Waveney Valley line that had replaced the Diss, Beccles & Yarmouth of the previous year but at the same time much suspicion of the London promoters and their chairman Mr Wilkinson due to the circumstances of their previous failure. At a Yarmouth meeting in early October called by the mayor, Wilkinson admitted that at a late stage in the parliamentary proceedings in the summer they had been persuaded to come via Reedham due to problems with a landowner on their planned route east of the Waveney near Burgh Castle. Now they had learnt better, had brought in a number of Yarmouth men as members of the committee and had resurveyed their line, now excluding Beccles. He denounced the Ipswich, Norwich & Yarmouth proposals as not in the interests of Yarmouth and the Norfolk plan for a line from Diss to Reedham as an unnecessary duplication of his own proposals and not a serious proposition. A vital factor in the new proposals was the Eastern Union's advance (under the auspices of the Ipswich & Bury) from the south and its informal undertaking to lease the completed line.

Those representing the fish merchants at the meeting strongly supported the line as a shorter route to their chief markets while others preferred it out of jealousy of Lowestoft which port it seemed to them the Norfolk favoured. As one asked, why on earth had the Norfolk leased the Lowestoft line ... £5,000 a year to get the trade of Lowestoft when they could have had the Yarmouth trade for nothing? Was it because Mr Peto had leased an estate at Somerleyton, and that therefore he must have a railway and had fathered it upon them? The Norfolk could be beaten and Mr Cory had done it. But others were more cautious; the Norfolk might prove best in the end. Should not matters be left to the promoters without involving the town as a whole?

There were now at least ten influential Yarmouth persons on the provisional committee of the line including shipowner George Danby Palmer, fish merchant Robert Hammond, and a Mr Samuel Paget. These three had apparently become railway enthusiasts and their names can be found on the management committees of two other proposals of that year for lines in Lincolnshire, in both cases along with Wilkinson. Perhaps because of their support the meeting ended with resolutions signed by the mayor to the effect that Yarmouth did not have an adequate rail connection, the Brandon route being too long and with an inadequate Yarmouth terminus, that the Norfolk should not be attempting to monopolise the town's communications with its Reedham to Diss route, that the Waveney line was the best option and that the town would support it.

It is perhaps appropriate to mention at this point one further proposed line in the Waveney valley, a line from Lowestoft to Beccles. It might have been thought that this, which could have connected to the Norfolk's Reedham to Diss or to the Waveney Valley or even to the Ipswich & Yarmouth, would have been supported by the Lowestoft company or the Norfolk itself. However, although Peto was the principal subscriber, there is no mention of it whatever in the minutes of either company and he appears to have been on what lawyers term 'a frolic of his own'. It followed more or less exactly the line of the later project of the 1850s (see Chapter 12) including a swing bridge over the junction of Lake Lothing and Oulton Broad at Mutford Lock. At any rate, while it went before Parliament, it was withdrawn there by the promoters without any evidence for or against being adduced.

The Norwich & North West Norfolk, also known as the Wensum Valley line, was the Eastern Union's puppet and its response to the defection of the Dereham Direct into the Norfolk camp. Surveyed by Locke it followed a considerably less direct line to Dereham making use of the easier gradients of the river valley. Its terminus in Norwich was to be close to river level at Coslany Bridge. From there it was to go through Heigham, past Hellesdon mill, via Costessy, Attlebridge, Lenwade and Lyng to Elsing. Here it forked with one line curving south into Dereham and the other north, still in the Wensum valley, past North Elmham and Ryburgh to Fakenham. A line from Dereham ran north to merge with the Fakenham branch. It does not appear to have planned for a junction at Dereham but, otherwise unconnected to any other railway, a branch from Heigham curved sharply south and climbed steeply to reach St Stephen's Gate more or less on the abandoned site of the Dereham Direct and in a position to connect end-on at Victoria Gardens to the Eastern Union line from Ipswich when eventually built.

Map A3   East Anglia, Actual and Proposed Lines 1846

Shows the position as at January 1846 after plans and Bills had been filed with Parliament prior to the forthcoming legislative season.

The Railway Mania is now in full swing and East Anglia is criss-crossed with railway projects. However during 1845 all that has actually been completed is the line from Norwich to London via Brandon, Ely and Cambridge. Building of the associated lines to be operated by the Eastern Union and the Ipswich & Bury is proceeding apace and a start has been made on the two lines south and east from King's Lynn.

Lines and proposals westward of Cambridge and King's Lynn are not shown except for the Peterborough/Ely branch of the Eastern Counties, still building, and the abortive plan for a connection westward from Brandon to Spalding and thence to the Midlands. Lines and proposals southward of Suffolk are shown only so far as they were or might have been relevant to developments in Norfolk and Suffolk. The boxed area is shown in more detail in Map B on Page 221.

Key

————————	Completed lines	/ Jointly
— — —	Lines under construction	// In competition
- - - - - -	Proposed lines	

Abbreviations of railway names

C&B	Chelmsford & Bury		LR&H	Lowestoft Railway & Harbour
D&C	Diss & Colchester		N&C	Newmarket & Chesterford
E&B	Ely & Bury		N&H	Norwich & Halesworth
E&S	Essex & Suffolk		NCC	North Coast Continuation
ECR	Eastern Counties		ND	Norwich Direct
ED&N	East Dereham & Norwich		NN	North of Norfolk
EUR	Eastern Union		NR	Norfolk Railway
I N&Y	Ipswich, Norwich & Yarmouth		NWN	North West Norfolk & Norwich
I&B	Ipswich & Bury		S&B	Spalding & Brandon
L&B	Lowestoft & Beccles		SV	Stour Valley
L&D	Lynn & Dereham		TB&N	Thetford, Bury & Newmarket
L&E	Lynn & Ely		WV	Waveney Valley
L&F	Lynn & Fakenham			

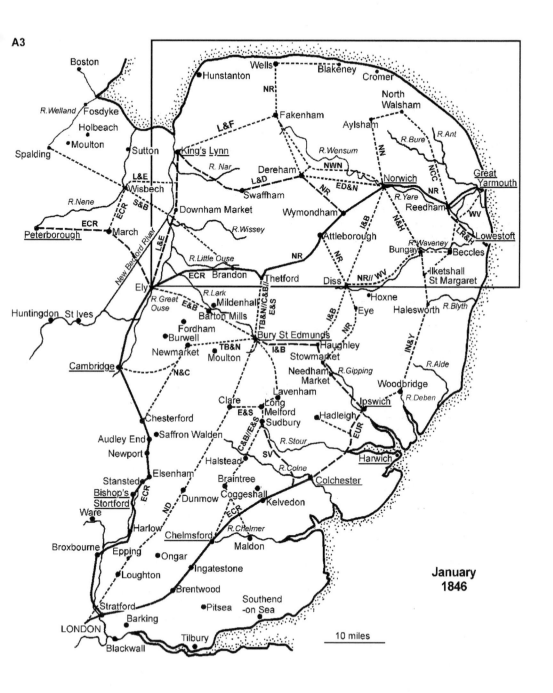

A3

Boston

R. Welland Fosdyke
Holbeach
Moulton
Spalding
Sutton
Wisbech
L&E
S&B
ECR
R.Nene
ECR
Peterborough
March
L&E
New Bedford River
Ely
R. Great Ouse
Huntingdon St Ives
E&B
Fordham
Burwell
Newmarket
Cambridge
N&C
Moulton
TB&N
Chesterford
Audley End
Saffron Walden
Newport
Halstead
Stansted
Bishop's Stortford
ECR
Ware
ND.
Harlow
Broxbourne Epping
Loughton
Stratford
LONDON
Barking
Blackwall
Tilbury

Wells
Hunstanton
Blakeney Cromer
NR
North Walsham
Fakenham
Aylsham
R.Ant
R.Bure
L&F
R.Wensum
NN
NCC
King's Lynn
R. Nar
Dereham
NWN
Great Yarmouth
L&E
L&D
ED&N
Norwich
NR
Swaffham
R.Yare
WV
Downham Market
Wymondham
Reedham
R.Wissey
I&B
N&H
LR&H
Lowestoft
Attleborough
R.Waveney
Beccles
R.Little Ouse
Bungay
NR
ECR Brandon
Thetford
Diss
NR//WV
Ilketshall St Margaret
Mildenhall
Hoxne
R.Lark
TB&N/C&B//
Eye
Halesworth
R.Blyth
Barton Mills
E&S
I&B
NR
Bury St Edmunds
Haughley
I&B
Stowmarket
IN&Y
Needham Market
R.Gipping
R.Alde
Lavenham
Woodbridge
Clare
Long Melford
E&S
Ipswich
R.Deben
C&B//E&S
Sudbury
EUR
Hadleigh
R.Stour
SV
Harwich
R.Colne
Braintree
Colchester
Elsenham
Dunmow Coggeshall
Kelvedon
ECR
Chelmsford
R.Chelmer
Maldon
Ongar
Ingatestone
Brentwood
Southend -on Sea
Pitsea

January 1846

10 miles

AMBITIONS, FRIENDS AND COMPETITORS   83

The initial list of provisional directors included Edmond Wodehouse MP of Thorpe, William Wilshere MP for Yarmouth (who was also on the committee of the Waveney Valley), J.C.Cobbold, two other railway directors from London, and thirteen others, all with Norwich or Norfolk addresses including John Sultzer of Norwich, an investor in and formerly a supporter of the Norfolk group. A month later the list had been augmented by four new names, all directors of other railways, actual or proposed. Such cross connections between railways were becoming common in 1845, the most extraordinary observed in advertisements in the Norfolk papers, although having no East Anglian connection, being the Erewash Valley Extension & Rochdale, Blackburn & East Lancashire Junction Railway which boasted a huge committee of whom over half had disclosed connections with other railways, fifty-nine different lines being referred to in the prospectus including several in Ireland and one in France. One of the ninety-two members was the ubiquitous Mr Wilkinson of the Waveney Valley.

The three projects connected with the Lynn based lines to Ely and Dereham (which in 1847 were to merge as the East Anglian Railways), an extension to Norwich, a line to Fakenham, and a line to Bury, probably never raised the initial subscriptions required and the two first never reached Parliament in 1846 or ever. Those East Anglian lines that were built were undercapitalised and were in no position to carry out the expansion plans implied by these proposals although the advertisements and prospectuses were as ever optimistic and the directors looked forward to connections westward to Spalding.

The last item on the list, the North Coast Continuation line, carried no conviction even in its most persuasive advertisement that referred to the 'well known intention of the Government to encircle the island with a continuous coast line' and assured the readers that 'a thoroughly practical engineer' had been secured and that a 'powerful committee' was forming in London. Later a large committee was named that included five respectable Norfolk residents from the area to be traversed but also many from London, most of whom were directors of other railways. The consulting engineer was to be J.U.Rastrick, who was also named for the Ely & Bury, and the acting engineer was one William Thorold of Norwich. All in all this appears to have been a prime example of a speculator's line for which there was no demand but whose shares when still partly paid might go to a premium giving a quick profit to those subscribers who sold out early. In this case it is doubtful if the initial subscription list was filled and the project is not heard of after 1845.

East Anglia already looked forward to a connection to the west via the Eastern Counties line from Ely through March to Peterborough that was now under construction while Peterborough was connected to the Midlands by the London & Birmingham branch from Blisworth. These existing or authorised links did not discourage promoters in the heady atmosphere of 1845 from planning more, and it must be admitted that some better route was desirable. The list in Appendix I includes all the railways (except the Grand Union – see Table A]) that hoped to come east to Peterborough or to Spalding and those that planned to cross the Fens to any point in Suffolk or Norfolk. So far at least as the area east of Spalding and Peterborough it must be observed that not one of these railways was built in the 1840s, if ever. Because of that it is unnecessary to consider any of them further. They are listed in Appendix I to demonstrate how confusing the prospects must have been for the Norfolk directors, let alone the average investor or speculator.

Matching some of the many advertisements were the usual notices of objection. Those placed in the Norfolk papers were, understandably, mainly concerned with the nearest lines, especially those to Dereham and Aylsham. There was a series devoted to the Wensum Valley line matched by an answering series signed by supporters. The contest seemed to be to collect the maximum number of signatures although prestige of those signing must also have been of importance. The series began at the end of September with just three landowners along the Wensum line objecting to the river route and supporting the Dereham Direct. The next week these had been joined by Lord Bayning of Honingham. By 18 October there were rival advertisements, the objectors list being half as long again as that of the proponents who however had at least forty names. Addresses given on both sides were generally in or on the margins of the Wensum valley. By the following week the supporter's advertisement had nearly twice as many names as the opponents though rather fewer 'gentlemen'. A week later the objectors ran just a short piece but had gathered as their trump cards the names of lords Leicester of Holkham, Hastings of Melton and Fitzroy of Sennowe.

The North of Norfolk had some influential Norwich supporters such as James Colman, Robert Chamberlain of Catton, John Norgate, Henry Staniforth Patteson, Osborn Springfield (son of T.O.), and William Stitt Wilson, all on its committee, as well as Peto's associate John Bagshaw who had subscribed over £12,000. Nevertheless the landowner opposition was strong. A meeting in late October chaired by Lord Orford on a motion by Sir Edward Stracey denounced the line as a project quite unnecessary and uncalled for. In the same edition of the paper that reported the meeting there appeared an advertisement for the New North of Norfolk, a reasonable parody of a railway announcement, that trumpeted that 'a Direct Communication from Norwich to Aylsham was of the utmost importance to the trade of Norwich' and that therefore a railway would be constructed half as long again as the present road going through certain 'important' hamlets instead of the 'insignificant villages' of Horsford, St Faiths, Hevingham and Marsham served by the road. Its Provisional Committee, it said, were confident that they would satisfy the claims that the most sanguine credulity of railway speculators could insist on.

The Aylsham line had an eloquent opponent in James Bulwer of Heydon who had clashed with the surveyors of the line for asking questions of his labourers and who may have been the author of the parody quoted above. He wrote, in one letter, that 'the legislature will surely no longer leave the victims of these projects utterly helpless, nor continue to overlook the monstrous injustice every day inflicted on the proprietors, compelled to incur an immense expense in opposing any, even the most visionary projects, which a parcel of gamblers in a back parlour in London may choose to start in a district'. This went to the nub of the problem that year and the next and shows why the more serious projectors worked hard to recruit local support and respectable local members to their committees.

The Waveney Valley line attracted fewer objectors and made especial efforts to show how well it was supported in the district. An advertisement in late October of those in favour headed its list with the Duke of Norfolk, four Privy Councillors from Norfolk (the High Steward of Yarmouth Lord Lichfield and lords Hastings, Berners and Suffield), a Bedingfield of Ditchingham and John Kerrick of Geldeston Hall as well as, from Yarmouth, four Palmers (the Recorder and three JPs) William Wilshere MP and the dissident Norfolk shareholder William Yetts. Trailing these were dozens of fish merchants and many of the Corporation, some duplicated under different headings. However by January some opposition had been mobilised, led by the same Mr Ferrier of Burgh Castle who had been instrumental in stopping the venture the year previous. At the same time John Kerrick was reported as chairman of a group in opposition to the Ipswich, Norwich & Yarmouth. The committee of the Thetford, Bury & Newmarket advertised that the Norfolk 'with the concurrence of the Eastern Counties' was to take a large share interest in their line and lease the Thetford to Bury section and warned the public not to believe any advertisement by Mr Eagle that a similar agreement had been reached with his railway.

An October editorial in the *Mercury* reflected on three looming disasters of the time, the failure of the wheat harvest, the failure also of the Irish potato crop and the railway speculation. Earlier railway booms and busts had merely recirculated money but this time there was a danger that many of the lines would actually be built, wasting the capital permanently. In particular the writer deplored the scandal of obtaining 'guinea pigs' as potential directors, names obtained by the promise of scrip to be sold if shares went to a premium but not taken up if they did not. Practical objections voiced in letters to the press included worry about the frequency of level crossings. This of course was a worry to the promoters too, for a level crossing meant a continued cost in terms of staff chargeable to revenue whereas a bridge could be charged to capital account and then ignored. The worst case was the short length to be built from Thorpe to Magdalen Gates and beyond to connect the main Norfolk line to the new branch railways. Seven public roads and one footpath must be crossed on the level in that short distance.

During November the Norfolk weekly newspapers carried formal advertisements for all the projects that affected the county, listing for each every parish that might be affected and necessitating supplements doubling their normal size. Most projectors also advertised that they had achieved the necessary minimum subscriptions to enable them to lodge the required deposits before Parliament reassembled. One advertisement was joint, for the Essex & Suffolk had at last merged with the Chelmsford & Bury. Both sets of plans had been deposited but it was those of the Chelmsford & Bury which would now be pursued. The *Norwich Mercury* quoted extensively from a famous article in the *Times* of London that had counted 1,428 railway projects going forward that year that would require an estimated capital of £701,243,208 on which £49,592,816 deposits must be paid. For those days these figures were astronomical and the country obviously could not afford it.

In the local papers for 6 December the Norfolk clerk of the peace reported the names of the companies that had duly lodged their plans as required by midnight on the 30 November. Everyone in Norfolk had made the deadline, though some by only minutes as can be seen by the times annotated on the deposited plans. The *Illustrated London News* made much play of the panic in London when several hundred agents for new railways had converged on the Board of Trade to lodge plans before the strictly applied deadline, a task made more difficult because the closing day was a Sunday when travel from the provinces could be especially difficult. In the preceding weeks previously unheard of rates were being demanded by the lithographers entrusted with the production of plans while extra specialist labour was being imported from the continent.

The parliamentary session of 1846 was the very vortex of the railway mania with more railway projects coming before the legislature than ever before or after. How the various committees managed to accord sufficient attention to each and every one defies imagination, and in fact they scarcely did. Nevertheless reasonable justice was done. To recapitulate, the Norfolk's proposals for the coming legislative season were for a line to join the Ipswich & Bury at Stowmarket, for the Reedham, Diss and Thetford cut-off, and for the extension of the Dereham branch to Fakenham, Wells and Blakeney. In addition there was the proposed financial stake in the Ipswich, Norwich & Yarmouth and an agreement to lease the whole of that line when and if it was built. Finally undertakings had been given to lease the Dereham Direct, the North of Norfolk and part of the Thetford, Bury & Newmarket were these successful in obtaining approval. All these had been confirmed at the half year shareholders' meeting in February 1846.

The board had instructed their parliamentary agents to oppose certain Bills, including those for the lines from Stowmarket to Norwich, in the

Waveney and Wensum valleys, and the Chelmsford & Bury branch from Lavenham to Stowmarket. There had previously been several meetings with the Eastern Union directors in an unsuccessful attempt to persuade them to stop the Ipswich & Bury line extension from Haughley to Norwich in consideration for which the Norfolk would have granted them running powers from Stowmarket into Norwich via their own proposed branch from Spooners Row (between Attleborough and Wymondham).

Examination of railway proposals in Parliament began in February and by the middle of the month there were already reports of second readings of some Bills while others were meeting difficulties in complying with standing orders. Shares of most existing railways were standing high on the markets. For example Norwich & Brandon shares, still only eighteen shillings paid, were quoted at twenty-five and three quarter shillings on 12 February. However reports of parliamentary proceedings concerning railways are rare between February and April when came news of the early casualties. The Wensum Valley line had failed at the starting post being unable to raise the required deposit. Subscription moneys would be returned to the subscribers after deduction of 2s 6d per share for expenses. Several of the western connecting lines had already been thrown out: more were to go.

In May there were three full days of hearings before a Commons committee concerning the Eastern Union/Ipswich & Bury line into Norwich with Samuel Bignold prominent amongst several Norwich persons giving evidence of need in favour of the line. The line to Ipswich was shorter and so should be faster, while the position of the proposed terminus at Victoria gardens in Norwich was said to be much preferred by Norwich traders and potential passengers. The Norfolk's and more especially the Eastern Counties' safety record and poor timekeeping told against them in contrast to the as yet untried line of the Eastern Union/Ipswich & Bury. Their engineering evidence given by Peter Bruff withstood all the challenges which could be advanced by 'the subtle Mr Bidder' as he was described by one newspaper. The only serious drawback to the project was that the proud town of Eye was to be by-passed. By contrast the inclusion of Eye on its route was one of the few points scored by the Norfolk's alternative of a line from Spooners' Row, near Wymondham to Stowmarket despite evidence in favour from Jeremiah Colman, the flourishing mustard manufacturer, and much talk about the otherwise deprived rural population to the east of Eye.

Also in May there were many hours of committee hearings concerning the Ipswich & Yarmouth and the two lines competing to build along the Waveney valley. It was apparent that none of the lines was likely to generate substantial local and intermediate traffic along their predominately rural routes while the coastal line suffered from a further disadvantage in that river and sea navigations could deprive it of a major part of even the agricultural freight of its hinterland. Landowner evidence, including that from Sir Shafto Adair, an Eastern Union director, centred around cheaper coal for their estates while James Bedingfield of Ditchingham and John Kerrick of Geldeston, although both on the Waveney Valley committee, seemed vague as to its actual route. All three lines promised Yarmouth a somewhat shorter route to London but two of them required Yarmouth to have a new station at Southtown. The main debates revolved around the advantages and disadvantages of this. It was apparent that, as ever, the citizens of the town were deeply divided. There was no question that the Norfolk's existing station at Runham was inconvenient and there was considerable scepticism over its latest proposals to bridge the Bure and to lay tramways on the quays although it was acknowledged that the paving commissioners had at last given consent for the tracks. Prejudice against the Norfolk and anything which might favour Lowestoft underlay much of the evidence. One witness for the Waveney Valley said that Yarmouth passengers for London preferred now to go by sea because of the poor reputation the Eastern Counties and Norfolk had gained through accidents.

A retired merchant, Mr Ambrose Palmer, explained that although the principal quay and shipyards lay on the east side, the timber yards and much of the main industry and many of the warehouses lay on the west which was also the side to which came the majority of the corn for export. For this reason a station there must be convenient. Against this it was pointed out that the site of the proposed station and the main quay space on the west lay upstream of the town bridge. Any increase of shipping to the western quays would mean greater periods of opening the drawbridge and consequent delays to road traffic. Also the opening in the bridge was too narrow for paddle steamers. Admittedly the bridge was in theory temporary pending the construction of a new permanent structure but had been in position for many years and as yet there was no immediate prospect of a replacement. Fish was landed either on the east quay or on the beach while the smokeries were also on the town side, all being closer to the Norfolk station. Some of the questioning bordered on farce. 'How, if you heard a friend was to come to you in Yarmouth', asked counsel of one witness, 'would you know which station to go to in order to meet him?' Behind the scenes some dirty work had been going on. One farmer had been told by a Waveney Valley representative that if his corn went via Reedham it would have to be transhipped there. Another party was petitioning for the Ipswich, Norwich & Yarmouth to be wound up and their deposits repaid: there was suspicion that these were also Waveney Valley subscribers.

By the end of May the score as concerns East Anglia was approval in committee for the Ipswich & Bury line into Norwich but the loss of the Norfolk's line to Diss, the Ipswich, Norwich & Yarmouth (and its associated alternative the Halesworth & Norwich) and the Waveney Valley (although the committee considered somewhat hopelessly that Yarmouth did deserve a better London line and Beccles and Bungay both deserved something of a railway). Despite support from the Lynn & Dereham, the Dereham Direct was also negatived by the parliamentary committee. The North of Norfolk line, though unopposed, was similarly dealt with and the Bill was withdrawn. Newspaper editorials were jubilant over the line to Ipswich, for the Norfolk remained unpopular with both Norfolk papers, and not overly disappointed about the loss of the Dereham Direct. The *Chronicle* referred to it as 'a failure which never could have occurred had the committee been put properly in possession of the merits of the case, or had they possessed the least local knowledge themselves'. Yarmouth, the paper admitted, had reason to be disappointed but should co-operate now with the Norfolk to gain a new terminal within the town. However at Yarmouth itself there was much frustration and a new meeting that resolved to petition Parliament. It was reported there that the failure of the Waveney line had caused great rejoicing at Lowestoft and once again the Norfolk was slated for failing to bring lines to the Yarmouth quays.

By the end of June the Ely & Bury, the Newmarket extension of the Ipswich & Bury and the Thetford, Bury & Newmarket had all failed before committee. It was reported that of ten different railway plans deposited the previous November for railways reaching Bury, every one had now been thrown out. However the Newmarket & Chesterford had succeeded. At its first meeting the new company announced its intention to apply for permission in 1847 to build also to Ely, Bury and Thetford. They reported that they had negotiated with the Norfolk for the latter to lease their line at six per cent on cost but that negotiations had been broken off when the Norfolk admitted that the lease would require also the permission of the Eastern Counties. Two months later a Newmarket director addressed a meeting in Thetford advocating a direct line thence from Newmarket which the Eastern Counties would lease however little the Norfolk would like it. This line would considerably shorten the western route from Norwich to London and would be superior to the Eastern Union since it would run direct through to Yarmouth. The Norfolk could still use their line to Brandon as a base of a link to the North. Thetford, he said, would have a great future as a railway junction.

The North of Norfolk advertised to say that they hoped the Norfolk would support a further try the following year, but meanwhile one pound a share would be returned to subscribers. Almost at once a meeting of subscribers described this as 'petty if not insulting'. The Norfolk itself, though its lines to Diss from Wymondham and Reedham had both been lost, at least gained approval for its extension from Dereham to Fakenham, Wells and Blakeney. By the time the parliamentary session closed in July the East Anglian approvals were limited to these and the Ipswich & Bury line into Norwich from Stowmarket. Everything else had been turned down except the Lynn extensions westward by the Lynn & Ely which in the event were never to be built.

The Norfolk shareholders were told at their August meeting that while the Lowestoft lease had at last been approved the directors had not proceeded with a plan for a new station in the centre of Yarmouth due to strenuous opposition from some of the inhabitants. The Reedham/Thetford line had failed to satisfy standing orders on trifling matters and would be resubmitted in 1847. Both the Ipswich, Norwich & Yarmouth and the Thetford/Bury lines had been rejected due to landowner objections. A brave face was put by the directors on losing the projected line to Diss, Stowmarket and Eye and it was prophesied that the Ipswich & Bury would be ruined by their direct line to Norwich. The Norfolk revenue was coming chiefly from local traffic and not from through bookings to London.

In mid-November the *Chronicle* was able to publish the line-up for the parliamentary session for the following year, noting with satisfaction that all the lines proposed for East Anglia were being put forward by existing companies. There was at last a check to the mania for new railways its editorial said. The projects listed were:

By the Norfolk Railway:

Norwich to Aylsham and North Walsham (the North of Norfolk repeated with some variations including a short tunnel through Chalk Hill rather than a line along Riverside)

Thetford to Reedham via Diss, as in the previous year with the addition of a branch to Halesworth.

Thetford to Bury

Wymondham southward as previous year but shortened to terminate at Diss

An alteration to the plan for the junction with the Lowestoft at Reedham to allow for trains from both east and west to cross the bridge.

By the Ipswich & Bury

A new Waveney Valley line from Diss to Yarmouth South Town via Harleston and Bungay

Bury to Thetford

Norwich via Wensum Valley to Dereham and to Aylsham

Ipswich to Woodbridge.

By the Lynn & Ely

Holbeach to Spalding (a leapfrog move beyond the Eastern Counties)

Ely to Bury.

By the Newmarket & Chesterford

From Newmarket eastward to Moulton, forking there into branches to Thetford and to Bury.

There were also to be Bills for the merger of the Eastern Union with the Ipswich & Bury and of the East Anglian lines into a single entity. The Eastern Union was putting forward eighteen Bills chiefly for lines in Essex, Cambridgeshire and Hertfordshire. The only ones affecting Norfolk or Suffolk were to give it power to purchase the Newmarket & Chesterford and the merging East Anglian railways. The paper omitted some further lines affecting the area. The Stour Valley Railway, that had reached Sudbury from the south, proposed to build on from there via Lavenham to Bury with a branch from Lavenham to join the Ipswich & Bury at Stowmarket. In direct competition the Ipswich & Bury itself was proposing a line from Stowmarket to Sudbury. It was also planning further moves westward to Newmarket and to Ely in competition with the Newmarket & Chesterford.

Subsequently a further plan was filed for a repeated version of the 'coast line' of the previous season, Ipswich to Haddiscoe via Woodbridge, Halesworth and Beccles, with power to sell to one or other of the Eastern Counties, Norfolk or Eastern Union. By or on behalf of whom it was filed is not stated but it must be related to a Norfolk minute in October where the board proposed to sponser such a railway if the Eastern Counties would bear half the cost. Later the company's lawyers advised that the line would better be promoted by an independent company with the Norfolk and Eastern Counties taking an interest in capital and leasing the line if an Act was obtained. Presumably the latter company declined doing this as nothing further is heard of the project.

CHAPTER 6

The Norfolk Railway:
1845 to 1847

Raising and spending capital

From its very formation by merger the company was suffering from a condition that was common to many railway enterprises at this time, undercapitalisation through a failure by the promoters to realise, or at least to allow for, the initial cost of their railway additional to the line itself. As explained in Chapter 1, not only were preliminary expenses such as legal and parliamentary costs and interest on capital during construction almost invariably omitted from estimates but sometimes also locomotives and rolling stock and such essential if ancillary structures as stations, sidings, signalling systems, housing for staff, and warehouses. If sufficient initial capital had not been raised for all these then the company would need to borrow and ultimately further capital would be needed, usually on terms much less favourable. Yet had the full cost been realised at the start it is probable that few railways would have been built at all. The Yarmouth & Norwich had ostensibly and unusually been bought as a complete package, but even here it soon proved that more land and structures were required at Thorpe while the land cost itself had been underestimated. Once Norfolk trains were running to London the need for rolling stock was greatly increased.

The initial capital statement of the Norfolk railway made up to 30 June 1845 and presented to shareholders in August was given in the following form:

	Yarmouth & Norwich £	Norwich & Brandon £
Accumulated costs to 30 June	259,040	312,777
Funds in hand	3,372	52,718
Total received from shareholders, loans etc.	£262,413	£365,495

While the total of approximately £628,000 capital raised appears to be more or less in line with the original estimates made of the costs of the two railways it must be borne in mind as regards this and all later capital statements that they were drawn up on a purely cash basis and therefore do not allow for costs incurred but not paid for, still less further costs effectively committed but not contracted for. On the other side the statements omit the amounts as yet uncalled on shares subscribed for and loans authorised but not taken up.

After the initial difficulties described in Chapter 3 in obtaining enough Yarmouth & Norwich subscribers it appears that little problem had been found from 1844 to 1846 in placing additional shares. The Norwich & Brandon shares authorised for the Dereham branch and Thetford diversion (22,000 shares of ten pounds each) had been offered to shareholders pro rata to their existing holdings. Nearly all railway shares rose to a premium during that time and were eagerly acquired when offered at par if only to be resold on the stockmarket. Subscribers had been obtained in early 1846 for most or all of the shares which the company planned to issue to pay for the ambitious construction programme put before Parliament and the deposits they paid in were the main source of sums in excess of £90,000 which the company was required to deposit. We have little information on just who subscribed how much for shares in 1844 but Appendix 2 lists some of the major subscriptions in 1845 and 1846 listing persons known to have connections to Peto or to the Norfolk lines. Certainly there can have been no problem in allotting the £300,000 of 5% guaranteed shares for the extension to Wells which were eventually all that were issued in 1846, particularly in view of the guaranteed dividend which had to be paid before any dividend was declared on the ordinary shares.

The report to 31 December 1845 showed a total capital spend increased to £775,987 including 'extensions' on which £68,823 had been paid out. A further £60,335 was in hand. Much of the cash raised must have come from calls made on the Dereham extension shares. In response to a questioner at the half year meeting Bidder, who as engineer attended all such meetings, said that the final cost would now come nearer to £14,000 per mile. He explained that much of the increase would be due to buying further land and buildings to cope with extra traffic, especially at Norwich. Also housing for staff was required as were more generous areas of land at all principal stations. There would also be the costs of additional locomotives now found to be required.

Six months later the capital account made up to 30 June 1846 showed the extent of the wild commitments the company had entered into that year. The accumulated payments made for land and construction had now reached £985,079 while in addition deposits lodged in Chancery for the proposed extensions totalled £99,161 and £34,500 in all had been advanced to promoters of the Spalding & Brandon, the Ipswich, Norwich & Yarmouth and the Thetford & Bury railways of which just £12,625 had so far been returned. There was only £26,773 in hand. Of the total of £1,132,889 raised from all sources £99,833 was in the form of temporary loans. Bidder's report noted that £80,000 had been added to the Norwich & Brandon estimates for doubling the track. In response to a shareholder who objected to the advance to the Ipswich, Norwich & Yarmouth promoters, Bidder admitted that he too found this unpalatable; the company was encouraging a line in competition with itself, but it had been done in self defence in the hope of scuppering the Ipswich & Bury alternative proposal of a direct line.

The various buildings belonging to the Norfolk were valued for insurance at over £60,000 in December 1846 which is some indication of the amount spent by then in addition to the cost of the line itself. The capital account as at the end of that month presented to the shareholders meeting in February 1847 was for the first time set out in considerable detail. The accumulated spend under all headings now totalled £1,199,689 including £136,367 for locomotives and rolling stock, £71,330 for land required for enlargements, depots, houses and warehouses, and £155,902 so far spent on the extension beyond Dereham. £1,228,791 had been raised through shares and loans of which just £29,102 remained in hand. Temporary loans had been reduced to £51,000 but ominously £156,163 had been raised already out of the £300,000 new stock intended to finance the Wells extension although no work had yet begun on site: most of this money must have been spent on other purposes.

Building extensions: to Dereham and beyond

Immediately after the formation of the Norfolk company Bidder had been instructed to proceed with plans for the Dereham branch earlier approved in Parliament and a committee of the board, including Mr Parker of its solicitors, had been appointed to negotiate land purchase along both that line and that of the Lowestoft Railway. At the shareholders meeting in February 1846 it was reported that the land for the line had largely been purchased and works had begun in the previous autumn. Grissell & Peto were the main contractors and supplied the rails with Merrett once again the site agent. This line, although short, was through more rolling country than the earlier works in Norfolk and substantial cuttings and embankments were needed along the route to contain the maximum gradient at even 1:110. Even so there were to be numerous level crossings. Initially single track would be laid but there would be room for double, and the route, as the rest of the system, was to have telegraph lines alongside.

Initial progress was slow. There was a considerable quantity of brickwork and much earth moving to be done, especially at the Hardingham cutting which, at fifty foot in depth, was probably the biggest work to date in the county. Many of the labourers at this isolated site lived in a nearby encampment. A newspaper item in August 1846 reported reasonable progress with some bridges erected and piles of bricks at station sites but, with so many railways now building, this and other lines, notably the Ely & Peterborough and the Lowestoft, all works by Peto, were delayed by labour shortages. (Even so Peto maintained in mid 1847 that his then labour force on all contracts of some eleven thousand men was smaller than it had been a year before.) The planned opening date in October was unlikely to be achieved. The company's own half year report noted that completion would be delayed because of need to alter the layout at Dereham to accommodate the extension to Fakenham and Wells. Another newspaper article in October spoke of a labour force of only five hundred and reported works well advanced with some sections complete with rails laid. Opening might, it was predicted, be in November, but even this proved too optimistic.

Early in December the works were sufficiently complete for an experimental trip to be made from Norwich to Dereham by a number of Norfolk directors, shareholders, engineers and Peto himself, all riding in an open truck. To judge by the enthusiastic description of the pleasant countryside, the well kept farms and the pleasing and ornamental stations, a reporter from the *Norfolk Chronicle* must also have been aboard. However all cannot have been entirely well since one upshot of the journey was the decision to dismantle and rebuild a bridge over the line, the arch of which was too flat. When a party of workmen started to remove the roadway the following week the whole structure collapsed, burying them in rubble. Surprisingly, although several were injured, only one required hospital treatment. The new government inspector, Captain Joshua Coddington RE, succeeding General Pasley, had been due to inspect the line immediately after the trial trip but could not attend, which in the circumstances may have been as well. However the line opened for goods traffic only a week later.

Passenger opening was deferred until late in February 1847. It appears that in the meantime several bridges had been taken down and rebuilt but at least the track bed had had enough time to become well consolidated. Railway openings were becoming a more commonplace event by now and ceremony on this occasion was muted. The first train from Norwich took an hour, and this time the main comment from the *Chronicle* reporter was that the road from Dereham station into town on a day of heavy rain was disgracefully muddy. The Norfolk company was host to no ceremonial dinner but the town was, although only one railway representative, Mr Clay, the traffic manager, was able to be there. Healths were nevertheless drunk to all involved, including to Till and to Peto, the latter having ensured some popularity by promising £100 for the town's poor.

Once parliamentary approval had been received in 1846 the engineers had been ordered to stake out the whole line onward from Dereham via Fakenham to Wells and an estate agent had been commissioned to proceed with the purchase of land. Five thousand tons of rails were ordered at the same time to be delivered to Yarmouth at just under ten pounds a ton at a time when ironworks were inundated with railway orders. At Fakenham itself objections were being raised over the proposed crossing of the main road on the level. Rather late to think of that noted the *Norfolk Chronicle* unsympathetically. In October the Norfolk board passed an unusually cautious minute to the effect that Peto should be asked to quote for the Dereham/Wells line exclusive of land and, if the board liked his quotation, he should be given the contract but otherwise 'the contract should be thrown open'. In any case the line should be completed only to Fakenham in the first instance. It was not until the spring of 1847 that a contract was placed (with Peto) to extend the line the further twelve miles to Fakenham for £62,000 plus £4,000 for a year's maintenance. This required little earthmoving and at £5,000 per mile was as cheap as railways ever came, even given that the price did not include land, stations or rails.

Building extensions: across the Bure into Yarmouth

In early May 1845 Cory's bridge collapsed in a famous and bizarre accident. A critical weld parted when the new southern footway became overloaded by a crowd rushing across to see a clown navigating the river in a washtub drawn by four geese. Several hundred fell into the river and seventy-nine were drowned. A temporary bridge must soon have been erected to replace it as some bridge was essential as the only means other than by ferry by which passengers could reach or leave the railway. In July 1846 the wreckage of the old bridge was being auctioned. There were eight tons of cast iron, including the piers which the buyer must dismantle, and eight of hammered or wrought iron which comprised the chains and rods etc. However it was not before late 1847 that Cory presented

The collapse of Cory's bridge

The ruins of the
bridge

the Harbour Commissioners with plans for a permanent replacement.
This, a wrought iron bridge of the iron arch or bowstring type, was to
last until the mid-twentieth century. Although radically different from
its predecessor it was normally also referred to as a (or the) suspension
bridge.

That same month a meeting of the Norwich and Brandon shareholders
had been told that the maximum total cost for the bridge at Carrow and
the works at Yarmouth including both a railway bridge and tramlines
on the quays would be £52,000. In August 1845 the first meeting of
Norfolk shareholders had ratified a new agreement with Cory whereby he
would give up his right to tolls in exchange for an annuity of £800 per
annum, redeemable for £24,000. At the meeting Mr Yetts, the Yarmouth
shareholder who the year before had objected to the merger, complained
at the delay in reaching the Yarmouth quays and at the attention being
paid to Lowestoft that he said was arousing fierce suspicions in Yarmouth.
He thought the Lowestoft line would never have been undertaken had not
Peto settled in the district. All rumours of the Norfolk being opposed to
Yarmouth should be scotched at once. As it was another party there was
for bringing in a competing line via the Waveney Valley.

Bidder had replied that the reason that Yarmouth was ill served was due
to opposition in and from the town itself. The Norfolk was anxious for a
bridge and for tramlines on the quays. He did not think he need defend Peto
but promotion of Lowestoft should energise Yarmouth and the Lowestoft
railway was, he said, a good defence against the Waveney Valley line. In
fact the company had not proceeded with its Bill to build the bridge on the
line ratified by the shareholders in the previous February. Although there

were no objections from the Harbour Commissioners most probably the collapse of Cory's bridge gave hope that a better line could be obtained. In February 1846 the Norfolk board were being told that both the Yarmouth Paving Commissioners and the Harbour Commissioners were now likely to agree the proposed line along the quays and to a fixed bridge near the station opposite the site of Paget's brewery (which had been demolished in 1844). In May 1846 the shareholders once again agreed to extend the railway to Yarmouth jetty and it was reported to the board in June that work on the quays was about to begin. A press report confirmed this and said that the railway wanted the bridge at the north end of the brewery site. In August the board agreed to buy the Paget brewery site for £3,000 plus an extra £500 if a further Act was obtained for a bridge. Bidder told the shareholders in August that he was optimistic over his latest bridge plan. He believed Yarmouth would have to agree to it once the Lowestoft line was open and providing competition.

In early October a press report said, 'there was now a good prospect of a bridge'. Late in October the Haven Commissioners finally agreed both to the Bure crossing site and to the plans of the railway bridge itself after a session in which Richard Till and the site engineer had addressed their meeting as had three prominent Yarmouth citizens presenting a supporting petition from the town. A crucial point was the agreement of the Norfolk to abolish tolls on their bridge. As the new iron rail bridge would take several months to prepare and erect the railway obtained permission for a temporary wooden bridge to continue in place. It was also necessary for a yet further Act to authorise changes from previous plans and permissions. The press greeted the news with pleasure anticipating a new terminus on the brewery site although this was never built. The *Chronicle* observed that Yarmouth was now being much more co-operative; could this be, the editor speculated, the salutary effect of the competing development of Lowestoft?

In February 1847 the board agreed to pay £26,000 to Cory for permission to own the site and abolish tolls. It was not explained why the price had increased. While Cory's bridge itself was to be toll free, the toll house was to be moved west so that, while travellers to the station by either bridge need not pay, tolls would yet be charged to any who were to take the Acle road. The board now estimated the total costs of the whole Yarmouth extension at £75,000, including the sum to be paid to Cory. Then in July the press reported that Cory was to receive only £21,819. The bridge did get built, although, probably due to the company's perennial shortage of cash, it was not opened until 1852. Described as constructed 'on the tubular principle' it incorporated separate passages for railway wagons and for carriages. No separate footway was added until 1876 at which time it was reconstructed into the bridge still visible today, the deck hung from three parallel wrought iron arches, disused except as a footway but preserved as a listed monument.

Map A4   East Anglia, Actual and Proposed Lines January 1847

Shows the position as at January 1847 after plans and Bills had been filed with Parliament prior to the forthcoming legislative season.

The Railway Mania is now in effect over although this may not have been evident yet to all. All proposals, few of which even if authorised were to be built for many years if ever, were being put forward by one or other of the existing companies. In the past year the main Eastern Union/Ipswich & Bury line has been opened from Colchester to Bury and a start has been made on the extension to Norwich. The Lynn lines are open south and west of Lynn for some miles but construction on the remainder of their system is proceeding but slowly. Elsewhere the link from Ely to Peterborough is open but not yet either the Lowestoft/Reedham line or the Norfolk's branch to Dereham. The later comers, the Stour Valley and Newmarket & Chesterford lines, have begun construction.

Lines and proposals westward of Cambridge and King's Lynn are not shown except for the Peterborough/Ely branch of the Eastern Counties, and the branches by the Eastern Counties and by the Lynn & Ely respectively north and west to Wisbech . Lines and proposals southward of Suffolk are shown only so far as they were or might have been relevant to developments in Norfolk and Suffolk. The boxed area is shown in more detail in Map B on Page 221.

Key

————	Completed lines	/ Jointly
— —	Lines under construction	// In competition
- - - - - -	Proposed lines	

Abbreviations of railway names

ECR	Eastern Counties	LR&H	Lowestoft Railway & Harbour
EUR	Eastern Union	N&C	Newmarket & Chesterford
I&B	Ipswich & Bury	NN	North of Norfolk
L&D	Lynn & Dereham	NR	Norfolk Railway
L&E	Lynn & Ely	SV	Stour Valley

A4

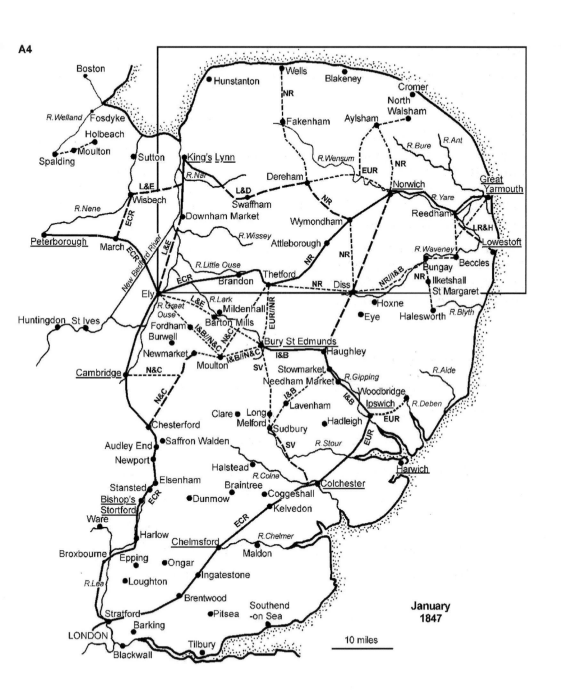

Boston

R.Welland Fosdyke

Holbeach
Moulton
Spalding

Sutton

King's Lynn

Hunstanton

Wells

Blakeney

Cromer

North
Walsham

Aylsham

R.Bure

R.Ant

NR

Fakenham

R.Wensum

EUR

NR

L&E
Wisbech

R.Nar

Dereham

Norwich

R.Yare

Great
Yarmouth

Swaffham

L&D

Reedham

LR&H

R.Nene

Downham Market

Wymondham

Lowestoft

Peterborough

March

R.Wissey

Attleborough

NR

R.Waveney

Beccles

ECR

New Bedford River

R.Little Ouse

NR

Bungay

NR

Ilketshall
St Margaret

ECR

L&E

Brandon

Thetford

NR

Diss

NR/I&B

Ely

ECR

Hoxne

Huntingdon St Ives

R.Great
Ouse

L&E

R.Lark

Mildenhall

Eye

Halesworth

R.Blyth

Fordham

Barton Mills

EUR/NR

Burwell

I&B/N&C

N&C

Bury St Edmunds

Haughley

R.Alde

Newmarket

I&B/N&C

Moulton

SV

I&B

Stowmarket

R.Gipping

Cambridge

N&C

Needham Market

Woodbridge

N&C

Clare Long
Melford

Lavenham

Ipswich

R.Deben

Chesterford

Sudbury

Hadleigh

EUR

Audley End Saffron Walden

SV

R.Stour

Newport

Halstead

EUR

Stansted

Elsenham

Braintree

R.Colne

Colchester

Harwich

Bishop's
Stortford

ECR

Dunmow

Coggeshall

Ware

Kelvedon

Harlow

Chelmsford

R.Chelmer

Broxbourne

Epping

Maldon

R.Lea

Ongar

Loughton

Ingatestone

January
1847

Brentwood

Southend
-on Sea

Stratford

Pitsea

LONDON Barking

10 miles

Blackwall

Tilbury

Competitors' progress

Competitors' lines were progressing too, if slowly. At the end of October 1846 the Lynn & Ely opened a passenger service between Lynn and Downham Market. Although this was only half the distance to be covered to Ely the event was greeted with enthusiasm by the press. A good deal of space was taken up with statistics for the trade through Lynn's port and how the railway could only enhance this. The reporter for the *Chronicle* was impressed particularly by the quality of the carriages. Even those for the third class were roofed, with windows and with backs for the seats (in sad contrast to those of the Norfolk). The three locomotives, all built by Sharp Bros of Manchester of a six wheel type warmly approved by General Pasley, were also commended by the reporter. Numerous Lynn worthies rode to Downham and back on the day and then to Narborough on the allied Lynn & Dereham railway.

These companies, shortly to merge as East Anglian Railways, had already severely overspent their budgets on getting as far as they had. It seemed likely that the further extension of both would prove hard going as the Ely line had yet to bridge the Ouse while the Dereham line had heavy earthworks ahead. The directors in December 1846 were playing for high stakes when they rejected an offer from the Eastern Counties to lease their lines in perpetuity at five per cent on cost of construction rising to six per cent but limited to the Eastern Counties own dividend rate less two per cent. Their shareholders insisted they return to the negotiating table insisting on not less than seven and one half per cent.

Earlier articles had emphasised the astonishing developments at Brandon and even more at Ely resulting from the railways. Ely was quite changing in character with a grand station and a new cattle market anticipating its coming role as a major railway junction. The Lynn line might yet be some time away but the Eastern Counties' line to Peterborough

Ely station

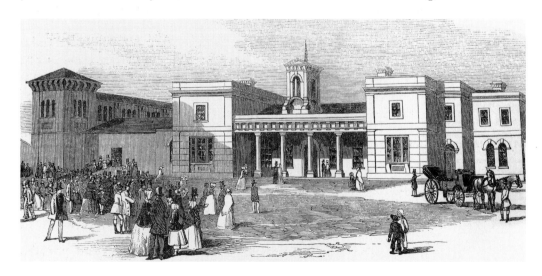

was nearly complete and meanwhile the weekly payroll for the navvies (who improvidently never saved their pay) was some £1,750, mostly money spent in the town. The latter line was proving difficult to build due to the soft and unstable nature of the Fen soils necessitating frequent viaducts and heavy piling. It should have been completed in September 1846 but several earth slippages prevented opening until December. Then, at last, it opened for goods, bringing for the first time East Anglia into rail communication, however imperfectly, with the Midlands and North.

The Eastern Union/Ipswich & Bury line north from Stowmarket had encountered severe difficulties in the marshy valley of the Gipping but was opened through to Bury at the end of November that year. Its line from Haughley Junction, north of Stowmarket towards Norwich was soon to begin construction and in December work began on its station site at Victoria Gardens in Norwich. Thus the Norfolk would face direct competition in the near future.

Running the line

From July 1845 and through the hectic period described in the previous chapter the Norfolk directors had an existing railway to manage, the continuous line from Yarmouth to Brandon plus, for the first eight months, the further section from Brandon to Ely that the Eastern Counties were temporarily unable to service. Neither the branch to Dereham or the Lowestoft railway were in full operation until 1847. In considering the results reported to shareholders reference should be made to the table below. However things were never as simple as the figures summarised there might suggest. Those for receipts are probably entirely factual and correct, growing with the increased traffic as the line lengthened and as branches were added. A small part of the receipts came from rents but over ninety seven per cent came from passenger fares and freight charges for goods, parcels and livestock. But as regards operating costs the position was different.

Throughout the short history of the Yarmouth & Norwich its trains were operated under contract by George Merrett, Peto's agent during construction, at a fixed £7,000 for a full year. In addition the company paid out about £1,000 a year for administration and office costs and fees and expenses of the directors. However immediately after the formation of the Norfolk the board decided that Merrett was to give up his contract and:

> Mr Peto [was to] be requested to take charge of the entire line, the management of the locomotive and carriage department and also the maintaining of the permanent way on or after 31 July ... The terms of the contract to be referred to Mr Stephenson for settlement ...

It is not clear if or for how long such an arrangement existed, probably

Norfolk Railway and predecessors Summary of operating results presented to shareholders					
Half year to	*Gross receipts*	*Costs*		*Operating profit*	*Half year dividend rate*
	£	£	%	£	%
Yarmouth & Norwich					
30 June 1844 (2 mos)	2,725	1,170	43	1,555	
31 December 1844	8,859	3,936	44	4,923	
30 June 1845	6,541	4,095	63	2,446	
Norfolk Railway					
31 December 1845	31,286	15,384	49	15,902	2.5%
30 June 1846	37,937	15,793	42	22,144	3.0%
31 December 1846	45,680	22,190	49	23,490	3.5%
30 June 1847	47,545	24,609	52	22,936	3.0%
31 December 1847	58,658	29,833	51	28,825	2.5%

no more than a few months and certainly not longer than a year. Merrett continued to be responsible for day to day maintenance, now for the whole line.

It was soon apparent after the formal opening that things were not going well. For a start there were not enough locomotives either on the Norfolk or the Eastern Counties to satisfy the timetable and to deal with breakdowns. Already in September 1845 an order was placed for twenty new locomotives from Robert Stephenson & Co. of Newcastle (to come by sea). A series of capital expenditure approvals dealt with such matters as cottages for platemen, a gas works, an engine house, a repair shop with smithy, and a goods shed at Norwich station, coal depots at principal stations, and purchases, sales and exchanges of minor pieces of land. Peto himself had been the original purchaser of some land, such as a wharf at Carrow, that were better in the ownership of the company and surveyors had to be appointed to fix a price as at arms length.

Despite the delegation of operating responsibility the board's traffic subcommittee was kept busy with such matters as staff salaries and terms of employment, passenger complaints of lost baggage and goods, accommodation at stations for cattle and coal depots, compensation for injured livestock and indeed everything except running the trains themselves. There were several disputes with landowners who believed they had rights to stop trains for their personal convenience. Some had, particularly at the Berney Arms and at Hethersett, but the company was anxious to evade any such obligation if it could get away with it. There were many complaints about the level crossing at Lakenham, just outside Norwich, where long queues of carriages, pedestrians and animals could build up if a train was late. On one occasion an impatient butcher forced the gates and the waiting crowd, including a flock of sheep, crossed notwithstanding that a delayed train was expected. Eventually a bridge, paid for partly by the railway, partly by the city, and partly by public subscription replaced the level crossing. The newspapers report several instances where trains were seriously late causing, for one example, farmers' consignments of animals to miss their market and in another fish wagons so delayed at Brandon that the merchants were claiming compensation.

There was general dissatisfaction with the Eastern Counties, especially the inefficiencies at the London terminus and the goods management there in particular. Nor was confidence in their partners increased by two accidents that had occurred in the summer to trains on the Eastern Counties section of the London line. In both cases the engine and in one the entire train had been derailed. In the earlier case the fireman had been killed when the engine rolled over and in the later both the locomotive crew had been thrown off, uncomfortably no doubt but safely into a pond. Both cases were agreed to have been caused by unsuitable wheels on the engine, incompatible with the profile of the rails, and this design of engine could not be used again for passenger work until the wheels had been modified by the makers. Clearly these incidents were not helpful to the reputation of the new joint enterprise, especially as the Eastern Counties had for long been notorious for accidents.

By January 1846 Adam Duff, Norfolk chairman, was seeking a meeting with Waddington, deputy chairman of the Eastern Counties, to discuss the 'disappointments experienced on their line' and possible means of mitigation. In the same month the *Mercury* ran a violently indignant editorial slating delays, accidents and the general incompetence of management and employees on the London route. It was suggested that Hudson, since October in control of the Eastern Counties, had cut both staff and wages. Nobody took responsibility. The trains were slow in the first instance and delays innumerable. Parcels took days. It was no excuse to say that the line had opened early. Other railways operated satisfactorily so why could not this one? The *Chronicle* was no kinder, concentrating on poor safety and untrained staff. Further all the management was in London except for one or two local directors with little power or knowledge of railway working, only one of these showing any interest at all. Nobody ever answered questions or probably could.

Both these editorials came in the wake of a spectacular accident on Christmas Eve 1845 when a Norfolk up train ran off the line near the Kilverstone bridge between Attleborough and Thetford, the engine having left the track and rolled over. Although no passengers were seriously injured both the engineer and firemen were killed. Earlier there had been comparatively minor accidents reported but nothing like this. The inquest at Thetford was a confused affair spread after adjournments over three days. There was a major conflict of evidence over the speed of the train. Bidder, for the company, said that the speed had been excessive over a length where a restriction was in force and the accident had occurred because steam had been shut off suddenly and the weight of the train had forced the engine to jump off the tracks. The guards, both of whom had been badly injured, maintained that the speed had been nothing like the 60 mph that others had alleged and that they had applied such brakes as they had. The implication from this was that there was track fault and it was acknowledged that work had been proceeding on the line due to subsidence of the embankment.

General Pasley, the Board of Trade inspector, having viewed the wreck, blamed the engine itself as being of an unsatisfactory design that could develop a dangerous oscillation at speed and which should therefore not exceed 40 mph. The engine in fact was one of a somewhat controversial new Stephenson six wheeled design that Pasley had previously criti-cised. Robert Stephenson subsequently wrote an extensive report to the company in justification of the design in which he backed Bidder's theory concerning the accident although it has to be admitted that history tends to side with Pasley. However the jury did not, with two members blaming both excessive speed and a dangerous engine, but the remaining twelve putting the blame solely on 'overdriving' that is to say excessive speed.

The widows of the dead engine crew were each granted ten shillings weekly by the board to run for three months 'and then reconsider'. It may be significant that the next order for passenger locomotives specified a four wheel arrangement. Just a week after the newspapers had carried reports on the inquest there was news of 'another awful smash' on the Eastern Counties, this one at Stansted where a broken down freight train was hit by another. Two months later there was another 'frightful accident' on the same line at Ponders End when a broken rail derailed a train on which Waddington was himself a passenger. No human lives were lost although a guard was critically injured and several valuable racehorses were killed. There were other accidents on the Norfolk. Some minor in shunting and switching but at least three fatal, one when a porter fell under a train at Eccles station, another when a company employee was crushed at Thorpe and a third when a ten year old child was killed on the line at an unguarded crossing. In February three porters at Attleborough were found intoxicated and were first suspended and later discharged and prosecuted. And despite the complaints at board level there were still disputes with the Eastern Counties as when that company insisted on stopping Norfolk Sunday trains at every station between Stortford and London.

At the half-year general meeting in February 1846 the accounts presented to shareholders for the six months to the end of December showed revenue of £31,286 (six months for the Yarmouth & Norwich but only five for the Norwich & Brandon). Operating charges of £15,384 were

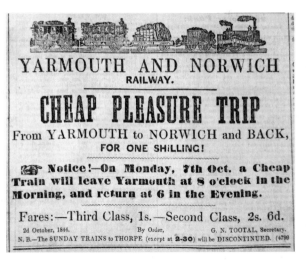

problematical. A charge of £2,999 payable to the Eastern Counties as rental for operating temporarily the section of line between Brandon and Ely was unquestionable. The balance of £12,385 was explained as being forty per cent of charges to customers, a rate the directors, 'after careful study', had considered appropriate, even excessive. What the true costs of working had been were not revealed although it was clear that they had been higher. The excess had, it appears, been charged to capital account, justified as being exceptional costs during an initial period of operation, what might today be called 'learning costs'.

The main adverse factors in the first period of operations had been the lack of the bridge at Carrow, the shortage of locomotives, and other operational teething problems including the fact that the electric telegraph was not yet in operation along the whole line. The directors hoped to have the further twenty locomotives by April which they thought would be sufficient. Interest charges absorbed £4,177 and the balance of £11,725 was virtually all paid out as dividend. What the true balance or the dividend would have been had all operating costs been charged is unknown. No provision was made for depreciation of either rolling stock or the line itself (or, indeed, ever was) an omission quite normal for that time. Complaints by members at the meeting over timetable irregularity were dealt with blandly and as to the Christmas Eve accident, why if the public demanded speed they must accept the occasional consequences!

There had been excursion trains to Yarmouth from the very earliest days of the Yarmouth & Norwich but once the Brandon route was complete there could be occasional excursions along the entire line between London and Yarmouth. In late June the press reported a somewhat disastrous occasion when some fifteen hundred persons from stations between Cambridge and Wymondham had been brought to Yarmouth for two night stays over the Whitsun period. Unfortunately Yarmouth was ill-prepared and not enough accommodation or even food was to be found in the town. Disappointed holidaymakers were to be found wandering the streets late at night or sleeping on the beach. Moreover when one return train broke down hungry passengers waited two and one half hours for a relief engine while the driver walked first to a farmhouse and then rode with a farmboy to Brandon, the nearest station.

A week later there was a report of another excursion, this time from London to Norwich and Yarmouth on a Saturday. Twenty-five carriages brought eight hundred persons to Norfolk, finding the inn-keepers this time ready and well stocked. The following Monday a train left Yarmouth joined by more carriages at Norwich and yet more along the line to produce a 'monster train' of fifty-two carriages carrying two thousand passengers to London. The *Norfolk Chronicle* described the people as 'mainly working class' paying just seven shillings and sixpence for a return valid for a week and spoke of the 'great happiness and gratification' of those looking forward to family reunions and the 'many happy faces peering from windows, beaming with delightful anticipation of pleasure in store'. As it was going to take six and a half hours from Norwich to London and as there were no refreshments on the train perhaps expressions had changed somewhat by the time of arrival. In the same issue of the paper one further excursion was reported, one where it is fairly sure that true delight must have ensued. This was a train to Yarmouth carrying some three thousand children from chapel schools in Norwich, Thetford, Attleborough and Wymondham at three pence per head for a day by the sea. Those from Norwich had first formed up by their schools and had then marched to the station in serried ranks. Thousands of spectators, it was said, cheered 'the happy urchins' and a further train followed on which parents and others could travel at one shilling each.

An unforgettable excursion took place that summer when a party came by train from London to Yarmouth to cross to Rotterdam on 'the Iron Steam Ship Norfolk'. Although this was publicised as a demonstration of a possible extended service to travellers there is suspicion that it was chiefly intended as a riposte to a similar and quite successful voyage organised by the Eastern Union from Ipswich to Rotterdam just a few   Brandon station

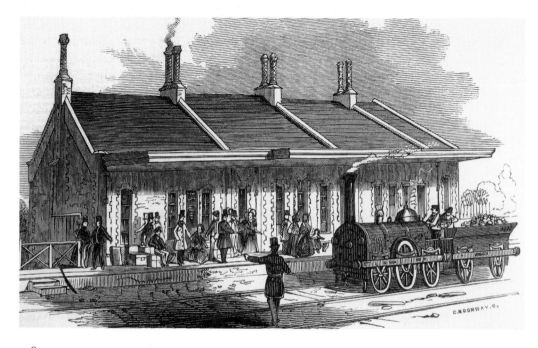

weeks before. The excursion train was scheduled to leave London at five a.m. on Thursday 22 July, arriving at Yarmouth at eight fifteen (unprecedented speed for the time), the ship to arrive at Rotterdam by five the same afternoon, and to return on Friday p.m., sailing through the night to allow passengers to be back in London p.m. Saturday. The fare was set at thirty shillings but only twenty for passengers joining at Norwich or Yarmouth. Some two hundred booked including guests representing the Eastern Counties, Eastern Union (J. C. Cobbold) and Norfolk railways, the mayor of Yarmouth, and Peto himself acting as impresario.

Little worked out to plan according to the reporter from the *Norfolk Chronicle* who was aboard. Departure from Yarmouth was delayed by more than an hour as nobody had briefed Customs who insisted on examining all baggage. When the ship eventually left a band aboard played bravely for a short while but the ship, being unballasted, rolled vigorously in the strong beam wind, and many were sick. Later in the day it was calmer and after dinner in the forehold during which the band played enlivening airs many felt better although the reporter noted sourly that the railway people formed a party of their own provided with bumpers of champagne and sherry cobbler. Unfortunately the skipper steered too far to windward over-compensating for a cross tide so that instead of making Rotterdam by five p.m. the vessel reached the mouth of the Rhine only when night had fallen and the tide had been lost. The pilot at first refused even to attempt an entrance and when persuaded to try found insufficient water on the bar at Brielle and so took the ship into Helvoetsluys. The ship having no sleeping accommodation and the small town, although well supplied with alcohol, being otherwise quite unprepared for two hundred visitors, most of the passengers spent a drunken night on the streets before rejoining the ship for a four a.m. departure.

On the early morning tide the vessel soon covered the twenty miles up river to Rotterdam, a town that much impressed the reporter as so many of the inhabitants spoke English. At two p.m. a grand dinner was held for the visitors and representatives of the town at which Peto was chairman and represented both the Norfolk and the Eastern Counties. In his inevitable speech he enlarged on the great prospects he could see for trade across the North Sea and especially between Yarmouth and Rotterdam. Alcohol again flowed freely and not only amongst the dinner guests as when they returned to the ship many of the crew were found to be drunk. One hand had to be rescued after falling into the harbour. Some passengers wanted to get off but were dissuaded and felt better once the ship steamed down river. Out at sea there was a big swell and a brisk head wind rising to a gale. With only twenty berths on board many sought shelter from the cold in the holds while others perforce slept on deck. The ship behaved well this time, Southwold was sighted at dawn and Yarmouth was reached in time for a late breakfast but again progress was delayed by a full scale Customs examination of all baggage. The returning train performed well enough to Norwich but outside Ely a boiler tube burst on the locomotive bringing it to a halt. The passengers, said the reporter, were by now philosophical and walked the remaining distance into Ely where a replacement engine was begged from an arriving train. London was reached at eight that evening.

Many of the passengers must have been seared by the experience and the *Railway Times*, no friends of Peto's, asked rhetorically 'Who would think of sending 250 persons to sea in a vessel with accommodation for only a dozen' and thought prospects of ferries from Harwich far better than anything from Yarmouth. However the Norfolk directors were far from daunted. Not long after they resolved to establish a company to open steam vessel routes between Yarmouth and Lowestoft and Hamburg and Rotterdam and to make an offer to the owners of the *SS Norfolk*, the Norfolk Steam Boat Company, to unite. William Johnson of Yarmouth, giving evidence in early 1847 concerning the positioning of railway stations at the town, referred to a new company of which he was a director, entitled the Yarmouth, Lowestoft, Rotterdam & Hamburg company, which is probably the same enterprise. At that stage it owned a building but had no ships. How far the project went is uncertain but in May 1847 we find an advertisement for The Great Yarmouth & Lowestoft Steam Packet Co that had chartered the steam ship *Norfolk* to run between Yarmouth & Rotterdam weekly until August when the company's two new steamers *Yarmouth* and *Rotterdam*, then building, would be launched. Enquiries were to be directed to the Steam Packet Office on Yarmouth South Quay or, significantly, to the Superintendent of the Norfolk Railway. The company was more probably a venture by Peto and others than by the Norfolk Railway itself, a forerunner of his Northern Steam Packet Company of 1851.

The Norfolk's revenue reported in August for the half year to June 1846 was £37,927 and a dividend at the rate of six per cent per annum was declared for the half year on the paid up value of the ordinary shares that were now to be converted to a single class of stock. Once again working expenses had been charged at forty per cent of revenue with the excess presumably being charged to capital. All comment by directors and shareholders was to the effect that forty per cent was too high. Bidder, by contrast thought there was little chance of it being less, even though coal should be cheaper once the Lowestoft branch was open. While agricultural wages in Norfolk might be low mechanics cost considerably more than in the north. He pinned his hopes on future growth of revenue.

In early September 1846 the newspapers carried an account of a robbery at Thorpe station when over £800 was stolen; a bag containing cheques, gold and coins had disappeared. While the thief was not found, despite a large reward offered and help from the London police, the incident led to the dismissal of two clerks and a ticket collector for gross negligence since the bag had been left in an open safe and empty room.

Norwich station

An article in the *Norfolk Chronicle* later in the autumn was devoted to a survey of the station at Thorpe. Buildings and tracks by then extended over fifty acres with a new goods warehouse, busy workshops and piles of goods seen stacked prior to movements onwards. Much levelling of the site had taken place, and roofs had been extended over the whole of the station. The signalling systems were working satisfactorily and delays occurred only when 'monster' trains arrived or departed, such as the London excursion noted above. One train a day was scheduled to reach London in just eight minutes over four hours although it was admitted that the normal time was closer to five hours or even more. There were now plenty of engines to maintain the timetable (a Board of Trade report in the summer recorded eighteen belonging to the Norfolk but by the year end there were far more) but it was noted that Norwich traders continued to find the location of the station inconvenient.

One of the principal reasons advanced in Norfolk for building its railway at all had been the ease of transporting fat cattle to London. At that time and for long before beasts had been driven slowly south from Scotland to fatten on the Norfolk marshes and then, when ready, onwards to London. Although the lack of a westward connection meant that young cattle were still for a while driven across the Fens, the new railway enabled the second part of their final journey to be done at ten times the previous speed. The Bird in Hand at Tasburgh, ten miles south of Norwich on the Ipswich road, that in 1845 had fed 9,300 beasts with fifty tons of hay, required in 1846 less than one ton. However there were problems with cattle transport. Beasts could leap out of the open trucks. Drovers were expected either to buy a ticket at full rate or travel with the cattle in open trucks. There was nowhere very suitable at the London end for the cattle to rest, as they must, before continuing on foot to Smithfield. If taken overnight on a Saturday, London regulations allowed no cattle driving through the City on Sunday mornings. When the railway attempted to raise fares for animal transport in November 1846 and to enforce certain stringent conditions farmers were in revolt while the *Chronicle* observed that such highhanded action by the railway showed how undesirable it would be if the railways of the region were ever to merge, so destroying any prospect of competition. A correspondent produced figures to show that rail carriage of cattle in eastern England was at approximately double the rate charged in Belgium.

At a meeting with farmers on 30 November Richard Till, general manager of the Norfolk, backed down. Instead of charging for 126 miles of railway transport the fare would be calculated on the direct distance of 108 miles, reducing the proposed charge per beast shipped at Norwich from 10/6d to 9 shillings. Some of the proposed conditions would be relaxed. For instance a proposed minimum number of beasts per farmer in any one shipment would be abandoned; they could send just one if they pleased. Just as soon as facilities were available cattle would be unloaded at Stratford rather than at Tottenham. But a month later some of the same complaints were being repeated. Would not the railway build proper accommodation at Stratford, and better still, a tramway from there to Mile End and Smithfield itself? Despite these and other complaints 1846 ended well for the Norfolk. Heavy snow blocked main roads in late December but the trains kept well to time, a single stoppage due to snow at Chesterford being soon cleared.

The cattle story did not end in 1846. Due to the continued number of injuries to animals the railway were proposing in December an abattoir at Trowse that would obviate live beasts being sent by rail at all. In March 1847 they were advertising for tenants of two slaughterhouses recently built, each capable of killing 100 beasts or 200 sheep a day. In the same month an advertisement appeared for a new company, that sought to raise £400,000 to purchase a new abattoir at the existing Islington cattle market, described in some detail and only a quarter of a mile from a railway which distance could easily be covered by a tramway. However, since the Northern & Eastern had long ago abandoned its original plan to terminate at Islington and had instead joined the Eastern Counties at Stratford, an abattoir at Islington could be of no help to the Norfolk. A few months later the company was advertising slaughter and packing of animals at Trowse as a service without charge.

The accounts presented to the February 1847 meeting for the half year to 31 December previous charged to revenue for the first time ever the actual costs of working the line, given in some detail. The percentage of total revenue was not forty but forty nine and, as one shareholder pointed out, if rents were excluded from revenue the percentage topped fifty. After interest charges there was only some £19,500 available for dividends which, because by now there was much more paid up capital, would require over £29,000 to improve upon the three per cent rate declared at the previous half year. There had been a surplus brought forward of some £2,250 and the difference was made up by charging to capital account £7,480 of interest paid on capital raised for the Dereham branch which had previously been charged to revenue. While not improper by the standards of the time and certainly not illegal this should have raised some purist eyebrows. As to the high rate of operating costs, the written report airily commented that this had already been explained. When a shareholder reminded the directors of the forty per cent estimate and quoted rates from other lines, the Midland at 32%, others at 33% and even the Eastern Counties at only 40%, Bidder explained that the Norfolk was running more trains than it needed to attract new traffic and ran them at twice the speed than had been customary even a few years earlier. He did not comment, as he might later have done, that the lines quoted in comparison were all managed by Hudson and the figures were more than likely to be unreliable. But whatever the reasons it was now becoming clear that the Norfolk was not a cheap line to run.

The meeting in August 1847 received a report for the half year to 30 June which showed only a slight increase in revenue and operating costs even further increased. Because the shareholders were more concerned with prospects of merger (see Chapter 8) and with the results of the recent parliamentary session, not much attention was paid to the results. Even though the dividend was cut back to three per cent this rate was only achieved by some further special credits and capitalisation of further interest on the Dereham line.

For the six months to 31 December 1847, the final half year ever published, the revenue had increased sharply but the ratio of working expenses to turnover remained high. The dividend was cut once again. Shareholders were assured that economies were being effected by reducing the number of trains run while increased revenue should result from the opening via Peterborough of connections with the Midlands but by now it was increasingly obvious that the line, without merger or significant extension, was not adequately remunerative. By the end of 1847 the capital raised, taking shares and loans together, was approximately £1,650,000 and as interest rates were generally around five per cent, the total annual charge for dividends and interest on loans would have been over £80,000. Even this ignores the charges being borne by the Norfolk on capital raised for the Lowestoft project (see Chapters 7 and 8). Based on the best half year experienced, the amount available to pay all this was less than £58,000. The circle was being squared by charging interest during construction to capital account. This was a common enough practice at the time. However, wherever charged, if cash is flowing out faster than revenue is bringing it in, the company is on a direct course to bankruptcy.

CHAPTER 7

The Lowestoft Railway and Harbour Company: 1844 to 1847

PETO has conventionally been called 'the father of Lowestoft' and so, at least as regards the Victorian harbour, fishing port and holiday resort, he is entitled to be. This was no case of philanthropy although Peto had a justified reputation as a philanthropic man. Undoubtedly he had vision. His vision for Lowestoft was of a handsome seaside watering place whose large harbour would form an important link in a commercial chain, if possible a Peto controlled chain, stretching from Manchester to the Baltic. Unfortunately he did not himself possess the means to bring this about but, for a few years at least, a great part of his objective was achieved.

The harbour

Prior to 1831 Lowestoft had no harbour. A fishing centre since the Middle Ages, its boats were worked off the beach where even shipbuilding was carried on. The eastern end of Lake Lothing was several hundred yards from the sea, separated by an area of shingle, while only the tortuous and narrow Oulton Dyke connected the western end to the River Waveney. Supposition that Lake Lothing constituted an old mouth of the Waveney since blocked by coastal drift contributed to the enthusiasm for creating a harbour that resulted in an Act of Parliament in 1827 authorising work to begin. This enthusiasm stemmed almost entirely from Norwich where the initial capital for the venture was raised. That city had been in years of dispute with Yarmouth about port and freight charges and the condition of the river Yare and welcomed the prospect of an alternative route to the sea. The full project involved building the New Cut to shorten the distance between the Yare and the Waveney, so avoiding the shallows of Breydon Water and bypassing St Olave's bridge; cutting a straighter and wider version of Oulton Dyke; building an embankment pierced by a lock at Mutford to divide Oulton Broad from Lake Lothing; and cutting through the bank at the eastern end of Lothing, building a sea lock in the cut made, bridging the cut with a swing bridge and constructing short sea walls extending on either side of the lock.

As customary with any major civil engineering project then or now the estimate of costs and hence the capital raised were inadequate. Extra finance was obtained on loan from the government's Public Works Commissioners and the harbour duly opened in 1831. However there were major flaws in design, especially at the seaward entrance. It was intended to keep the channel open by periodic sluicing from the sea lock. That is to say that normally Lake Lothing was kept at high tide level but occasionally the lock gates would be opened near low water and the lake's contents would pour in a strong stream outward to drive away the shingle, sand or mud that had accumulated. The intention was to clear a sufficient depth of water in the lock approaches for ships to enter, while at the next tide the lake would be refilled.

Two major problems were found. Firstly the harbour walls did not extend far enough seawards to reach deep water and, against the predictions of the engineer, the accumulation of material outside the walls was prodigious. Sluicing was initially successful in driving this matter away but not far enough to prevent a bar being formed so that while the lock was clear enough the channel to seaward was nevertheless still obstructed. More frequent sluicing than had been anticipated meant that successive refilling of the lake actually brought in substantial quantities of mud in suspension that precipitated at slack water to silt up the channel in the lake itself. Harbour use did increase and small seagoing ships did indeed work up to Norwich but revenue from harbour dues was inadequate to defray the expense of maintenance, especially dredging, that fell into arrears. The lock itself deteriorated and the gates were attacked by shipworm and so severely damaged that they had eventually to be left open making sluicing no longer possible.

The company that had built the harbour and navigation had insufficient revenue to service the government loan and the lenders foreclosed. The harbour was put up for sale but no buyers were found until 1842. Then a local consortium paid just under £5,000 to take on the near derelict and unprofitable enterprise, the Loan Commissioners writing off more than £70,000 in debt and lost interest. The new proprietors did not find their acquisition any more profitable. According to one of their number they spent on maintenance over two thousand pounds in excess of harbour dues received during the two years of their ownership.

The project of 1844

The first public indication of any plan to build a railway from Lowestoft was a notice in the local press on 21 September 1844 calling a meeting in the town to consider the expediency of a railway from thence to Reedham. This was less than six months after the opening of the line from Yarmouth via Reedham to Norwich and almost a year before Norwich was connected by rail to the rest of the country. Only a few weeks earlier the newspapers had carried a note of the purchase by Peto, by now well known in the area, of the Somerleyton estate close north of Lowestoft.

The meeting had, it transpired, been called by Peto himself. Held in the town hall on 28 September, it was attended by 'a large assembly' of which some thirty were named in the report in the *Norfolk Chronicle*. Amongst those present in addition to Peto, the main speaker, were baronet Sir Thomas Gooch of nearby Benacre, who took the chair, Edward Leathes, once a director of the Eastern Counties and brother of J. F. Leathes of Herringfleet Hall whose lands stood squarely across the likely route of the line, and Thomas Morse, whose family owned a Lowestoft brewery. These three later became directors of the company. Also present were Richard Till, then treasurer of the Yarmouth & Norwich company, and J. W. Hickling, related to B. W. Hickling, one of the consortium that had acquired the harbour.

Peto spoke optimistically of the prospects for a railway. There would be no engineering difficulties. Where the route was not a perfect level materials were at hand to ballast the line. He had already had an encouraging response from Mr Leathes concerning acquisition of the necessary land. There might be some difficulty concerning a bridge at Reedham but he did not see why the Yarmouth Haven Commissioners, responsible for the river navigation, would object. The main danger was jealousy from Yarmouth merchants and shipowners yet the line would do no more than place Lowestoft on a par with the other port. Norwich should certainly have no objection. Having spent over £150,000 during the previous decade on opening a navigation to Lowestoft and constructing a rudimentary harbour there, the city would surely wish that harbour saved from the dereliction with which it was threatened.

There would be no problems with the Board of Trade. He knew the people there and the whole matter could be agreed within half an hour. Big gainers would be the Yarmouth & Norwich and the Norwich & Brandon railways that would obtain direct access to a port, something they did not yet have at Yarmouth where so far the railway terminated on the west side of the Bure. But the biggest gainer of all must be the Lowestoft fishing industry for when all the lines now building were complete their fish could be in the industrial Midlands and North on the same day it was landed. Were the line not built the Lowestoft boats must go either to Yarmouth or to Harwich to dispose of their catch.

The line, he believed, would pay on its own, but it could be worked more economically if it merged with the other two railways. Their directors were prepared to take a lease but awaited the decision of the Lowestoft proprietors. Shares would be offered in the first instance to local interests but he, his partner Grissell, and other large proprietors in the other railways would take up any shares that Lowestoft did not. There should be no difficulty with acquiring land. He, himself, had in the past three months negotiated the purchase of all the land needed by both the Norwich & Brandon and the Eastern Counties for their connection to London and the latter's branch to Peterborough. Not once had it been necessary to resort to a jury hearing.

Very little was said about the harbour. What was stressed was the ease and speed with which Lowestoft fish and local agricultural products could be brought to markets, especially those of the industrial north. Lancashire, said Peto, was a market as important as London and the railway would carry fish to Manchester in seven hours. The weaver would be able to buy and eat fish one evening that had been landed that same morning. Passengers could be carried to London in five hours, but it was the northern connection that was emphasised.

There was no dissent expressed. The popular local vicar, the Reverend Francis Cunningham, replied to Peto. An enthusiast for railways, he pointed out how poorly placed were now those ancient towns, such as Northampton and Kingston on Thames, which had declined a railway and had been bypassed. But, he pleaded, could Sunday traffic please be kept to a minimum? Edward Leathes said that he and his brother would look sympathetically at the plans when available. If fairly dealt with they would be happy to see the railway pass through their land.

The Lowestoft company

As with all railways detailed plans had to be deposited by 30 November of the year preceding that in which Parliament would consider a Bill to authorise the line and the formation of a company. That this was accomplished on behalf of the Lowestoft projectors by 30 November 1844 reflects credit on the speed with which surveyors had worked but also suggests that work had begun even before the October public meeting. The short line, being largely level, appeared to offer no great difficulty, and the land ownership was spread amongst comparatively few persons. Significant, in the light of later recriminations, was a sketch of the proposed outer harbour forming part of the plans showing a considerably smaller area than was later enclosed. However the sketch shows in addition to the harbour walls an impressive detached breakwater outside the entrance. Robert Stephenson was officially consulting engineer but the work was in the event done under the direction of George Bidder,

Another action taken early was that in October Peto 'took possession' of the harbour and navigation. In fact he bought it from the local syndicate for £12,500 but it is unclear when it was paid. Initial payment was either by the Norfolk company or a predecessor as in October 1845 the Lowestoft company reimbursed the Norfolk for that sum. By that date, when evidence on the state of the harbour was under review by the parliamentary Tidal Harbours Commission, an engineer had already been appointed by Peto and a considerable amount of dredging had been undertaken in the rivers and in Lake Lothing. Although this work was eventually paid for by the company, it was described as having been carried out on behalf of Peto himself. It was not until March 1846 that Peto reimbursed the company for the capital cost of £12,500. For two years thereafter he charged a rental to the company of £1,000 per annum but subsequently and until 1852 this charge was neither paid nor recorded. However the deed of conveyance of the harbour to the company required it to redeem the rent charge at the end of ten years for a capital price of £25,000.

A prospectus for the proposed Lowestoft company to reconstruct the harbour and build the railway was issued in early 1845 and special meetings of the Yarmouth & Norwich and Norwich & Brandon shareholders to approve the proposed leasing were called for February. The prospectus looked for £120,000 in share capital in 6,000 shares of £20 each. The initial deposit was to be just £1 5s 0d per share but the whole of the subscription was to be paid up by midsummer 1847. The proposition to the two Norfolk companies was that they should jointly lease and operate the Lowestoft line and harbour for a rental of four per cent of a fixed cost plus half the profits of operation. There does not seem to have been any opposition at the meetings of the two Norfolk companies to the proposed leasing arrangements but then the proposition put may have been less than precise and in any event, until the Lowestoft Company obtained its Act and was incorporated, there could be no contract.

This being 1845, with the railway mania gathering way, there was no difficulty in obtaining subscribers for shares. Three receiving banks were employed to receive share applications and deposits, two local, Gurneys in Norwich and Lacons in Yarmouth, plus Glynn, Halifax, Mills & Co in London. Except for the largest applications we do not have the addresses of the applicants but the local banks received less than twelve per cent of the deposits demonstrating once again the degree to which outside finance paid for the early Norfolk lines. By the end of February 1845 applications had been received for 5,196 shares, over the necessary three quarters of those to be issued, and a deposit was then paid of £5,196 to the Bank of England, curiously at five per cent rather than the normal ten per cent of the full value of the shares. Applications continued to come in, eventually for a total of over 7,500 shares which necessitated refund of deposits. It is not known on what system the abatement was carried out and so, while we have information on applications, it is not possible to give precise details of the numbers eventually allotted to specific individuals.

Appendix 2 shows the majority of the larger subscriptions. Altogether there were some 250 applications ranging from Peto's 500 down to a single share. In addition to those shown in Appendix 2 which cover 3,410 shares there were 36 applications for more than 25 shares. It must be remembered that these were twenty pound shares and at that time even one share would have been a substantial commitment for someone less than well off. The three men who were to become local directors, Sir Thomas

Gooch, Edward Leathes and Thomas Morse, did not even apply for the full amount (25) required to qualify as directors but presumably acquired more later. Other nominated directors were Adam Duff and Charles Tyndale of the Norfolk and Francis Mills, banker and major investor. A further director was nominated by the company's Act, Sir Francis Holyoake Goodriche Bt then residing near Watton, but he never acted as a director and applied for no shares. Other local men who invested but who do not appear on Appendix 2 were B.W. Hickling of Lowestoft, 100 shares, Charles Cory of Yarmouth, 40 shares, and John Sultzer of Norwich, 50 shares.

By April 1845 the Lowestoft Bill was before Parliament and in May was examined before a committee of the House of Commons. Edward Leathes gave evidence on the project generally, especially as to the advantages for transport of cattle, agricultural products and above all fish. He proved rather embarrassingly ignorant about the fishery itself and the proposals for the harbour but the opposers of the Bill, mainly the city of Norwich and the Yarmouth Haven commissioners were more concerned with engineering matters and bridges and he was given an easy ride. Bidder spoke to both potential passenger traffic and to the detail of the railway itself, describing the line by reference to an Ordnance map. The line would be just over eleven miles long, would cross the Waveney near Somerleyton by a swing bridge with a thirty foot wide opening and the Yare at Reedham by a larger swing bridge with an opening of forty-four feet. These widths had been chosen so as to be no smaller than the proposed new bridge at Yarmouth (in the case of Reedham) and that over the New Cut at St Olave's in the case of Somerleyton. The inspecting engineer for the Admiralty (James Rendel) had approved the plans for the harbour and the bridges as had the Hydrographer of the Admiralty, Captain Beaufort (he of the scale of wind force still in use) although approval of the outer breakwater had been reserved and it was possible that the Admiralty would undertake that itself so that it could shelter a man of war.

Concerning the harbour itself, Bidder planned that the new outer harbour would be sufficiently large and protected for silt brought in by the tides to be deposited there. Any that reached the inner harbour would need to be dredged but that in the outer harbour could be cleared by scouring from higher up. He assured counsel for the Yarmouth commissioners that no water would escape from the Waveney other than that lost through the operation of Mutford lock. The estimated costs were £80,000 for the railway and £40,000 for the harbour; hence the capital required of £120,000, but in addition the company was to have borrowing powers of £40,000. Asked if he had contractors to take it for these sums he replied, 'That is positively agreed on.' To a further question, 'For the railway?' he answered, 'And the harbour too.' As we shall see, the second part of the answer was untrue.

Counsel for Norwich started to ask questions concerning the bridge proposed at Reedham but was told by the chairman that Norwich had no standing in the matter, its jurisdiction not reaching so far down the river. Unabashed the counsel explained that he acted also for Yarmouth and so continued, attempting to demonstrate that Bidder had not explained the matter fully to Rendel. In view of the later disputes it is worth noting Bidder's statement, 'I intend to erect a bridge which shall have two openings of 44 feet to leave that part of the channel open which shall be found most useful. The other will be part on [over?] the river and part on [over?] dry ground.' The design would be the same as his previous bridge at Carrow.

His evidence of likely passenger traffic was vague although he had studied the present numbers travelling to Norwich via Yarmouth by omnibus ... and had doubled it. However he justified the entire project by its value to the Norfolk line and the other lines further on. He doubted if it would make a profit but neither did he think it would make a loss. Yet he went on to explain how much the traffic between Yarmouth and Norwich had been stimulated by the existence of the railway with 200,000 passengers being carried in the first year of operations and held out hopes that growth at Lowestoft would be commensurate. It has to be admitted that this was scarcely a bullish report and it is surprising that he got away with it. Less surprising is that the report in the *Norwich Mercury* is garbled and implies that he was forecasting substantial operating profits.

Counsel for the main objectors, Yarmouth Harbour Commissioners, withdrew when it became clear that the bridges would not impede the river navigations to Beccles and Norwich. There was substantial government approval for the harbour part of the project that promised to provide a much needed refuge for coastal shipping at no cost to the taxpayer (Neither the Admiralty nor the company ever built the offlying breakwater). The remaining stages of parliamentary process gave no trouble and the Bill was duly converted to become an Act. Richard Till, by now secretary and general manager of the Norfolk, was secretary. At the directors' first meeting on 23 July 1845 it was recorded that it was intended to lease the undertaking to the Norfolk company but the terms of that lease were not recited. And, although it was not apparently discussed, there was a snag in that the recently formed Norfolk company had not taken any powers to lease the Lowestoft in its originating Act and so could not do so until a further Act could be obtained in the following year.

It is a puzzle just what the true relationship of the companies was and what it was understood to be. Neither held shares in the other. Peto was initially a director of neither yet appears from the outset to have dominated both. It was to a board meeting of the Norfolk that the terms of the proposed contract to build the railway were submitted in December. The rental under the lease was frequently referred to as four per cent on a fixed cost of works plus fifty per cent of operating profits. In practice, perhaps because there were never any profits to share, this became a guarantee by the Norfolk of a four per cent dividend on the Lowestoft first issue of capital which, although duly paid, was not recorded in the Lowestoft accounting records at all.

Building the railway and harbour

The specific requirements in the company's Act for the bridge at Reedham merely asked for, 'a good and sufficient draw or swivel bridge ... Which when opened shall leave a clear and uninterrupted waterway for masted vessels directly following the present channel of the river of at least forty four feet clear span ... ' This asks for no more than Bidder had already said would be provided. The plans submitted with the Bill showed that it would be sited some 1200 feet west of its present position and that the line across it would then curve west to join the main Norwich/Yarmouth line in the direction of Norwich. This must early have been perceived as too inflexible and in October 1845 Peto attended a meeting of the Yarmouth Harbour Commissioners seeking their permission to move the bridge site 1200 feet down river which would allow the railway space on the north bank for the line to split, one arm to curve west and the other east, both joining the main line. Permission was granted, although not without opposition. An amending Bill was prepared to go before Parliament in 1846 but by April of that year the Harbour Commissioners had changed their mind and, after finding that the Admiralty had no objection to the new bridge site, were nevertheless instructing their clerk to take steps to oppose any bridge at Reedham at all.

Under the contract submitted to the Norfolk board on 1 December 1845 Grissell & Peto offered to construct the railway as a single line but with room for double track, including land but excluding stations, for £80,000. Bidder, on behalf of Stephenson, approved and recommended the terms to which the Norfolk board agreed. Nothing was mentioned about the harbour except that it was agreed to purchase certain lands adjoining it. There was certainly nothing recorded concerning a significant omission from the contract for the railway. As it was afterwards revealed the price did not include rails or other materials for the permanent way itself. By the end of February 1846, when the half-yearly shareholders' meeting was held at Lowestoft, work was already quite well advanced on the railway. The contract with Grissell & Peto was reported. Already all the necessary land had been purchased, half of the earthworks had been completed and most of the permanent way material had been delivered. The chief difficulties expected would be with the bridges. Casting their main components was going ahead in London and delivery was expected in July. It was hoped that the line would be open in the autumn by which time the Ely/Peterborough link should be completed also and so there would be a continuous connection to the Midlands. The harbour plan of works was said still to be before the Admiralty which somewhat contradicts the statements made earlier in Parliament by Bidder but could be a reference to doubts about the external breakwater.

Exactly what was to be done to the harbour does not seem to have been publicly reported by the company but there was no secret since a preliminary plan had accompanied the railway plans deposited in November 1844. A revised version of the plans, omitting the breakwater, had been presented to the Tidal Harbours Commissioners in November 1845. The existing sea lock was to be repaired (although in later years it was removed) and the existing seawalls left in place but they were to be surrounded by new seawalls stretching out from the shore some 1,000 feet to reach deep water and to form an approximately rectangular outer harbour, over 500 feet wide, of some twenty acres that would serve primarily as a protection and as a harbour of refuge. The fish wharves and market would be built on the northern side of this area. Within the lock many hundred feet of wharves would be constructed on both sides of Lake Lothing while both inner and outer harbours were to be extensively dredged. A Mr James Hodges had been appointed site engineer by Peto to work under the general supervision of Bidder.

On the north side of the inner harbour there were to be constructed coke ovens by which imported coal would be processed to produce coke as then used by railway locomotives and, as a vital by-product, creosote. Nearby a further plant was to be constructed for the purpose of impregnating timber with creosote necessary for protecting harbour wall piling from rot and worm and also required for railway sleepers. These plants were needed early in the project since driving the timber piling was the first stage of building the harbour walls, later to be faced and infilled with stone. The whole concept could be described in modern terms as 'state of the art' for the 1840s. How any competent engineer could have imagined that all this, even given the limited area planned for the outer harbour as compared with that finally constructed, could be completed for £40,000, or even £80,000 if all the proposed borrowings were applied to the harbour, defies imagination. There is no question of Bidder's competence. He had spent ten years before 1835 much engaged on dock projects and was later to design London's Victoria Dock, in its day the largest enclosed dock in the world. Possibly he underestimated the difficulties of working on an exposed shore but it seems more likely that, with the crushing burden of work that he was then engaged in, the harbour had been given inadequate consideration.

At no time until the end of 1847 was any revised costing on the harbour works reported to either board. In January 1846 Bidder recommended to the Lowestoft board that the works should be carried out by Peto at a fixed profit of ten per cent of cost as evidenced by engineer's certificate. Both parties agreed but in fact it does not appear that Peto or Grissell & Peto were ever concerned with the harbour works or earned profit at ten

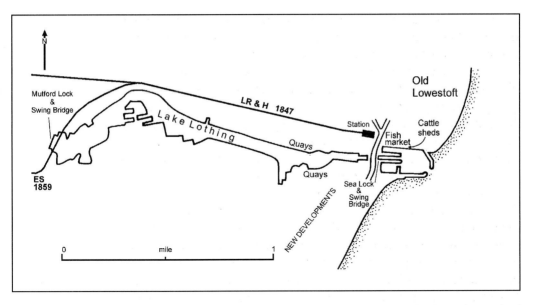

Lowestoft harbour as first completed

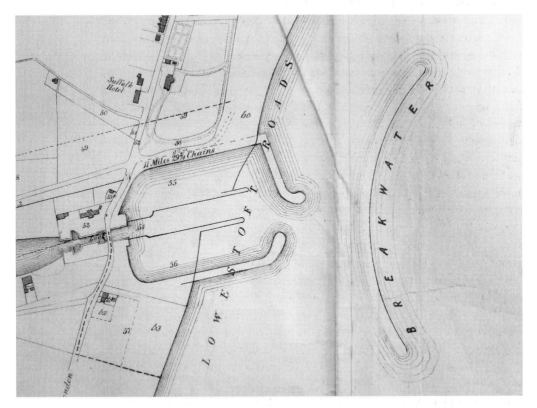

Sketch plan of proposed outer harbour as included in original deposited plans, 1844. The plan shows the suggested outer breakwater which was never built. The outer harbour as eventually completed was more than double the size shown.

per cent or any other rate. Rather Hodges appears to have performed the work directly on behalf of the Lowestoft company periodically drawing cash from the company's bankers that he used to purchase materials and pay labour, apparently including himself. By contrast the railway construction proceeded under a conventional system of financial control with Bidder issuing periodic certificates for the value of work done and land purchased that were paid to the contractors in cash or bills after the deduction of a ten per cent retention. This continued to November 1846 at approximately monthly intervals after which there was a gap of over eighteen months before the final contract account was drawn up.

The *Norfolk Chronicle* had an enthusiastic correspondent who made two visits to the works in the summer of 1846. In the typical flowery style of the day he wrote appreciatively of the 'swarthy and robust' workmen engaged on a project of no common importance and of numerous separate trades united in a common purpose. He was especially impressed with Hodges's pile driving gear which ran on rails above staging mounted on existing piles and could hammer down three piles simultaneously, each sixty or more feet in length from twenty to forty feet into the beach. Creosoting was performed in cylinders eighty feet in length and six feet in diameter into which piles were run on small iron carriages. The cylinders were then evacuated by steam power that sucked creosote from a tank below to fill the cylinders and force the fluid into the wood. Another product of the coke ovens was gas that was used to illuminate buildings such as the smithy and the engine house.

In July he visited the bridge site at Reedham and described the base circles of immense piles on which was to be placed a caisson sixteen feet in diameter to carry in turn the turntable and rollers forming the pivot for the swing bridge. The bridge was to stand twelve feet above high water and the clear waterway would be fifty-five feet in width (although both these dimensions were somewhat exaggerated. It should be noted that the bridge was to pivot on a base close to the north bank of the river: the present bridge, well known to Broads sailors, which replaced the first bridge in 1904, pivots on the southern side.) At that time there were 400 men at work on the harbour.

However that summer a new difficulty had arisen concerning the bridge. Norwich Corporation was at that period engaged in a renewed dispute with the Yarmouth Haven Commissioners concerning the navigation of the River Yare. Norwich had long wanted the navigation improved to enable seagoing ships to come all the way to Norwich. The attempt to build a route via Lowestoft having largely failed attention had returned to the lower Yare. Here ships larger than wherries were not only impeded by the narrow opening through a temporary town bridge at Yarmouth, renewal of which was long overdue, but also and fatally by inadequate depths at the upper end of Breydon Water which required aggressive dredging. The majority of the Commissioners were not sympathetic to

Norwich and retained most of the substantial harbour dues to pay for the new bridge. Now, in the middle of this ongoing dispute, it was conceived that the Reedham bridge would impose a further obstacle. Late that July the chairman of the Norwich River Committee was telling the main council that although the railway had obtained Admiralty permission for bridges at alternative sites at Reedham, the City had objected to one and persuaded the Admiralty to withdraw permission. Now the railway were building at that site anyway without either Admiralty or Parliamentary permission. They had agreed to build at fifty foot width but there would be no 'sideway'. The result would be a constriction of the river as at Carrow. His statement seems to have been incorrect as regards the Admiralty but it is the case that the company's 1846 Bill to authorise the changes had been withdrawn, perhaps due to Yarmouth's opposition, and work was indeed proceeding without statutory permission.

When the *Chronicle* correspondent visited again at the end of August 1846 to attend the half year meeting the pace of work on both the railway and the harbour had slackened somewhat which was put down to shortage of labour but which in fact was probably due to shortage of cash. On all his visits he expiated on the attractiveness of Lowestoft as a holiday resort. A native of Yarmouth, he envied Lowestoft its cliff and reported good lodgings and inns but warned the townspeople that they would do well to remove the pool of stagnant sewage at the bottom of the town. On the commercial side he not only admired the works but the fact that the railway would run direct to the docksides and the fish market. He called on Yarmouth to wake up and take notice.

At the shareholders' meeting on 29 August it was reported that rails had been laid from Lowestoft to Somerleyton, the line from Somerleyton to Reedham was ready for ballasting, good progress had been made with the bridge foundations and approaches and the bridge castings had been made and shipped. The harbour works were now proceeding at increased speed with the north pier pilings now extended 700 feet seawards and the south pier 550 feet. It was reported also that the Act for the 'transfer' of the undertaking to the Norfolk Railway had received Royal Assent. In fact the Act allowed the Norfolk either to buy or lease the undertaking, apparently at its own option. Forty thousand pounds were to be borrowed since it was possible to raise a mortgage now that half the share capital had been paid up. As regards the bridge, the shareholders were told that the Admiralty had asked for another five feet of unobstructed waterway at Reedham and that this would require modification to the bridge components already built and consequently some delay. Reference was made to the dispute with Norwich but it was said that while there would have to be some negotiations with the Norwich River Committee there was no ill feeling and the company's engineer would be meeting the city's engineer the following week. A blot on the record had been the number of serious accidents including a double fatality in the week previous to the meeting.

Local vicar Francis Cunningham had spoken of the serious accident rate and appealed to the company for a subscription to the infirmary that he had set up getting £100 from the company that Peto promised personally to match. The money was needed principally to provide food for the infirmary inmates. Otherwise they must be fed by their mates who brought supplies highly unsuitable for invalids. He considered that the accidents were in no way the company's fault but arose from the labourers being unfamiliar with their work!

As at the end of June 1846 a cumulative total of just under £60,000 had been raised from all sources, mainly calls on shares, and only £52,000 had been paid out. But by 31 December the accounts presented to the half year meeting in February 1847 showed expenditure risen to £165,000 and although £26,000 more had been raised from calls £78,000 had been borrowed of which £18,000 had been advanced by the Norfolk company. Moreover the project was not finished. The railway had not opened and there had been difficulties at the Reedham bridge including landslips although it was now in place and ballast trains were using it. The harbour was far from finished but at least the work so far had survived the winter gales without serious damage. The piling was nearly complete and about half the stonework was in place. Much wharfing was complete and in use and a further, larger dredger was being acquired.

However the dispute over the bridge site had certainly not ended with a calm discussion between engineers in September. Instead, according to the minutes of the River Committee, Norwich had gone to court and obtained a bill of indictment at the autumn Assizes against the Norfolk Railway for impeding the navigation and had then applied for an injunction to stop the works. Nevertheless, after a site meeting in November, the company had agreed, the Press reported, 'to so widen the river as to allow two arches, each with a span of fifty feet'. The

report noted that this would involve much earth moving on the north or Reedham side which, looking at the site today, was an understatement. The agreement was formalised in March 1847. What the agreement and the subsequent Act required was very precisely stated. On the north or Reedham side of the river the company was to excavate the bank and dredge the area excavated to a depth of nine feet for some 270 yards either side of the bridge so as to form a navigable channel fifty feet wide on the north side of the cylinder of the bridge and thereafter keep a navigable channel of fifty foot width on each side, north and south, of the cylinder and one of 100 feet for a distance of 500 yards to the east and west of the bridge. But whatever the agreement or the Act might say, the company's attitude was simple. It took no notice.

Although it takes us ahead in time it may be as well to bring this particular piece of the story to an end. Between 1849 and 1855 Norwich Corporation was insisting on the promised widening of the river at Reedham bridge and obtained a writ of Mandamus in 1850 to enforce the undertaking given in 1847. In October 1850 the bridgemaster told the Yarmouth harbourmaster, who was discussing a temporary obstruction, that the railway company was about to excavate the bank to enlarge the waterway. However he was either misinformed or ingenuous for the Norfolk Railway had no funds to do the work which in any case meant that further land must be acquired. Its protest that according to locals the work would only make the navigation more difficult was brushed aside by the Norwich River Committee but the latter lost their case before the Court of Queens Bench in 1851 as the company's powers to acquire the necessary land had expired. The work was certainly never done and all Norwich achieved was a sum of £500 as liquidated damages against which it had to set considerable costs.

CHAPTER 8

Frustrated hope, looming disaster: 1847

F ROM THE BEGINNING OF 1847 it is desirable to draw together the threads of the previous three chapters into a single narrative. From about this time the affairs of the Norfolk and of the Lowestoft become inextricably entwined and little pretence continued of them being separate entities. Although regular shareholders meetings of each continued to be held, the directors meetings of the Lowestoft after 1847 became largely formalities with all matters of importance regarding the line and harbour being dealt with at board meetings of the Norfolk. Operations on the main line continued much as before although Norwich continued to look forward to the time when a better route to London opened via Ipswich despite suspicion, fuelled by rumours, that the railways might amalgamate and leave the city at the mercy of a single operator.

Prospects and plans

At the end of 1846 the Norwich board minutes were still full of optimism. In December the Norfolk board put forward the following estimates of capital required for the Bills going to Parliament:

	Estimated cost £
Wymondham to Diss	160,000
Reedham via Beccles, Bungay, Harleston & Diss to Thetford	560,000
Thetford to Bury	140,000
Beccles to Halesworth	90,000
North of Norfolk (Norwich to Aylsham)	250,000
Yarmouth extension (including Bure bridge)	75,000
	£1,275,000

To finance all this they would seek authorisation to issue more 5%

guaranteed shares similar to those created in the previous summer to finance the extension to the north coast. The expensive Reedham/ Thetford proposal showed that there was still hope of some co-operation with the Newmarket & Chesterford or some other Thetford bound company whereas Thetford to Bury shows that if necessary they were prepared to build the link themselves. Beccles to Halesworth obviously depended on the Reedham to Beccles link. What does not appear to have been put before the board was any statement of existing commitments, creditors and resources. With much of the 1846 expansion share issue already paid up and spent despite little progress on the Fakenham line it is hard to see how they could have been so confident about the future. Bonds and other loans were also falling due and in February 1847 new ordinary capital, £197,000 in new £20 shares with £5 payable as deposit, was created and placed with existing shareholders to provide funds for loan redemption. But after that issue, with the first symptoms of what became a national financial crisis looming, it became for some time more and more difficult to raise further capital whether by way of shares or loans.

Even late in 1846 there had remained an unsatisfied demand for shares from subscribers to those lines that had failed to gain parliamentary sanction. Conversely companies such as the Norfolk that had supported the promotion of failed lines had seen an opportunity to widen their capital base by offering new shares in their own company to disappointed subscribers to those lines. The earliest example of this practice had been in August 1845 when the Norfolk board decided that former subscribers to the Diss & Colchester and to the Wells & Dereham (ex Wells & Thetford) could have options to subscribe to the Norfolk's proposed new expansion shares even though it would be many months before such shares could be authorised by Parliament. The Wells subscribers could have one new £20 share credited as two pounds paid for each two of their own and get fifteen shillings cash returned from their subscription moneys. Alternatively they could have ten shillings returned on each old share subscribed for, being all that would be left of their deposit after payment of legal and other expenses. The Diss & Colchester shareholders were to have similar terms. This gave the Norfolk the opportunity to hold onto their original subscription moneys for a further year at least. There were over twenty thousand pounds in a Diss & Colchester bank account taken over by the Norfolk in 1845 but also some sizeable bills to be paid.

Through the Autumn of 1846 recriminations continued amongst the subscribers to the North of Norfolk. In a series of meetings and advertisements it was pointed out that they had been induced to subscribe on the understanding that London financiers, all members of the provisional committee, would be taking up more of the shares while the entire enterprise had the backing of the Norfolk which, it was alleged, was to pay half the expenses if the project failed. Now it turned out that some of the shares reserved for these people had not been allotted once it became clear they would never remain at a premium. Had allotment been made and deposits paid there would have been over three thousand pounds more cash available to meet the legal and other costs. J. H. Tillett, solicitor and secretary to the committee, stood uncertainly as the pig-in-the-middle of this dispute, trying to pacify local subscribers while negotiating with London solicitors to moderate their bills.

One committee member, Robert Chamberlain of Catton, maintained that the reason he had taken up few shares was because the demand from Norwich had been so great that he voluntarily stood aside when at the time he could have had a premium of a pound per share. He now regretted he had ever become involved and hoped, he said, for a legal action which would enable him to clear his name. A subscriber riposted that Chamberlain could perfectly well have taken up more shares later when the premium fell away and if he had done so there would not have been over one thousand unsubscribed. All the decisions had been taken, it was alleged, by three (unnamed) members of the committee who were also Norfolk Railway directors. Two of these were probably Adam Duff and Charles Tyndale as it is known that both had been substantial subscribers.

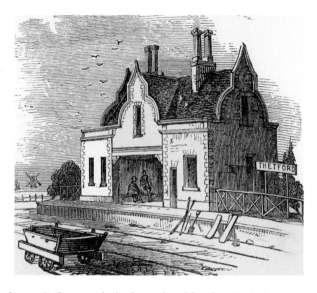

Thetford station

Then an advertisement in October 1846 revealed that the North of Norfolk line had 'been taken up by the Norfolk Railway' and the subscribers to the previous project were to be given a privileged chance to subscribe for Norfolk shares. For every five North of Norfolk shares subscribed for they were to be offered six new Norfolk £20 5% guaranteed extension shares, credited as forty shillings paid, on payment in cash of only thirty shillings per share. Six thousand of these shares were to be created in 1847 for the purpose, all of which were to be taken up by North of Norfolk subscribers. Five per cent guaranteed dividend was not too bad a return at a time when the speculative value of ordinary railway shares was rapidly disappearing, while by 1847 the Norfolk was grateful to get fresh subscribers on any terms whatever.

The disappointed subscribers to the Waveney Valley line were another source of capital the Norfolk hoped to tap. An advertisement in late October 1846 said that the Norfolk and the Waveney Valley would go jointly to Parliament in the 1847 session in support of the Norfolk's line Reedham to Diss and Thetford. Waveney subscribers who agreed could subscribe for one new Norfolk £20 5% guaranteed extension share for every share in the Waveney enterprise for which they had originally subscribed, paying in thirty-five shillings per share and being credited with forty shillings paid. Moreover they would get five shillings cash returned should the new line achieve its Act. This might be seen as a clever move by the Norfolk to outflank the Eastern Union that had proposed to lease the Waveney line, but in the event the Eastern Union riposted with their own Waveney proposal.

Another company seeking capital via access to disappointed subscribers was the Ipswich & Bury, in one case from the subscribers to the Dereham Direct which held a liquidation meeting in late October 1846. The committee had spent a total of nearly fifteen thousand pounds over two years, the majority in legal and parliamentary costs and less than four thousand on engineering. However the Norfolk was blamed for the engineering cost being even this high since they had replaced Gravatt with Borthwick who had insisted on doing the work all over again. The costs so far had virtually eaten up the share deposits and there were only some fifteen hundred pounds left with bankers. Edward Willett, chairman, was claiming £1,362 from the Norfolk, who he held morally responsible for the debacle, and if this claim succeeded there would, after payment of the remaining creditors, be enough to return four shillings per share to subscribers (after long argument the Norfolk settled for £600). There were hard words spoken by one subscriber about the level of legal costs but others pointed out that the Lynn & Dereham had fared no better (although they at least had a railway under construction).

Four shillings per share was not all the subscribers could hope for. Willett, a director of the Ipswich & Bury, had come to an arrangement on their behalf with the latter company which was to receive all the engineering plans and drawings so that a further attempt could be made in future to build the Dereham line. In consideration the Dereham subscribers would have the right for each cancelled Dereham share to subscribe for one Ipswich & Bury share of £25 with a guaranteed five per cent dividend. For this they must pay forty shillings deposit but would be credited with having paid fifty shillings. Of course ultimately they would be due to pay all but ten shillings of the full twenty-five pounds, but even as late as October 1846 most railway shares still stood at a premium.

Merger or sell out?

In mid February there was a major new development when Cobbold of the Eastern Union approached the board with an offer of a merger. His company had already agreed a full merger with the Ipswich & Bury with which it had always acted in concert but as yet the necessary statutory authority had not been received and so any further merger was conditional on the separate assents of the shareholders of each company. Nevertheless, although the Norfolk directors were wary of Cobbold, being uncertain how much authority he carried, yet so far had their confidence apparently slipped in the previous two months that the prospect of a rescuer was welcomed. After some initial misunderstandings a detailed draft agreement was put together of which the following were the main terms:

1. The Norfolk capital, including debentures, was not to exceed £1,067,000.

2. The Eastern Union would pay the Norfolk 7½% on that capital from 1 July 1847 in perpetuity. However Norfolk shareholders would have an option to be paid off at £150 per £100 stock in debentures redeemable in cash over three years or take £100 stock in the merged company.

3. The Eastern Union would also assume the existing Norfolk guarantee of Lowestoft capital.

4. The Norfolk would withdraw its Bills for the lines Thetford/Bury (in favour of the Eastern Union's similar Bill) and for the Reedham/Diss/Thetford line (but if a full amalgamation was to go ahead the Eastern Union might build in the Waveney valley and allow the old Waveney subscribers the opportunity to subscribe).

5. Both companies would withdraw their Bills for lines to the north of Norwich.

6. The Norfolk would go on with their Wymondham/Diss Bill and the Eastern Union would not oppose it. They would also continue their bridge and line into Yarmouth.

7. The merged operations would be managed by a joint committee of four Eastern Union and three Norfolk members but further capital expenditure would be the responsibility of a finance committee with three members from each side

A rental of seven and a half per cent or a pay off of fifty per cent over par was or should have been extremely attractive and it is hardly surprising that the Norfolk directors were in favour. But looking at these terms in the light of the financial information presumably already available to the Norfolk board and published only a few days later it is clear that they were unworkable. For the accumulated Norfolk capital at the previous 31 December (see Chapter 6) already exceeded by more than £150,000 the maximum figure they were guaranteeing, while further capital would be necessary if even the limited projects referred to in Item 6 of the heads of agreement went ahead. It is impossible to tell whether the Norfolk directors were in ignorance of their own position, did not understand it, or were just hoping for the best.

Notwithstanding that this had many of the marks of a take-over of the Norfolk rather than a true merger, the basic terms (but not the limit on

Norfolk capital) were put to shareholders of both companies at their half yearly meetings in the same month and generally welcomed. But it could not be voted upon nor implemented at once since first the merger of the Eastern Union and the Ipswich & Bury must be fully consummated by the issue of a certificate from the Board of Trade's railway commissioners and that was not to be forthcoming for many months. The influential journal, *Railway Record*, welcomed the proposals as an end to ruinous competition, exactly the reason why it was greeted with some dismay in Norfolk towns. Construction of the Ipswich & Bury line from Haughley to Norwich had begun only at the end of February. Despite elaborate ceremony, speeches and of course dinner on the occasion of the cutting of the first sod just outside Norwich, suspicion was voiced that perhaps no terminus would be built at Victoria Gardens.

Shortly after the main agreement was reached there was a substantial amendment. The Norfolk realised that they were so contracted to the former Waveney Valley shareholders and so pledged in the Waveney district that they must necessarily go forward with their line from Thetford via Diss to Reedham. The Eastern Union's Waveney promoters also felt obliged to go before Parliament. So it was agreed that both sides should continue with their promotions but that if the Norfolk succeeded the section Diss to Thetford should not be made. Further if no amalgamation should proceed, then the Eastern Union would claim the Diss/Wymondham line, leaving a final settlement to arbitration.

Prior to the public announcement of the intended merger the main item of local railway controversy reported in the press was a series of public meetings successively in Yarmouth, Beccles, Harleston, Bungay, Diss and Hoxne to debate the relative merits of the two competing Waveney valley proposals. The Yarmouth meeting, understandably, had the largest attendance and revealed the bitterest divisions. Mr T. F. Steward rehearsed the history. In 1845 the Diss, Beccles & Yarmouth line with a proposed terminus in South Town, promoted by a syndicate headed by Mr Wilkinson, opposed by the Norfolk and with virtually no local subscribers, had run into late opposition to its route near Burgh Castle, had then done a late deal with the Norfolk to go by Reedham and, now opposed by Yarmouth, had failed in its revised bid for parliamentary approval.

Subsequently a new company formed by Wilkinson had obtained substantial local support for a line approximately on the original route and a promise from the Eastern Union to lease it. However it, too, had failed before Parliament in 1846, the main objection being that of having two railways on parallel routes only a few miles apart though separated by Breydon Water. In addition it appears that the Admiralty had objected to the proposed fixed railway bridge over the Waveney as being an obstruction to navigation even though it had the approval of the Yarmouth Haven Commissioners (who believed all bridges impeded navigation and could exacerbate flooding but were not averse to obstructions that stopped seagoing ships reaching Beccles).

At a late stage in the parliamentary proceedings Mr Steward and others present had gone to London to support Wilkinson's line, but finding this a hopeless prospect had negotiated with other interested parties. The Eastern Union, although friendly disposed, had been unable to help, Wilkinson's company had no further resources, and so a tripartite agreement had been reached with Wilkinson and the Norfolk whereby all parties would support in 1847 the Norfolk's revised Waveney route from Diss which would join its main line at Reedham and enter Yarmouth across the Bure with a new terminus in the town. Shipowner G. D. Palmer and the leader of the fish merchants R. Fenn both supported Steward, the latter simply on the basis that it really did not matter which way the line went if the fares were to be the same. J. E. Lacon, on behalf of the Norfolk (though he was not a director), confirmed that the railway would not charge less from Lowestoft to Norwich (or anywhere else) than the rates that applied to Yarmouth, an assurance that satisfied some doubters.

Mr Dowson led the opposition. He didn't trust anyone but especially not the Norfolk Railway. It was inefficient. He instanced a turkey delivered the day after Christmas, a consignment of flour delivered wet and a recent experience of a seven and a half-hour journey from London. The tramlines on the quays were dangerous. What he wanted was a direct line to London, the route a crow would fly. His seconder slated the Norfolk as a terrible company and a promoter of Lowestoft. Why give in? Ipswich was no rival. He held shares in the Waveney line but all railways were a curse and would bring death to the coastal trade, and then where would the Navy recruit its men?

Now, for the first time, there were speeches in support of the Eastern Union's new alternative. Mr Clowes, a solicitor for that line, spoke of its advantages, particularly a terminus close to the quays on the west side of the river. Cobbold himself pointed out how his line was the shortest and assured Yarmouth that Ipswich was no rival as a port or wished to be. However Mr Ferrier, the man who had stopped the 1845 version of the line, objected that the Yarmouth supporters of the Eastern Union line were mostly people who had property to sell in Southtown. Moreover it would depress the value of property that was not sold while it would result in excessive traffic on the temporary town bridge. As to the quays on the west side, they would be poorly served since the railway had to be four yards from the quayside. Mr Wilkinson spoke in support of Ferrier and in defence of his own conduct throughout, despite a barrage of boos and hisses that was only halted when the chairman ruled that no one would be called until Wilkinson had been heard. He and his syndicate had exhausted their resources in trying to build a Waveney line. Now it would be best to accept the line via Reedham and a new terminus at

Paget's brewery; the line to Southtown would never be permitted and the Eastern Union was too demanding.

Eventually a vote was taken and it was found that the majority still rejected the Norfolk line and would support that of the Eastern Union. This was also the conclusion at the meetings at Bungay, Harleston and Diss. At Bungay the matter was decided on a question of reputation; which railway best looked after their passengers? It was emphasised also how much shorter it would be to London via the Eastern Union than by the Norfolk although the latter was marginally shorter from Bungay to Norwich. At Harleston the chief objection to the Norfolk version was that it left out the important village of Dickleburgh. For Diss the problem with the Norfolk was too many level crossings and possible susceptibility to floods. The reports of the first two of these meetings suggest that the Norfolk had not sent representatives to argue their case. Likewise at Beccles, but here the vote was strongly for the Norfolk version since the Eastern Union was not going to come to the town, proposing instead a station on the north side of the river. Finally by the time of the Hoxne meeting the proposed merger of the two systems had been announced. Lacon attended to explain its effect and that a choice still existed in the Waveney area. In the event the Hoxne meeting voted for the Norfolk version because it would provide a station at Brockdish (and seemingly because it would not go to Dickleburgh).

The Lowestoft company half-year meeting took place at the end of February, a few days after the meeting of the Norfolk at which the proposed merger had been announced and approved. The financial position at 31 December and the state of the works as then reported were described in Chapter 7. If anything was said about the agreement with Norwich Corporation to widen the river it was not reported. Mr Cory asked how the proposed merger would affect the shareholders' interests and was assured by Richard Till that while full details were not available their interests would be fully protected. A Mr Gowing was anxious that the railway would be open by May as otherwise the fish merchants would need to charter a ship to take the catch to market. Peto promised him that the line would be open for goods by 1 April. He also spoke with satisfaction about the Eastern Union merger which would be of advantage to all. Because the 1846 Bill to authorise the change of bridge site had not been proceeded with an amending Act was needed to sanction the move and the line through the Reedham hills. The shareholders' minute book is silent but it is a fact that the Bill to Parliament in the summer of 1847 also requested authorisation of a doubling of the share capital.

After the main meeting and before a special meeting to approve the new Bill Peto offered an informal and most bullish report. The coke ovens and the harbour dues together were already bringing in £5,000 a year despite the lack of a rail route. (Nothing was said about harbour costs.) There was over twenty feet of water in the outer entrance at low water and no more silt and sand was coming in than they could sell as ballast. (While this may have been true at the time, today there is less than fifteen feet.) As to the holiday potential a large hotel and sixteen new villas were under construction by developers near the south esplanade.

East Anglian developments

A crowded meeting at Bury in early March debated the town's attitude toward the competing lines in the area. There were the Newmarket & Chesterford proposals referred to above, the proposal by the Stour Valley company to extend to the town from Sudbury via Lavenham, and the Ipswich & Bury's planned extensions from Bury to Thetford, to Newmarket and to Ely, and also from Stowmarket to Lavenham and Sudbury. At the meeting Cobbold, for the Ipswich & Bury, offered to surrender their extensions to Newmarket and to Ely to the Newmarket & Chesterford if the latter would abandon its line to Thetford, withdraw its opposition to the Thetford/Bury link, and allow the Ipswich & Bury running rights over the line from Bury to Cambridge (they already having such rights to Chesterford). This the Newmarket & Chesterford refused, whereupon the meeting expressed its support for the Ipswich & Bury's lines in preference to those of the Newmarket & Chesterford.

All of the lines in East Anglia were experiencing financial pressure with money markets drying up. The Newmarket & Chesterford had begun the construction of their original line to Chesterford in September 1846 apparently in the hope that it could be leased either to the Norfolk or to the Eastern Counties. The first proved impossible and in February 1847 negotiations for an Eastern Counties lease also broke down. They were left for the time being to go it alone and did so, buoyed up for a while by rumours that the Great Northern, planning a branch east from Hitchin, might meet them at Chesterford. The line to there from Newmarket opened early in 1848, but no junction with the Great Northern ever materialised and how the company could possibly raise the capital to build its proposed extensions to Thetford, to Ely and to Bury was obscure.

The Lynn & Ely, after its swift advance to Downham Market, was severely delayed in reaching Ely by the extent of works in the soft fen ground and especially by the difficulties in building viaducts and bridges to cross the rivers Wissey and Great Ouse. Delayed construction meant extra costs while the land in the area proved unexpectedly difficult and expensive to acquire. In February 1847 the board appeared to have settled at last with the Eastern Counties to work their line, not at the hoped for seven and a half but at just five per cent on cost much to the dissatisfaction of some of the shareholders who attempted to unseat two retiring directors. The chairman himself admitted that he had opposed the deal, which in the event fell through when Parliament refused to approve. The *Norfolk Chronicle* deplored the prospect of another line controlled by the

The opening of
the Great Ouse
bridge for the
Lynn & Ely

Eastern Counties. Far better the editor thought if competition could be preserved by a lease to the Great Northern. In March an enquiry was held at Lynn into the company's proposals to build docks immediately south of the town with James Rendel, in his capacity as harbour specialist, as engineer. There was local support but by now it was unlikely that the necessary capital could be raised. It was to be another twenty years before docks were built at Lynn, and then at a site north of the town.

The line eventually reached Ely in October 1847. The celebratory dinner was attended by the secretary of the Eastern Counties who spoke of a spirit of co-operation but with no lease in prospect the company was left to operate the line itself. By then its projected line to Bury, for which there was in any case little prospect of financing, had been turned down by Parliament. The Lynn and Dereham reached Dereham in September, but was opened initially for goods traffic only. The works here too had been difficult and costly and at the last stages the main contractors had gone bankrupt leaving stations and other works unfinished so that the opening for passenger traffic was delayed.

In the previous July the amalgamation of these two lines and their orphan cousin, the Ely & Huntingdon, had been effected and several of the original directors, including west Norfolk magnate Sir William Folkes of Hillington, had resigned. At the first general meeting of the new company, East Anglian Railways, in early November 1846 it was stated that total capital expenditure stood at just over £900,000, many thousands over estimate, the biggest excess arising from extra land costs on the Lynn & Ely line. The Ely & Huntingdon was only ever built for a few miles of its intended length so that the sixty-five miles in total of the network had averaged nearly £14,000 each. This was far from the eventual total. Although no more mileage had been built, by the early 1850s the total capital spend, including huge sums for capitalised interest, amounted to over £1,600,000. By then the railway had passed through receivership and an abortive lease to the Great Northern Railway, and was being worked after all by the Eastern Counties.

Lynn itself had the possibility of a further railway in 1847. The newly emergent Great Northern, now with authority to build all the way from York via Peterborough to London, was considering also a line across the fens and river mouths from Spalding to Lynn which opened the prospect of a far more direct connection between Norfolk and the North. An Admiralty enquiry took place in March to consider the effects on the river navigations of bridges proposed over the Welland at Fosdyke, the Nene at Sutton and the Ouse at Lynn. The chief objector was the port of Wisbech notwithstanding that the Welland and Nene bridges proposed would swing to allow the passage of masted ships. Robert Stephenson gave evidence, advising against the line mainly on the grounds that, as the Admiralty would insist on the bridges remaining open much of the time, the operation of a railway would be impossible. He could see no need for the line in any case since all traffic could very well go via the Peterborough/Ely link. As Stephenson acted on occasion for the Eastern Counties and often for the Norfolk it cannot be said that his evidence was truly independent. The Great Northern line was not built then or for many years, failing to gain permission for the bridge at Sutton. The Eastern Counties completed a branch from March to Wisbech in 1847 (Peto being the contractor) and the Lynn & Ely branch from Magdalen Junction, near Watlington, met it there the following February although the Eastern Counties insisted on separate stations. No further railway building took place in the northern Fens for several years, the Eastern Counties' successful application to build from Wisbech to Spalding not being followed up by construction.

In March the first reports were arriving of parliamentary proceedings in examination of railway bills. The Norfolk, following the terms of its agreement with the Eastern Union, withdrew its Bill for a line between Thetford and Bury. By April there was the somewhat surprising news that the Newmarket & Chesterford proposals had all been approved in committee while those of the Ipswich & Bury and the Lynn & Ely west and north of Bury had all been turned down. As a result neither the Norfolk nor the Ipswich & Bury were to build a line connecting Thetford to Bury. The latter company, which had gained running powers over the Newmarket & Chesterford, had also withdrawn its Bill for its branch from Stowmarket to Sudbury. At the end of April the proposal by the Stour Valley Railway for a line Sudbury to Bury was examined. Mr Eagle gave evidence to the effect that Bury really wanted a better line altogether but had to admit that he had been the projector of such a line that had failed to gain either parliamentary permission or adequate financial support. A few months before it had been reported that Eagle was being sued by an unpaid lithographer, the very last sighting of his abortive Norwich Direct. There was strong opposition to the Sudbury line from landowners at the Bury end although their main objection was that insufficient money was being offered. Despite a later report that an accommodation had been reached with the landowners this line too was turned down.

In the Waveney Valley the renewed competition between the Eastern Union and the Norfolk was resolved by the end of May in favour of the Norfolk after the parliamentary committee had heard hours of evidence concerning the desirability or otherwise of two Yarmouth stations and the lingering (and correct) suspicions of some in Yarmouth that the Norfolk would never build a station in the town itself. Nevertheless the Norfolk at last obtained permission for the whole line Thetford, Diss and Reedham including the branch to Halesworth. Once this was certain the Norfolk withdrew its Bill for the North of Norfolk line. They were of course obliged to do this under the agreement with the Eastern Union but had persisted with it for several months, perhaps as a bargaining point.

Summer and autumn 1847; the end of merger prospects

Things were not going well amongst the lawyers concerning the merger. It was considered that Parliament would not accept the term allowing Norfolk shareholders to be bought out at a premium. However major Norfolk shareholders considered this essential and the lawyers were instructed to leave it in the Bill that was in preparation. A guaranteed rental from 1 July 1847 was also thought inadvisable given that no Bill could be before Parliament until 1848 so that condition was struck out. Finally the boards were advised that they had no power to delegate the management of their lines to a joint committee prior to amalgamation so that too was given up. The former Waveney subscribers were worried that parliamentary standing orders had recently forbidden interest being paid on capital during construction. The Norfolk board determined that they would satisfy these subscribers somehow but if they could not do so their deposits would be repaid as soon as possible.

Meanwhile it was reported that Peto and Bidder had gone over the Lowestoft line and had pronounced it fit for goods traffic for which it opened on 3 May. The delay from the confidently promised date of 1 April had been caused by some landslips along that section of the route that ran through marshes. How the fish merchants had coped was not reported. It was not expected to open for passenger traffic for a further two months to allow opportunity for the embankments to consolidate further under the weight of the frequent trains carrying coke that were expected. The line eventually opened for passenger traffic at the very end of June 1847 after inspection by Captain Coddington for the Railway Commissioners. Bands played at Lowestoft harbour where ships were dressed overall. The ceremonies were brief. A special train from Lowestoft went to Reedham and then on to Yarmouth, stopping on the way at Reedham where passengers for Norwich joined a train from Yarmouth. The reporter for the *Chronicle* was, as ever, enthusiastic for the line and gave fresh description of the bucket lifts at the harbour for unloading coal and the rail system for transporting coal to feed the thirty coke ovens from above. He eulogised the handsome stations, especially that at Somerleyton. He commented that the rail route from Lowestoft to Yarmouth was circuitous but 'as the people of Yarmouth wish to have as little to do with Lowestoft as possible, it is not of much consequence'.

The newspapers in July were much preoccupied with a general election campaign and especially with the contest in Norwich that is of especial relevance to this history as Peto was a candidate. Since the previous election the city's two seats had been divided between a Tory, the Marquess of Douro, son of the Duke of Wellington, and Mr Benjamin Smith, Whig and a son of a previous Whig member for the city. Elections in Norwich were notorious for bribery and that in 1841 had proved expensive for the successful candidates. Whether for that or another reason Smith declined to stand again and it was doubtful at first whether Douro would do so either. Perhaps in the hope that a contest could be avoided a group of nonconformists in Norwich nominated just one man, Peto, and for a while it appeared that no third candidate would stand, encouraging Douro to come forward again. However Peto, in an effort to square his position with the substantial group of Church of England Whigs concerning his attitude to church schools and property managed to alienate his original supporters. They, now disliking also the suggestion of an electoral fix, nominated a third, more populist candidate whom his detractors traduced as being virtually a Chartist.

The election, that for once appears to have been fought without excessive violence or bribery, resulted in an overwhelming victory for Peto with Douro taking the second place, though well behind. Douro indeed might have fallen behind the third candidate Parry had he not on polling day issued a declaration to the city's Protestant group that, while in favour of toleration of the Roman Catholics, he would ever oppose subsidising their schools or seminaries. Amongst Peto's nominators and friends at his post election meeting were T. O. Springfield, and Edward Willett, both directors of the Ipswich & Bury, as well as Norfolk Railway directors Horatio Bolingbroke and Sir William Foster. Douro's nominators included Samuel Bignold, Eastern Union director, and banker partners Major General Sir Robert Harvey, his son R. J. H. Harvey and R. Kerrison, all investors in railways. The leaders of the nonconformist and radical group that had supported the third candidate included Jeremiah Colman, latterly a supporter of the Norfolk and J. H. Tillett, the secretary of the North of Norfolk committee, and future Liberal MP for the City.

From the beginning of August the Eastern Counties announced what were described in the Norfolk boardroom as swingeing increases in fares on the line to London. The Norfolk board at first felt they had necessarily to follow suit not only on journeys past Brandon but also those purely on the Norfolk. A week later they were having second thoughts. Bidder, attending the Traffic Committee, doubted if the Eastern Counties increase would hold; meanwhile Norfolk customers were alienated. Miscellaneous capital outflow continued. For example £3,500 had to be authorised for corn and salt warehouses and a coal staithe at Norwich.

The capital account made up to 30 June presented to the half-year meeting of the Norfolk in August showed that spend had further increased bringing the total up to £1,375,633. Locomotives and rolling stock now stood at £150,542, additional land came to £119,412 and the Dereham extension to £174,989. Expenditure on the Wells extension had risen to nearly £100,000 including £25,000 for land and nearly £40,000 for rails and other materials but still no work had been done on site. Meanwhile the calls received on the 1846 extension stock had risen to £209,000 out of £300,000 and there were still £55,000 of temporary loans to repay.

Several shareholders at the meeting were unhappy. A Mr Anderson objected to virtually all the items in the accounts and queried others. He recommended reducing the proposed three per cent dividend for the half year. He was supported by one Major Court, the first recorded appearance of a man who was to cause the directors endless problems in later years. Mr Yetts strongly queried the continued growth of the expenditure at Lowestoft and the need there now announced for £120,000 more capital, the annual six per cent dividend on which was to be guaranteed by the Norfolk. Another shareholder proposed that the capital account should be closed, a problem with all railways he observed, objected to the Lowestoft expenditure, saying that no harbour ever paid, and thought the line north from Dereham should be stopped at some point to which it might pay. Till, in a weak speech, defended the capital outflow. They must service the district with branches, especially in an agricultural area such as Norfolk. He admitted that the dividend would exceed the half-year's results by some fifteen hundred pounds but that rate of dividend should be covered by the results for the year as a whole. Duff, chairman, told the meeting that relations with the Eastern Union remained excellent, their directors were fully informed as to the Norfolk's affairs and that there was not the slightest doubt that the merger agreement would be ratified.

Bidder admitted that little progress had been made on the extension to the north coast but vigorously defended the Lowestoft railway and harbour. The railway had been surprisingly difficult to build despite being virtually level but was now complete. The harbour, when finished, would be the finest on the East Coast. It would be some time before all the new capital need be called, if indeed it was all required. Much of the rising cost related to new warehouses. The harbour itself had used a great deal of timber but that was protected by the creosoting process which in the long term made a timber/stone construction much cheaper than one entirely of stone. With shareholders still attacking the Lowestoft venture the board had to make a further defence. The Lowestoft project had 'grown out of the Norfolk'; it was in fact a branch. Every railway wanted a port and here they had acquired a good one with revenue already at the rate of five thousand pounds a year. There was twenty foot of water on the bar; indeed there was no bar and no tendency for one to build. The outer harbour was usable now and the inner one must be finished. Eventually the accounts and report were approved by a narrow majority.

The results of the parliamentary session were summarised. To pay for the Reedham/Diss/Thetford line further extension capital of £400,000 with a five per cent guaranteed dividend was created reserved for subscribers to the former Waveney Valley project. At the same time another £105,000 of extension capital, for which the guaranteed rate had been increased to five and a half per cent, was created, £75,000 specifically for the extension into Yarmouth and, as later admitted by the directors, an extra £30,000 merely because it seemed opportune. That a preferred stock had to carry a five and a half per cent coupon was indicative of the tightening money market, a point further emphasised in that the Lowestoft had needed to offer six per cent notwithstanding a Norfolk guarantee.

Although they had also received permission for their line Wymondham/Diss there was now no immediate prospect of construction. They had hoped that the subscribers of the previous year to the North of Norfolk would be providing the capital for it and these people had already paid a two pound deposit on £120,000 of Norfolk 5% guaranteed extension stock but there was now no capital required. There was no problem with repayment in this instance but a solicitor was asking for five shillings cash per share in addition, a balance from their original subscription to the North of Norfolk itself. At an earlier board meeting the directors had hit on a plan to allow the Waveney subscribers a discount on their first call equal to five per cent interest on paid up calls until the completion of the line. Given that this was because precompletion interest had been declared illegal and as the issue of shares at a discount was itself possibly illegal it is not surprising that nothing further is heard of the scheme. Because it was later decided not to proceed with the line the whole affair presented the Norfolk with a continuing series of problems for many years. The subscribers did not want repayment, they wanted income dating from when they first paid a deposit. Eighteen thousand, four hundred and ninety of these twenty pound shares were applied for on which a two pound deposit had been paid but as the line was not built it was never possible to call the further eighteen pounds per share. However the same Act permitted over one hundred and fifty thousand pounds of borrowings which were in due course raised although there was no new line to secure them. This expedient was one of the means which enabled the company to stay afloat, perhaps longer than it should have.

Unusually the Lowestoft half year meeting was held after that of the Norfolk, a week later on August 28. There had been some £40,000 of expenditure on the harbour since the last meeting largely financed by further calls on shares. A detailed report was given on the state of the harbour and of the works in progress. The outer harbour wall was still unfinished but there was hope it could be before the equinoctial gales in order to provide a harbour of refuge by December. Other works included the rail sidings for the coke ovens, wharfing in the inner harbour, including a coal wharf with cranes, and a fish wharf in the outer harbour. An old pier was being removed to provide a beach onto which vessels running in before a gale could safely bring up.

Although the new Act, which dealt also with the new layout of the railway at Reedham, had been discussed by shareholders six months before it seems to have come as a surprise to some that it included provision for £120,000 of new share capital even though the need for additional cash had then been evident. The new capital was to be divided into 6,000 twenty pound shares guaranteed a six per cent dividend to be offered as rights to existing shareholders. However the shareholders taking up new shares were to give up the right attached to their old shares to participate in half the operating profits.

Attendance at the meeting was low but both Peto and Cory were present, as was Bidder. When Peto moved the creation and issue of the new shares, Cory queried whether a shareholder who did not take up his rights could still participate in profits as before. Nobody seems to have known although Bidder, no lawyer, opined that the majority would bind the minority. Cory then moved that the harbour should be completed at the expense of the Norfolk which should guarantee the shareholders five per cent on their old shares in lieu of their profit sharing rights. For this he found a seconder but little other support and his motion was lost. Then Peto proposed that the Norfolk would guarantee the six per cent on the new shares provided the entire profit sharing arrangement was cancelled. This was passed with just Cory voting against and the meeting then went on to authorise the borrowing of a further £40,000.

Two weeks later a meeting of dissatisfied Lowestoft shareholders was held in the offices of a Norwich stockbroker. One-fifth of the capital was represented in person or by proxy. John Sultzer, chairman, said that the company's funds had been applied for purposes other than those for which they had been raised. He suggested that the money spent additional to the original capital was the responsibility of the Norfolk and the second share issue appeared to be an afterthought. Cory said he had been to all the meetings and the first time he had heard about the new capital was at the most recent. He repeated his proposal for an increase in the guaranteed dividend to five per cent on the old shares leaving the Norfolk to complete the harbour. It was resolved that a deputation should put this to the Norfolk directors.

Through the later summer negotiations with Cobbold had been going badly. The main problem was that the Norfolk capital kept rising with the Yarmouth bridge project and Lowestoft harbour's insatiable requirements. Could the Eastern Union really be expected to pay seven and a half per cent on the rising total? At the beginning of October the Norfolk board minutes refer to a statement of liabilities and assets being read to the board and being referred to the finance committee. No such entry had ever previously been recorded. The tone of the minute suggests that the situation appeared unpleasant though not so as to trouble those directors less financially aware, but we have no knowledge of what it disclosed or what the finance committee thought to do about it.

On Friday 29 October a fateful meeting of the shareholders of the Ipswich & Bury Railway was held in London, called on the requisition of a number of northern shareholders who wished to rescind the provisional agreement with the Norfolk. There the leader of the dissidents pointed out that based on the figures previously given and compared with the results of the Norfolk published at its last half year the seven and a half per cent proposed lease would cost the Eastern Union combine vastly more than the present earning capacity of the Norfolk and could not be justified. His case would have been even stronger had he known the Norfolk's latest figures for capital spend. The meeting bowed to his logic and resolved to pull out of the deal notwithstanding the probability that the Norfolk would most likely fall into other hands.

This decision must have been known at the Norfolk board meeting the following Monday although no reference to it appears in the minutes. Things were bad enough without this additional blow. A new financial statement was read. Peto attended, saying he held two bills from the company, each for £30,000, the one due the following week and the other in early December. He asked for a mortgage bond for £30,000 as collateral that would enable him to roll over both bills for a further period. Others were lining up for payment. Sir Edmund Lacon said his Yarmouth bank would like their overdraft paid off. Bidder was looking for £3,150 for three years parliamentary expenses but would take 5½% stock at par in payment. This was not a good day to hear that Mr Sultzer and a deputation of Lowestoft shareholders wanted a meeting with the board.

By the board's December meeting the advantages of having a tap stock available had sunk in. The claim by the North of Norfolk subscribers for a refund of deposits was met by issuing to them £12,000 of 5½% stock credited as fully paid plus interest from 4 October. Merrett had lodged claims for £25,000 that were under consideration by the engineers. Peto on Merrett's behalf, said that if £12,500 of the new stock was issued in part satisfaction he, Peto, would ensure no claim for the balance for six months and would hold over his own claims until the authorised capital was further increased. The board agreed to these terms but stipulated that the stock should not be sold under par and if not sold at the end of six months would be redeemed at par. This was all very well but if the stock were thus employed in satisfaction of old debts it would raise no cash for current works. As a final gesture the board passed to a sub-committee the task of considering a general reduction in staff and their wages.

CHAPTER 9

Dismay, surrender and the immediate aftermath: 1848 to April 1851

I N DECEMBER 1847 the Norfolk board had received the deputation of Lowestoft shareholders led by Sultzer who complained that the new issue would devalue the existing shares, as indeed it was likely to. The question was deferred to a meeting to be held in Lowestoft later that month to be attended by shareholders of both companies. No minutes of that meeting have been found but a brief summary is contained in the Norfolk directors' minute book. It was made clear that the harbour works were proving expensive and that in the short term the revenues from railway and harbour were not going to be adequate to service the capital. However the borrowings (*sic*: no doubt both shares and borrowings were meant) were guaranteed by the Norfolk company. Thus the Lowestoft shareholders were in a better position than those of the Norfolk so it was hardly likely that more could be done for them. The resolution to deny the old shareholders any part of the profits if they took up new shares must stand. It was agreed to set up a joint committee of shareholders to consider the whole future of the enterprise.

The committee, which included George Stephenson, now beginning the last year of his life, visited Lowestoft in January 1848 and heard reports from Bidder and Captain Andrews, the newly appointed harbour master. Both spoke of the huge advantages the completed project would bring to the Norfolk Railway as a source of traffic but it was concluded, with the project still in its infancy, that it was impossible to make a sensible judgement. The estimated final cost of railway and harbour together was put at £317,737, £122,610 for the railway, £174,516 for the harbour and £20,611 for ancillary costs including the creosote works and interest paid during construction. It was not explained how this had risen from the original £160,000. It seemed inevitable that the project must be taken to conclusion given the progress already made. The only decision arrived at was that a joint committee of five from each company (later amended to five from the Norfolk company but only three from Lowestoft) should be set up to manage the project to completion. Meanwhile, with cash still short, the weekly wage bill at the harbour was being reduced to two hundred pounds a week and work slowed accordingly.

At the Lowestoft shareholders' meeting in February the directors for the first time in their report were less than bullish. In its first six months of operation the railway had carried some 43,000 passengers and 19,000 tons of freight and had made a profit of about £800. However the harbour was still not open, not even for purposes of refuge. Shareholders were given the January figure of £317,737 as the estimated cost for the entire project, still in fact somewhat short of the eventual outturn but quite sufficient to alarm. Finances appeared in a better state as over £75,000 had already been raised from the issue of new shares. However it been necessary to repay loans as further mortgages had proved impossible due to 'the late pressure on the money market'. In fact during the latter part of 1847 the country had been in a state of growing financial panic, partly the result of earlier speculation in railways. Lack of ready cash was given as the reason for the delay at the harbour and most of the labour force had been laid off.

How had it been possible to raise £75,000 on the new shares when money was so tight in the markets? The shares were to have been offered as 'rights', that is to say to the existing shareholders pro rata to their existing holdings. Admittedly the coupon at six per cent was attractive yet the guarantee by the Norfolk company could not have been particularly reassuring given that company's own desperate finances. Certainly the previously supportive Norfolk directors could not have thought so. Only two of them subscribed at all for a total of 68 shares between them although the engineers Robert Stephenson and Bidder had rallied to the cause taking 100 shares each. Some commissions were paid to brokers who brought in subscribers, some small shareholders took up their allocation and two larger holdings were placed with investors who had not previously featured prominently if at all. These were a Mr Lowson who took 383 shares and a Mr Wellington who splashed out on 500, the full £10,000 paid on subscription. What story had these men been told?

So far as can be determined Peto personally took up a total of 3,715 shares, a commitment of just short of £75,000, a truly staggering sum, approximately sixty per cent of the whole issue. Much of this came in cash to the Lowestoft company, in some cases via a bank or finance house, the two named in the accounting records being Lawrence & Co (probably stockbrokers Lawrence, Cazenove & Pearce) and the London Joint Stock Bank. A single sum of ten thousand pounds was noted in the Lowestoft journal as coming from the Norfolk company 'in part payment of his (i.e. Peto's) bill drawn on the Norfolk Railway' which of course did not bring in any fresh cash to the combined enterprise. One has to assume that Peto raised the bulk of this money on loan. Rumour in the City had it later that year that Peto had borrowed an extra £140,000 as a result of the 1847 crisis bringing his total borrowings to well over £300,000. Of course he had many commitments other than those at Lowestoft.

Despite the comparative restoration of finances the directors did not have an easy time at the meeting. Vociferous critics included Cory, Sultzer, Gowing and a new name, Stead. Cory's main question, astoundingly never asked before, was how was it that costs had risen to double the original estimates? When Till responded obliquely that they now had the power to raise additional capital, Cory pressed his point. Bidder, who had been responsible for the original estimates, was conveniently absent 'with a domestic affliction' and Till was left to talk vaguely of considerably lengthened harbour piers, the necessity of creosoting the timbers, more dredging and the building of coal lifts. In any case he said most things had cost more than expected, 'something that happened everywhere'.

Peto came to Till's aid with more precise particulars of the degree to which the piers had been lengthened and the resultant call for large quantities of ever longer piles. Those to seaward were seventy-five feet in length compared to those inshore which were only forty feet. Cory asked when the decision to lengthen had been made? Till again hedged; it had been a gradual development, but fully realised when more money was required to which the shareholders had assented. When Cory said that there was nothing in the February 1847 report Till said that Bidder had then explained it all (although no record appears of any such explanation in the minutes or press reports). (It is a fact that the south, the straighter pier, extending only some 900 feet to seaward in the earliest plan and 1,000 feet in evidence to the Tidal Harbours Commission in 1845, ultimately reached to 1,300 feet taking it into considerably deeper water.) Cory, well briefed, now pointed out that the very first report had said that contracts had been placed. Till then blundered by saying that all the work had been done without contract and without profit. On this Peto intervened a second time to say, correctly, that there was a contract but for the railway alone and that the harbour work had been done by the company itself without contract.

Cory was understandably not satisfied and he and Sultzer wanted to know just who had made the decision to extend the harbour. Till said it had been done by the two boards in consultation but admitted that the shareholders had not been consulted. Mr Stead observed that if Yarmouth, with no debt to service whatever, spent the whole of its £12,000 a year harbour dues on maintenance, it was scarcely possible that Lowestoft, with annual dues estimated at only £5,000 before any allowance for harbour maintenance and with accumulated costs of over £300,000, could ever pay a dividend at all, let alone four per cent. Till's reply that 'that was question which every gentleman must answer in his own mind' was hardly reassuring. Mr Gowing said that the harbour in its present state could not pay and must be finished.

There was much discussion on the need for dredging. Captain Andrews said there must inevitably be a regular charge. Peto, as usual fluent and in apparent command of the facts, explained that Yarmouth had a bar and much river silt falling from suspension so that there was a constant need of dredging. Lowestoft had no such problem. While some dredging would be needed in the outer harbour it would be needed in the inner harbour only if it was decided to leave the lock open due to the volume of traffic. In any case soil produced by dredging was necessary to backfill the quays. All of which might be true, but did not contradict Andrew's statement that there would be a charge.

Cory and Sultzer brought the debate back to their main points, Cory that the harbour had been enlarged without proper authority, Sultzer that the six per cent share issue was invalid and that it was beyond the company's power to deprive the dissenting shareholders of their profit share. Till's defence to the former was still merely that the shareholders must have assented to the expenditure since they had assented to the share issue. Sultzer had also asked whether in the directors' opinion the six per cent dividend was a charge before arriving at the profits to be shared. Neither Till nor the chairman, Gooch, knew the answer and when Sultzer pressed further the company's solicitor advised the directors against giving any answer at all.

Joseph Lawrence, head of the stockbroking firm that had supplied Peto with so much money and an original shareholder in the Norwich & Brandon, saying he represented several new shareholders, spoke against the dissenting shareholders. They had declined to take up new shares and, now the new capital had largely been spent, wanted half the profits that would result. They could have sold out and taken a profit. Their obduracy had resulted in the need to maintain a separate board and administration. Sultzer put two motions, the first to cancel the creation of new shares; the second to ensure that Till could not be secretary of both companies. Both were defeated, though narrowly, after Peto had made a typically emollient speech urging inter-company friendship.

This account of Lowestoft proceedings has taken us ahead of other matters concerning the Norfolk Railway. In January its board was considering a draft agreement with the Newmarket & Chesterford that had been proposed by the latter. This was predicated on the Newmarket company building their line from Newmarket to Thetford and some form of joint operation by that company and the Norfolk over the line that would then exist from Thetford through to Chesterford, a considerable cut-off as compared to the route via Brandon, Ely and Cambridge. The section Thetford/Newmarket was to be jointly managed and neither company was to have an arrangement with any other company without mutual agreement. At a board meeting in early February Duff had stated that 'several influential proprietors' had looked for two to three influential gentlemen to join the board in order 'to strengthen the hands of the directors' and for a start proposed Peto. Consideration of this was deferred until the next meeting. The sub-committee charged with reduction of staff costs had reported but 'their proposals were considered too trifling to bother with'. All that could be agreed on was that new staff should be offered lower salaries. At the next meeting, also in February, Peto, though not present, was elected to the board.

The report rendered to the half-year meeting of shareholders in late February heard of improved revenues but the directors emphasised that working expenses were unacceptably high as a percentage of revenue, an inevitable result of operating over too restricted a mileage (see table in Chapter 6) However better results could be expected when the Midland Railway line from the west opened to Peterborough. Meanwhile the number of trains run had been reduced. The Lowestoft line had got off to a good start and most of its goods traffic had gone to destinations on the Norfolk. Capital costs at £1,624,151 at the end of December were stated to be £380,000 over original estimates due to expenditure on 'carrying stock, engine houses, goods depots, sidings and cottages'. Since 1845 there had been regrettable costs incurred in fighting off competition in a 'district legitimately belonging to the Norfolk Railway'. It was now hoped that the Yarmouth bridge would be complete in three months. Work on the line to Fakenham had been suspended for the previous four months due to financial stringency but it was hoped to complete by the autumn. Peto's election to the board was reported.

After a brief introduction by Duff, Bidder supplied a comprehensive report on the history of the line so far and its prospects for the future. He estimated that the final cost of the line as at present contemplated would be £1,750,000 made up as follows:

	£000	£000
Lines, including land and all associated costs		
Yarmouth & Norwich		250
Norwich & Brandon, as a single line		380
Wymondham/Dereham branch		120
Extension Dereham to Fakenham		120
Yarmouth bridge and tramways		105
		975
Doubling line over 70 miles and taking in Thetford		200
		1,175
Stations and other buildings not in original estimate	250	
Locomotives and rolling stock	170	
Interest paid to shareholders during construction	60	
Abortive parliamentary spend	40	
Miscellaneous	55	
		575
		1,750

Everything, he assured the meeting, had been absolutely necessary. This is probably the most objective summary of the capital costs ever presented for this railway; unfortunately there was a good deal more expenditure to come than he allowed for (see Appendix 3) and his figures for capitalised interest and miscellaneous costs, presumably mainly legal and parliamentary, were seriously understated. As to the recent results he admitted receipts had fallen below his earlier estimates. This was something suffered by every line in the country due to the general trade depression which had especially impacted on Norfolk passenger traffic, particularly holiday traffic. He went on to give a quick survey of prospects, contemplating an annual revenue of £150,000 once all lines and connections were open. While they would lose some London passenger traffic to the Eastern Union they would gain via the Peterborough connection to the west. The Lowestoft guarantee was a cost but from that line they would gain much traffic, especially coal, in the process killing off the river trade. Blithely taking working expenses at forty per cent he forecast a future annual dividend at five and a half per cent.

Several shareholders were predictably unhappy including Mr Yetts and Major Court. The latter objected to nearly everything in the accounts and, according to the *Railway Times*, made 'a speech of considerable length involving minute statistical details'. Amongst other points he noted that the accounts were not signed by anyone and complained that he could not reconcile them with those of the previous half year. He suspected that the dividend at the half year had not been covered by profits [true, and admitted at the time]. He asked for details of the latest capital expenditure and complained that many sums charged to capital should have been deducted instead from profits [probably true]. He failed to obtain any answers. Other shareholders concentrated especially on Lowestoft as a bad and unnecessary investment. Bidder defended Lowestoft harbour as a valuable adjunct to the railway and complained that the whole system had suffered extra costs due to opposition by 'most inhabitants of Norwich and Yarmouth, almost to a man'. Peto also defended the Lowestoft venture, saying he was prepared to lease it himself at four per cent on the outlay, increasing that to five per cent when lines should reach Halesworth and Bungay. Mr Lawrence looked for some new and more assiduous directors. Mr Yetts proposed a motion calling for a committee of shareholders to examine the accounts but found little support.

The meeting was then declared special for the purpose of approving the Newmarket agreement. Its advantage as explained by the directors would be that the company would be managing 116 miles rather than 81 with a consequent greater spread of overheads. In any case it would be a valuable bargaining point in negotiations with their 'great neighbour'. How this would have played in the light of the Norfolk's existing agreement with the Eastern Counties is unclear but in any case of no importance since although the terms were agreed by the shareholders they related to a line

Peterborough station

that had not been built and was not in fact ever going to be built during the lifetime of the Norfolk company.

Early in March Duff proposed to resign as chairman and suggested Peto in his place, but this was too much for some directors and Duff remained in the chair. The question of finding more principal share-holders willing to join the board was again deferred. (Although no minute has been found it would appear that Edward Ladd Betts was in fact appointed before May, but nobody else.) It was reported that the Newmarket shareholders were to have a special meeting to chose between draft agreements with the Norfolk and with the Eastern Counties. One director suggested that a triple merger of the three companies might be a solution to their problems. The precise extent of those problems was not spelt out in the minutes or apparently discussed. Nevertheless the urgency of some action was recognised and Mr Newbery proposed that a subcommittee of three, he Peto and Duff, should be appointed to meet representatives of the Eastern Counties.

In early April the board was discussing a report from the subcom-mittee on prospects of merger with the Eastern Counties that referred to a preliminary arrangement for an amalgamation of the capital 'on equal terms'. A rough draft of an agreement from the Eastern Counties lawyers was on the table. The next minutes record a meeting on 26 April of four Norfolk directors, including Peto, with Waddington of the Eastern Counties and with lawyers from both sides. The Norfolk's financial state must indeed have been desperate as Waddington was offering to lend certain securities to discharge the Norfolk's more immediate and pressing liabilities in consideration of the transfer of the Norfolk plant and stock to be held as security. The meeting carried on over two days with the main attention being given to a statement of the Norfolk's liabilities. It was vital that this was complete, as the Eastern Counties would assume responsibility for the stated total and no more. Once the agreement came into effect the Eastern Counties would hold the railway and the only source of any further funds would be from the Norfolk's shareholders.

A special meeting of the Eastern Counties was held on 2 May to approve not only a merger with the Norfolk but also with the Newmarket & Chesterford. As regards the Norfolk, Hudson, presiding, stressed the economies which would be gained by merging the locomotive and other departments of the two companies and predicted appreciable through traffic to Norwich once the lines from Ely to the Midlands via Peterborough were open. He also made a curious comment to the effect that the Norfolk had, without merger, no interest in sending its London traffic via the Eastern Counties having just as much interest in sending it by water from Yarmouth. The real danger, he said, was of the Norfolk falling into other hands. The acquisition of the Newmarket company was justified as chiefly a defensive measure against the penetration of Eastern Counties territory by the Great Northern.

On Thursday 4 May 1848 a Norfolk board meeting was held to approve finally the agreement and a report to go to a special meeting

Pub. by Mess.rs Jarrold & Sons. Norwich.   *Eng by Newman & Co 48 Watling St London*

The Foundry Bridge & Railway Station, Norwich.

of shareholders that day. At the shareholders meeting Peto (in the chair in Duff's absence) put the best possible face on what was to happen, emphasising the prospect of an eventual full merger and explaining that the high costs of operation of the Norfolk on its own meant that the operating profits were simply too low to meet the interest on the various loans, to satisfy the large amounts guaranteed on preferred shares and still to provide an adequate return to ordinary shareholders. There would be substantial cost savings which he estimated at £25,000 in a full year.

Major Court was suspicious and had no confidence in the directors due to their past extravagant expenditure. He now doubted the need for amalgamation. Why not simply lease the railway to the Eastern Counties for seven years and discover what were the true comparative results? Mr Yetts seemed well informed and thus aware that future dividends were of less importance than immediate rescue. However he pointed out that the Norfolk shares were all fully paid up whereas the Eastern Counties shares were not. Mr Newbery, a director, made a good speech in favour of the merger plan. They had a dilemma. It was undesirable to talk down the company's value but they were in a jam. They needed about £200,000 but did not want to go to the shareholders. Their stock had been on a par with the Eastern Counties' but was now falling whereas the latter's was holding steady. He thought the Eastern Counties indifferent to the Norfolk and that their attitude was now 'take it or leave it'. The terms could not be improved. His own stock had been bought at £150 for £100 nominal but he saw his loss as inevitable. Several others, notably Sir William Foster, spoke in favour. Peto assured those present as to the Eastern Counties that 'there was not a line more efficiently, more soundly run, or more honestly managed' and asserted that he had full knowledge of its affairs. No doubt as a major creditor of the Norfolk he had an interest in completing the merger but in the light of later events and revelations this seems to have been going way too far.

Following the special meeting there was a further meeting of the Norfolk committee appointed to carry out the agreement that confirmed that the railway would be taken over by the Eastern Counties on Monday 8 May. That this action lacked parliamentary sanction was ignored in the emergency. What had been agreed? The following is a summarisation of the main terms of the agreement of 2 May:

1. The Norfolk would lease its line to the Eastern Counties the management of which would become forthwith the responsibility of a joint committee comprised of four members from the Eastern Counties and three from the Norfolk. [The first action of the joint committee was to dismiss the entire Norfolk staff and replace it with Eastern Counties men.]

2. The lease proposed would run for seven years from 9 May 1848 or until an earlier amalgamation. Both parties would apply to Parliament

in the next session and from time to time thereafter if necessary to procure a full amalgamation. (It would be necessary also to apply for authorisation of the lease.) The parties would work in harmony until the amalgamation the terms of which were not to disfavour the Norfolk stockholders who would be treated on equal terms with those of the Eastern Counties.

3. The lines handed over were defined as the 82 existing miles between Yarmouth and Brandon including the Lowestoft and the Dereham branch, plus the eleven miles of the extension from Dereham to Fakenham and that into Yarmouth. The latter works would be completed under joint control. No further extensions were to be built without the agreement of the Eastern Counties and in particular three authorised branches – Reedham/Diss/Thetford, Diss/Wymondham and Fakenham/Wells/Blakeney – would not be constructed.

4. An inventory would be made of working stock, plant, materials, tools, furniture and other articles that should be handed over to the Eastern Counties. The latter company to use them but must hand them back after seven years 'in like condition, reasonable wear and tear excepted.' These items (which included some forty locomotives and had by now cost £182,972) were later valued at £161,112 by Robert Stephenson who was appointed arbitrator for this and other purposes.

5. The Norfolk's and Lowestoft's combined called up capital was stated to amount to £1,999,295 including £444,450 of debentures. No further capital would be raised except that previously uncalled capital should be called up and the company must sell off any unwanted property, the proceeds to be used to complete the Lowestoft harbour and the Fakenham line. The Eastern Counties might advance money as necessary to the Norfolk on the security of the plant and stock taken over to complete the latter company's works and to pay off its liabilities.

6. The Eastern Counties would pay interest and guaranteed dividends for which the Norfolk was liable and would pay to the Norfolk ordinary stockholders a dividend at the same rate as was paid from time to time on the Eastern Counties' consolidated stock.

A month later it was found necessary to draw up a supplementary agreement. The share and loan capital of £1,995,295 was recited but, as there were also substantial further but unsecured liabilities, the combined total of all capital and liabilities was now quoted as £2,268,307 including £73,000 estimate to complete all works in progress. An alternative version, showing the position when all capital that could be called up had been, came to a total of £2,287,563. In the light of these figures the

Norfolk undertook to fix a maximum of £2,300,000 for all liabilities and capital, less current assets, this to be the maximum on which the Eastern Counties would be called upon to pay dividends and interest. Appendix 3 demonstrates how the total of £2,300,000 was never in fact exceeded in the remaining years of the company's history although the exact make-up of the capital structure varied. The capital structure immediately prior to the final merger of the company is detailed in Appendix 4.

Initially it must have seemed to the Norfolk board that they had reached a safe haven after their increasingly stormy voyage of the past year. Their last dividend to ordinary stockholders had been at an annual rate of five per cent, not the six per cent that they had been promised the previous summer, and they were having to pay five and a half on the most recent extension stock and six per cent at Lowestoft. Given that they had invested nearly £2,300,000 into their railway and the harbour at Lowestoft they would have to earn some £115,000 annually to service the capital and loans with even a five per cent dividend. So far they had never earned half of that. Now the Eastern Counties would pay all their interest and preferred dividends. In addition they were currently paying four per cent to their own ordinary stockholders and so must pay the same to those of the Norfolk.

There were snags, some obvious from the start, some revealed within the first year. The Eastern Counties was notorious for inefficiency and was habitually short of cash. Since Hudson had been elected to the board in late 1845 the company had been paying ordinary dividends as high as six and a half per cent but even though the rate had declined more recently to four per cent it was hard to see how this was being earned. The real problem was that it was not. The annual rate declared for the half year to 30 June 1848 was again four per cent but for the following half year it was nil. Hudson's practice of declaring whatever dividend he fancied, irrespective of profits, had been found out. It can be shown that the dividends for the time since his appointment should have been at less than half the rate actually declared, one reason why the company suffered from a cash shortage.

The Norfolk half-year meeting in August 1848 was chiefly concerned with explaining the agreement with the Eastern Counties. Peto repeated that the annual savings in working expenses due to the combined operation would be £25,000 a year but as the Eastern Counties subsequently issued only combined accounts for the two lines it was never possible to verify this. He was apparently delighted with the co-operation being received from Hudson and Waddington, both 'always a pleasure to meet'. No revenue account was presented, not even one up to the date of the Eastern Counties takeover of operations. The capital account showed that spend on a cash basis had risen to £1,736,208 for the Norfolk alone but it was more important to be sure that the final spend, including Lowestoft, would not exceed the £2,300,000 limit of which Peto at least was confident.

Lowestoft station
as rebuilt in 1855

Several shareholders were far from happy with such figures as were presented. Not only did Mr Yetts repeat his call for a committee of investigation but Major Court moved that the accounts be not accepted until audited. Mr Kennard, for the board, countered that as accountants for the Eastern Counties were going through everything anyway an audit was not essential and Court on this occasion did not press his point. Yetts made a long, angry attack on the directors for everything in the past, especially Lowestoft, all of which had combined to reduce them to their present extremities and surrender. Another shareholder countered that the deeds were done and how did it matter now? Newbery pointed out that Yett's attack could only devalue the company when it came to fix the terms of amalgamation. Kennard and others questioned the motives of Yetts; perhaps he was for his own reasons damaging the company deliberately. They moved that he be no longer heard.

Without a railway to run the chief concern of the Norfolk board over the next few years was to consolidate the arrangements with the Eastern Counties into a full merger. A secondary but often more pressing matter was to obtain cash by whatever means to finish the outstanding works, especially at Lowestoft harbour, to pay off borrowings as they fell due, and to meet the continual series of claims on their resources that had been forgotten or ignored in the past. Apart from calling up previously uncalled capital which was subject to various legal and timing restraints, their only source of cash had to be the Eastern Counties which company, as a matter of policy, never paid when payment could be avoided. In particular it proved difficult to extract the cash due for the sale of rolling stock as the Eastern Counties for long insisted that it must retain the entire proceeds against the possibility that the stock might be repurchased at the end of seven years. Even when the main part of the cash had been paid over a twenty-five per cent retention, over forty thousand pounds, was held back.

Progress towards a merger was slow and unsatisfactory. A Bill was prepared in the autumn of 1848 and at the half yearly meeting at the end of February 1849 Peto was optimistic as to its chances, while he remained confident that the limit of £2,300,000 capital expenditure would not be exceeded. But simultaneously a stormy meeting of the Eastern Counties shareholders, from which Hudson was inexplicably absent, not only set up a shareholder's committee (chaired by William Cash) to investigate the financial affairs of the company but also passed a resolution denying any intention to amalgamate with the Norfolk. The latter immediately replied with a public advertisement regretting the Eastern Counties resolution, praying for reconsideration given that the railway had been in their hands for ten months, and saying that the Norfolk directors would rely on the justice of Parliament.

The report of the Cash committee in April laid bare all Hudson's manipulation of the Eastern Counties accounts and the gross overpayment of dividends throughout the period he had been chairman. By early May a shareholders' protection association was demanding the resignation of all the directors and of the company's solicitor and the withdrawal of the Bill for amalgamation with the Norfolk (although the Cash report had said this should go forward). A petition was lodged with Parliament asking for an inquiry into the conduct of directors who were also MPs (Hudson himself, Waddington and John Bagshaw of Harwich). At the same time another meeting of the Eastern Counties, chaired by Waddington amid merciless heckling, heard that the board as a whole were to resign.

Although an amalgamation Bill did eventually go before Parliament that session, the Eastern Counties being bound under the earlier agreement to promote it, it is hardly surprising that its counsel betrayed no enthusiasm before the parliamentary committee while the Norfolk shareholders were far from unanimous in support. At a special meeting to approve the Bill Major Court said he opposed the amalgamation because he could not understand it. He believed it rested on a fallacy. He proposed that the meeting be adjourned while 'an intelligent accountant' investigated the accounts. Joseph Lawrence in response pointed out that everyone had agreed to amalgamate and they should now just get on with it. A Mr Baxendale spoke at length effectively accusing the directors of negligence. Just two or three of them should devote their whole time to running the railway, which should be operated under contract. They should institute detailed branch and product accounting. He was not surprised that the annual dividends had fallen steadily to the present unhappy state. Peto, however, saying he and his family had £100,000 in the concern and that he had consulted the other principal shareholders, pushed through a resolution in favour. In an impassioned speech he admitted that, following a recent letter, the Eastern Counties might be trying to repudiate the agreement, but if they could and did he was confident that the Norfolk could go it alone. There was no prospect of any committee of enquiry; that was not on the agenda.

Parliament did not pass the Bill. At the August half-year meeting Duff as chairman explained that it had failed due to a late opposition got up by the Newmarket and East Anglian companies. In consequence there had now to be a supplemental agreement with the Eastern Counties which took the form of an endorsement of the original document. This reiterated the intention to amalgamate, both parties to use their 'utmost endeavours' to procure an Act. Instead of a lease of the Norfolk as originally contemplated the Eastern Counties was to have running powers over the line and, in addition to the payments required to service preferred stock and interest, was to pay the Norfolk enough to maintain the railway, buildings and works in working order. (In practice this appears to have been ignored, such maintenance as required being paid for directly by the Eastern Counties on the authority of the joint committee.) The Norfolk must complete Lowestoft harbour 'as then designed' out of its own money for the Eastern Counties to work it (which makes it fairly clear that the earlier estimate of costs to complete was insufficient.) A revealing detail was that the Norfolk company was enjoined to procure a proper lease of the Lowestoft railway from the Lowestoft company. Apparently this important formality had been left in abeyance since the opening of the line two years before. The remaining points related largely to undertakings by both sides to pay sums to each other as were due in accordance with a settlement to be arbitrated by Robert Stephenson.

Major Court made another intemperate attack on the directors referring to the 'cooking' of the accounts since 1846. As a result he said a public [i.e. professional] auditor had been appointed on behalf of the Eastern Counties. Richard Till defended the board, saying the appointment of this man, Mr Quilter of Quilter, Ball & Co, [one of the early leaders of the accountancy profession] was largely because of the aspersions cast on the accounts by Major Court amongst others. However Court had some support and after much discussion he was appointed auditor along with stockbroker Joseph Lawrence. An Eastern Counties meeting the same day was typical of the noisy and quarrelsome meetings of that company in those years in the aftermath of the ejection of Hudson. A merger with the Norfolk was especially unpopular and one shareholder suggested it was worth not one third of what they paid annually on its behalf. Several shareholders made stringent criticisms of the directors and the chairman, Edward Betts who had succeeded Hudson, was personally insulted and accused of being no more than Peto's representative, an attack to which he replied with much spirit. R.W. Kennard, although no longer a Norfolk director, spoke to the meeting on behalf of that company but was shouted down. Ultimately the accounts and report were approved on a show of

Edward Ladd Betts

hands and although a poll was demanded and was to take place it would appear the board prevailed.

Norfolk directors' meetings after May 1848 were for some months rarer and two of the directors left the board. Whereas Peto, Betts, Newbery, Stephenson, Bolingbroke, Foster, Tyndale, Wardell and Anderson were all in attendance at the May meetings, and Duff sent apologies, Stephenson (who died that year) and Foster (whose attendance record was poor) are not referred to in the minutes after 1848. Lacon had been active on the board as late as March 1848 but is similarly not referred to again while Maitland had dropped out at some earlier date. Kennard appears to have left the board in late 1848. Betts had resigned from the board in August 1849 on becoming chairman of the Eastern Counties and at the same time Newbery resigned on moving back to Manchester. Till thereupon resigned as secretary, being replaced by a Mr Hutt at a lower salary, and joined the board.

Peto, Duff and Newbery were the initial Norfolk members of the joint committee but after these changes the membership altered to Peto, Tyndale and Till. In January 1850 Duff resigned as chairman giving as his reason that he was not on the joint committee and therefore was not in touch with events. Major (formerly Captain) Tyndale took his place, but it was Peto who acted as the chief contact with the Eastern Counties. During 1850 the board was augmented first by a Mr Arthur Mills (of 34 Hyde Park Gardens and probably connected with the bankers Glynn Mills), then by a Mr Jonah Smith Wells (of Milner Square, Islington and 75 Old Broad Street, 'supported by some large and influential share-holders') and finally, after Captain Wardell had resigned, by Mr Alfred Kingsford Barber (broker of Upper Clapton and 'a holder of a large quantity of the company's bonds').

Through 1848 and 1849 the minutes of both the Norfolk and the Lowestoft companies and also the accounting records of the latter demonstrate the extreme difficulties being experienced in satisfying creditors. Forty thousand pounds of Lowestoft bonds had earlier been authorised for issue but could not be placed in the market; instead they were used in large quantities as general currency to pay long outstanding contractors' and solicitors' bills due by the Norfolk. Obligations to repay loans falling due were met by short-term borrowings from bankers or by persuading the lenders to extend the term for a few months. When the Eastern Counties finally paid over the bulk of the cash for the rolling stock etc. it quickly vanished as loans were repaid. The retention was still unsettled as late as January 1851 but was eventually paid over, when it, too, was swallowed up by loan redemptions. It was found that there were legal obstacles in the way of calling up the outstanding five pounds per share on some 9,000 £20 shares issued in February 1847 specifically for the redemption of loans. Any call was at first put off for two years and later abandoned.

Several claims on the company proved especially troublesome at this time. The Waveney Valley former subscribers were bringing an action for a return of their original deposits plus interest, a matter that was not finally settled until 1855 and then at a cost of over three thousand pounds. It was agreed that their subscription moneys towards Norfolk shares would remain as Norfolk share capital but that no further calls would be made. Lord Leicester was claiming for damage sustained on land that was to have been acquired for the extension to Wells and had brought proceedings against the company. Other landowners, Lord Hastings and Mr Lee-Warner, had similar claims. It was established that these sums were not part of the £2,300,000 declared as the Norfolk's capital and liabilities and were eventually settled by the Eastern Counties. Finally Merrett, who had already received substantial payments, had further claims for maintenance work on the lines during the Norfolk's period of operation. The Eastern Counties would not accept liability and the matter ran on for many years.

General meetings of the shareholders continued to be acrimonious during 1850 largely due to the activities of Major Court who became what the directors must have considered to be a thundering nuisance. One day before the meeting to be held on the 28 February Court's audit report was published in *The Times*. Many of his points were perfectly legitimate but the undue publicity had the primary effect of hitting the share price as they suggested a major scandal. He considered that £19,000 of expenditure that should have been charged to revenue (and thus paid for by the Eastern Counties) had been charged to capital. He objected to stamps on shareholders' proxies being paid for by the company, and rather more importantly, he objected to some £3,000 that had been paid out to the former North of Norfolk subscribers in addition to the shares issued to them. Further he observed that the balance on the Eastern Counties account in the Norfolk's books and that on the Norfolk's account in the books of the Eastern Counties differed by some £50,000 . He suggested that there should be a monthly audit of all expenditure and that all legal bills should be taxed [a court procedure for assessing the value of the work done] before being approved for payment.

At the meeting the directors raised an objection to the publication but several shareholders said that it was a legitimate proceeding. No special answer was made to Court's points except to say that Mr Quilter was proceeding with his own examination but that his report was not yet available (it appears that it was still outstanding a year later and, if ever received, does not appear to have been published). Mr Lawrence, joint auditor with Court, thought the company's accounts were kept in an excellent manner. He knew Court from elsewhere; he had a great fancy for going minutely into accounts, much more than he, Lawrence, considered necessary. It was eventually agreed to print Court's report alongside that of the directors. It was reported that it had been agreed not to attempt a further amalgamation Bill in the 1850 session and that instead joint working over a longer time would enable the relative values of the two companies to be better assessed. The Eastern Counties dividend had been slashed and only fifteen shillings per £100 stock was available for the Norfolk ordinary stockholders.

Prior to the next half-year meeting in August 1850 Court excelled himself in publishing what *The Times* referred to as a 'very elaborate report'. On this occasion he had constituted himself as what one share-holder described as 'a one-man committee of investigation' and had attempted to audit all transactions from 1846 onward, in particular comparing all capital issues with the authorising Act of Parliament. His most wounding point was his contention that the issue in 1847 of £105,000 of guaranteed stock was 'illegal', not having received specific parliamentary authorisation, and even if authorisation by the share-holders was sufficient could not be entitled to a preferential dividend. He was aggrieved that he had not been allowed to extend his examination to the records of the Lowestoft company. He pointed out that there was now a vast difference between what the Eastern Counties showed in their accounts as due from the Norfolk and the equivalent balance in the Norfolk's own accounts. He had many less material points too.

Not surprisingly the meeting that followed devoted most of its time to consideration of Court's report. Tyndale, chairman now, said that it had done immense damage to the company and was full of errors and false deductions. He declined to read it to the meeting but Court insisted on reading it himself. He wanted it printed but his fellow auditor Lawrence said his point on the illegality of the 5½% stock was too serious to be printed without an accompanying rebuttal on behalf of the board. Several shareholders supported Court. Peto, swiftly pointing out that he had not been a director when the stock was issued, explained that the many items in dispute with the Eastern Counties were being arbitrated upon by Stephenson or were being settled directly with the company by himself. He would have hoped that Court would not have published before meeting the proprietors. Eventually, on the motion of Mr Wells, it was agreed that the report would be passed as regards the (miserable 10 shilling per £100) dividend and that Court's report would be published along with a detailed commentary by the directors, the rest of the report to be considered at an adjourned meeting.

A special meeting was held after the half-year event solely to sort out the position of the Waveney shareholders. They had been dissatisfied with the proposal to issue them with Norfolk shares and had gone to court to recover their deposits and the interest they claimed, but had lost their action. This brought out high feelings with our old friend Wilkinson saying that no fraud committed by Hudson approached that which the Norfolk had perpetrated upon the Waveney applicants, a remark that was replied to by Tyndale in terms that *The Times* declined to report and which came near to resulting in a challenge to a duel before both parties withdrew and apologised. Moreover the complex problem could not be resolved and this meeting too was adjourned.

It was not until November that the half-year meeting was reconvened prior to which Court's report had been duly printed and distributed along with the directors' rebuttal. Basically the directors explained the circumstances in which the various share issues to which Court objected had been made, said they had never acted but on the best legal advice, and pointed out what harm would arise in attempting to undo matters at this late stage. Court's most material point of all was that, in raising over £150,000 of borrowings under the authority of the Act for the Reedham/Thetford line which was never built, the directors had exceeded their powers: it was as well that the directors were able to show that they had legal advice to the contrary. Nevertheless their reply brought to light some transactions they might have preferred to remain confidential such as costs of over £17,000 that had been incurred long before (and capitalised) in connection with the Diss & Colchester and Wells & Dereham applications to Parliament and an issue of £2,000 worth of shares to Till as compensation for the loss of his job as secretary. Another revelation was that £30,000 of the £105,000 share issue had been made for no greater reason that it had been convenient to do so at the time.

Tyndale started off the meeting with a bullish statement of the company's potential in any merger, its revenue now at £120,000 per year. If the working costs were fixed at £50,000 (and he said independent contractors would charge no more) in contrast to the far larger sums the Eastern Counties were declaring, then there would be ample surplus to pay all interest and a larger ordinary dividend than they had ever yet received from the Eastern Counties. Lowestoft harbour was beginning to benefit from trans North Sea trade thanks to the 'untiring energy' of Peto in organising a steam packet service. Major Court's interventions had been of little help and would he please refrain from further damaging comments. Court, unrepentant, read his reply to the directors' rebuttal of his earlier report, making no concessions. He wanted a committee of shareholders to be formed with the task of going over in detail everything that had been done in the past and to nominate new directors to the board.

He gained some support despite a riposte from his co-auditor Lawrence who told the shareholders that they had now 'felt the evil of admitting Court to the office of auditor' and the shares had fallen as a result. Peto, clearly for once exasperated, said he would be quite glad if the shareholders did throw out the board. He was neglecting more interesting matters to attend to their affairs. The firm of Quilter, Ball was looking at the accounts of both the Eastern Counties and the Norfolk. Shareholders should wait until they had finished and could then further investigate if the directors had done anything wrong or could throw them out if they then had not their confidence. Meanwhile they should look at the commercial prospects. He was all for connecting the Norfolk to the Eastern Union at Norwich. Then the number of trains being run, at present ten or eleven into Norwich each day by each company, could be halved. Ultimately Major Court's proposals were heavily defeated, at least one director threatening to resign were it passed. Through the autumn and winter there was extensive correspondence in the railway press concerning the relationship of the Eastern Counties and the Norfolk. The Eastern Counties had issued a statement asserting that large losses were being made in running the Norfolk section of the system and there were suggestions of repudiating the lease, if indeed there was a lease, which was disputed. The *Railway Times* ran an editorial mocking Peto which would have done credit to *Private Eye* in the present generation but admitted that Court's fumbling and inarticulate approach was Peto's salvation.

In January 1851 Peto was authorised by the board to negotiate with the Eastern Counties and the Eastern Union for a triple merger, or just with the Eastern Counties alone if the Eastern Union was unwilling to join in. By now Bett's brief period as chairman of the Eastern Counties was over after he suffered a severe accident, his place being taken by engineer Joseph Glynn. By the end of January the three boards had agreed terms to be put to their shareholders in the following month. Under these the Eastern Counties would take over the working of all three railways; £60,000 would be allowed annually to the Norfolk and £72,000 to the Eastern Union to cover their preferred stocks and guarantees; and the balance of profits would be divided between the companies for their ordinary shareholders in the ratio 6:1:1. This arrangement would endure for fifty years during which the three companies would remain separate legal entities if necessary but all undertook to work towards a full amalgamation as soon as possible.

David Waddington

Special meetings of proprietors were to be held in February to approve these terms but that of the Norfolk had to be adjourned until late March when it was learnt that the Eastern Counties shareholders had referred the agreement to a committee of shareholders for consideration. The adjourned Eastern Counties meeting on 18 March was the usual noisy affair, which lasted seven hours. The shareholders' committee had reported adversely on the merger proposals but had put forward no alternative. There was contention for places on the board. Ultimately those in favour of the amalgamation lost and left the board while those objecting to the terms won the day and amongst others Waddington rejoined the board. Glynn resigned as chairman and Waddington succeeded to his place.

The Norfolk meeting met ten days later in an atmosphere of disappointment and recrimination. Major Court delivered a further critical report and declared his intention to resign as auditor because he held a wider view of an auditor's responsibilities than did the company. Many objected to a fresh statement made by some Eastern Counties members that their company made a loss in running the Norfolk line. Peto insisted that unless the three companies came together running costs would inevitably continue at an excessive rate. There was no need for two stations in Norwich and two competing lines to London. He wanted either a complete amalgamation, or at least the present agreement extended in perpetuity. Otherwise they should withdraw from the agreement and work the line themselves. Indeed he could produce someone who would run the line at far less than was being done by the Eastern Counties. Many companies incurred only half their running costs per mile. At the earlier meeting he had hinted that the Great Northern company might be their salvation if the Eastern Counties declined to merge. Now he said that he would if necessary run the local traffic himself which at present was being subordinated to through trains. Perhaps because of these bold statements a board meeting later that day elected Peto to the chair in place of Tyndale.

CHAPTER 10

The railway under Peto: 1851 to 1856

Dealing with the Eastern Counties

With the apparently decisive rejection of a merger with the Eastern Counties, just four years of their lease with guaranteed income to run, an immense load of debt shortly due for repayment, claims mounting up against them from all sides and claims on the Eastern Counties for which they were unable to obtain satisfaction, it might have been thought that the directors of the Norfolk Railway were in a hopeless position. Yet this was not entirely the case. For if they lay at the mercy of the Eastern Counties, yet their railway, whatever the Eastern Counties shareholders might say, was essential to that company's strategy so long as the Eastern Union and the Norfolk blocked their access to Norwich, Ipswich and the ports. And in Peto they had a resourceful chairman at the height of his powers, possibly insolvent but persuasive, influential, well connected, and far from ready to give up his burgeoning plans for Lowestoft, North Sea shipping and railway lines on the Continent.

During the early 1850s, as will be described, he was engaged in setting up both a major shipping line for North Sea and Baltic trade and a railway company in southern Denmark. Yet this is not to suppose that these matters and the Norfolk railway itself represented more than a minor part of his affairs during that time. For with money less tight than in the late 1840s and railways in demand Peto was operating as contractor but still more as financier on a larger scale than ever before whether alone or in partnership with his brother-in-law Edward Betts and his former rival Thomas Brassey. There were railways built in Lincolnshire, in Essex and in the west of England, docks in London and Birkenhead, the Marsh Cut on the River Ouse, a railway in Norway and above all the Grand Trunk Railway in eastern Canada with its associated fabrication and locomotive plant in Liverpool, the great Canada Works. It is astonishing that Peto could spare time for the tiny Norfolk, yet he seldom missed a board meeting.

The railway itself was of course under the management of the joint committee dominated by the Eastern Counties although Peto, Tyndale and Till represented the Norfolk. One of the first matters to pursue was the amounts that the Norfolk maintained were due from the Eastern Counties including the £40,000 retention on the rolling stock purchase, over £26,000 for work at Brandon station where the two lines joined and for joint working there, £7,000 for other works, £13,419, being a share of the costs of promoting the Diss & Colchester years before and £4,000 to recover a charge that had been made for carrying stone to Lowestoft harbour. The total in October 1850 had been over £100,000 apart from which there was delay in passing over moneys to pay guaranteed dividends. In addition there were claims on the Norfolk that the Eastern Counties had agreed to pay but would not such as damages on the aborted line to Wells, landowners' claims in that area for land purchases not completed and the subcontractor's claim in respect of delayed completion of the Fakenham line.

Although there was certainly additional capital expenditure on the Norfolk line over and above the amount allowed for in 1848 this was paid for in the first instance by the Eastern Counties although included in the counter claims being made on the Norfolk. Few items were now being capitalised in the Norfolk's books apart from legal and parliamentary expenses. Even the cost of a new dry dock at Lowestoft, over £10,000, was being paid for by the Eastern Counties while some surplus land and equipment at Lowestoft was sold. Peto's shipping company took a short lease on several of the Lowestoft harbour facilities including the cattle sheds and yards, the creosote works, the new graving dock and a shipyard that a previous tenant had vacated.

Norfolk Railway 0-6-0 *No.* 21 (*E.C.R. No.* 225) *built* 1845

In mid-1851 Peto was meeting with Quilter, the accountant acting for the Eastern Counties, in an attempt to achieve a settlement. By the following spring the two were said to have reached an agreement but the result had to be submitted to lawyers for both sides. Initially it had been agreed to refer everything to Robert Stephenson as arbitrator but when this was done the Norfolk was dissatisfied with the answer and arguments continued. There are references in the Norfolk minutes to talks with Quilter and an 'award' but in the Norfolk's accounts to 31 December 1852, the first we have other than as brief extracts, identifiable open accounts and other claims on the Eastern Counties totalled over £138,000 although some items sound dubious in the extreme. The total was much the same at the 1853 year end but by December 1854 all the claims had vanished from the accounts. As the main compensating change was to increase the amounts capitalised as the cost of the railway it would seem that the Norfolk had given in on most points.

More successful was a grand refinancing authorised by an Act of 1852 that permitted the issue of 50,670 new debenture shares of £10 each carrying a perpetual interest charge of four per cent. These were to be issued in the main to existing shareholders, the proceeds to be used to repay the large sums of mortgage loans falling due over the next two or three years, much of which had been borrowed at higher interest rates. However £25,000 of new debentures were to be issued to Peto himself in consideration of his giving up his rent charge on Lowestoft harbour. It may be recalled (Chapter 7) that he had originally paid £12,500 for the harbour and river navigation. He had then leased it in 1846 to the Lowestoft company for £1,000 per year (although the rent had been collected for two years only). If the initial rental at eight per cent on £12,500 was reasonable then its conversion to four per cent on £25,000 was not unfair. In mid-1852 the company had £479,000 of secured debt. By the end of 1855 debenture shares in issue totalled £447,000 but debts had been reduced to £69,000. Had it not been for the extra £25,000 issued to redeem the harbour rental the combined total would have been little different. The balance of the increase was mainly represented by the continued capitalisation of legal and parliamentary costs, a constant drain on every railway company.

Throughout the period 1851 to 1853 the Norfolk board and their lawyers kept an eye on the possibility of forcing a merger with the Eastern Counties. An opportunity occurred when in 1852 the Eastern Counties took over the running of the East Anglian lines. This required an Act and the Norfolk's lawyers succeeded in inserting a protective clause to give the company a right within twelve months to amalgamate with the Eastern Counties at a price to be determined by arbitration. Eventually the Norfolk decided not to attempt this since exercising the option would at once determine the existing agreement without allowing advance notice of what terms an arbitrator would settle upon. However Peto worked to cultivate Waddington, chairman of the Eastern Counties. Although the latter had been reappointed to his board on a policy of rejecting a Norfolk amalgamation he was far from hostile to such a move. Both being MPs, he and Peto would have had frequent contact, and by 1851 he had been roped in as one of Peto's colleagues as a patron of the annual Lowestoft regatta, as had his co-director Lord Alfred Paget. No doubt they also enjoyed the hospitality of Somerleyton Hall.

The Eastern Union Railway, still entirely independent, was in constant dispute with the Eastern Counties which refused to make it easy, indeed hardly practicable at all, for the former to run fast through services from Norwich and Ipswich past Colchester to London. Like the Norfolk in 1848 the Eastern Union was in increasingly difficult financial straits as it began to build its branch to Harwich although it continued to make aggressive moves in several directions. In 1851 it was once again promoting a Norwich/Dereham line. In the following year it flirted with a proposal for a line connecting Yarmouth to Lowestoft although this never reached the form of a Bill. It agreed to work, should it ever be built, a new, locally promoted, version of a Waveney Valley line, which had obtained an Act in 1851. In 1853 Cobbold and Bruff were involved in a partially successful bid to build a link between Norwich and Spalding, largely running over other lines but building for itself in the Fens. Only the section Spalding to Wisbech obtained permission (the first link in the later Midland & Great Northern Joint Railway) and only the section Spalding to Holbeach was built in the 1850s.

By October 1853 the financial situation was such that the Eastern Union board felt it could no longer carry on and pleaded with the Eastern Counties for a temporary working arrangement to be followed by a full merger. Early in November Peto, whose ear must have been close to the ground – after all he was in partnership with Brassey, an Eastern Union director and its main creditor – reported to the Norfolk board that an arrangement had been concluded between the two companies for working the joint lines and sharing the revenue and that a similar arrangement with the Norfolk was possible. He and Bidder were authorised to confer with Eastern Counties, and promptly did so. By the end of the month they were outlining to the board the terms of a proposed agreement.

This agreement, which would require the approval of members in special meeting and subsequently ratification by an Act of Parliament, was said to be very similar to that already concluded with the Eastern Union. It was not an amalgamation, and would not alter the fact that the combined railway would continue to be worked by the Eastern Counties although under the control of a revised joint committee that would have two Norfolk members, two from the Eastern Union and four from the Eastern Counties. Instead of the existing arrangement whereby the Eastern Counties simply paid the Norfolk's dividends, from 1 January 1854 the revenue of the combined operation, after allowing the Eastern Union forty-six per cent for working expenses and after certain other charges, would be divided into seven parts of which the Norfolk would have one, the Eastern Union another and the remainder would be retained by the Eastern Counties.

All claims either way were to cease (though it is hardly surprising to find from later minutes that they did not). All rolling stock would become part of the property of the joint enterprise (and so no question could arise of the Norfolk having in future to repurchase it). All Norfolk capital expenditure authorised before the 19 November would continue to be paid for by the Eastern Counties and capitalised in their books. Interest on the accumulated total would be charged to the joint revenue account before division of the balance. However, although this arrangement was part of the agreement, it became subject to extensive argument later on. Moreover the Norfolk was somewhat rashly continuing to authorise further capital expenditure in the following year in the full expectation that the Eastern Counties would fund that too.

A list of the capital items in progress in November was contained in the minutes. The main items were at Lowestoft including enlargement of the station, the new graving dock, resiting the coke ovens (smoke was causing a severe nuisance) a new fish market and removing the creosote works. Other stations were also being enlarged including Yarmouth and Fakenham. A special meeting of the shareholders in December readily approved the new arrangements. When the Bill to authorise them was put to Parliament in 1854 a clause was inserted in the eventual Act that bound the Eastern Union to put forward proposals for a full merger not later than 1862. Appendix 5 summarises the Norfolk's earnings and dividends for the eight years from 1854 until the company was merged into the Great Eastern Railway in 1862.

The new agreement did in fact subsist right up to the final mergers although not without trouble. So long as Peto was chairman of the Norfolk and Waddington of the Eastern Counties most disagreements could be smoothed out and although the railways had a poor record for efficiency, comfort, timing and safety the operations under the control of the joint committee continued without serious difficulty. Later, after both chairmen had departed, relations declined. This period will be dealt with in the final chapter. Meanwhile, even before the new agreement had been negotiated, the Norfolk board, perhaps emboldened by its successful refinancing in 1852 and now entirely dominated by Peto, had been contemplating investment in new lines. One of these projects, a new line to Aylsham, was being surveyed in November 1853 but was abandoned since it was unacceptable to the Eastern Counties. Two others, the Wells & Fakenham Railway and the Halesworth, Beccles and Haddiscoe company, which developed into the East Suffolk Railway are dealt with in the ensuing sections.

The East Suffolk Railway

The first involvement of the Norfolk in new lines started when Peto and others, including Betts and Edward Leathes, promoted the Halesworth, Beccles & Haddiscoe Railway in 1850. This line more or less duplicated one part of the abortive 'coastal line', the Ipswich, Norwich & Yarmouth of 1846, but it is hard to see what its economic justification might have been. Beccles, it had been said by a parliamentary committee, did deserve some railway connection but this would seem likely to have been better served by a revived Waveney Valley route giving it a more promising connection to London. Halesworth was, if anything, a less important centre than Beccles. A junction with the Lowestoft line at Haddiscoe gave only an indirect connection to Lowestoft. However much now desired by local landlords experience everywhere already showed that lines through purely agricultural areas were unlikely to pay. The best explanation that can be suggested is that in the minds of the promoters this was the first step in building a through route from Yarmouth and Lowestoft to Ipswich, perhaps a Peto plan to extricate the Norfolk Railway and more especially the town of Lowestoft from their dependence on the Eastern Counties if attempts at merger failed.

There is little about this line, which obtained its Act in June 1851, in the Norfolk minutes but the following year a further Act gave the Norfolk power to acquire or lease and to work the railway. Two months later a special meeting of the Norfolk shareholders approved the terms of an agreement to do just this, the price in case of purchase being fixed at £150,000 and in case of rental at £6,000 per year 'or such other consideration as may be agreed upon'. The agreement was not sealed by the Norfolk until the following January. Meanwhile Peto had received a letter from solicitor Charles Palmer of Yarmouth warning that the Eastern Union were planning a railway from Ipswich to Lowestoft and Yarmouth that he thought the Norfolk ought to prevent, criticising the existing arrangements at Reedham and advocating a direct line between Yarmouth and Lowestoft that he thought would be popular and used for exchanges of summer visitors.

Peto's reply, a copy of which is preserved in the Norfolk minute book, doubts the value of either the local link or a further line to London. He wrote that

> The present lines are all the district needs and Yarmouth is much better off with one good line four hours to London every day than it would be with two, neither of which could then afford your expresses. Besides, though you need not be jealous of Lowestoft, you don't want it nearer to London than your own town. The local line you speak of will not pay working expenses. While I retain the chair of the Norfolk, it is not my feeling to promote lines to disappoint those who embark upon them; but by a careful utilisation of the traffic of the district, in friendly alliance with other companies, to benefit largely the towns of the district and give a dividend at the same time to my own shareholders.

How he could square this with the Halesworth proposals is questionable. Three years later he wrote in a letter to the Norfolk board that he had promoted the Halesworth line as a protection for the Norfolk against a threat by parties with adverse interests. Whether or not this meant the Eastern Union that company did not proceed with their version of the coastal line except to obtain permission in 1854 for a branch from Ipswich to Woodbridge.

Construction of the Halesworth line was not begun until 1853 but was complete over its originally planned length by November 1854. In the meantime the project had greatly expanded. In August 1853 Peto explained to the Norfolk board his plans to extend the Halesworth line south to Ipswich, referring to a pledge by him to Lord Stradbroke to induce the latter to withdraw his support for a line proposed the previous year (perhaps an Eastern Union plan?). The Norfolk board minuted their support for such a line to be under the joint direction of the Eastern Counties, Eastern Union and the Norfolk itself and approved an application to Parliament. By an Act of 1854 the Halesworth, Beccles & Haddiscoe changed its name to the East Suffolk Railway and was given permission to build to Woodbridge where it would meet the new branch of the Eastern Union to come from Ipswich. It seems to have been generally assumed that the Eastern Counties would work this line as it was already bound to work the line to Halesworth under its arrangements with the Norfolk.

The engineer on the East Suffolk line was George Berkeley and the contractors were the partnership of Peto, Brassey & Best. The authorised share capital of the company, as enlarged in 1854, was £450,000, plus £150,000 borrowing powers. The Norfolk did not subscribe for any shares and had no fresh agreement with the East Suffolk but was nevertheless required to apply its seal to the Bill of 1854. Later that year Peto, on behalf of the promoters, made a curious proposal to the Norfolk board. He offered to abrogate the terms whereby the Norfolk had an option to purchase the Halesworth line

Norfolk Railway 2-2-2 No. 6 (E.C.R. No. 46) built 1845

(only: there was no option to purchase the new extension south) and to leave the question of purchase open until after three years of operations at which time some 'competent parties' could fix the real value. However in the meantime the Halesworth company needed 'a loan of debentures to the extent of eighty per cent of the previously fixed purchase price' which would be secured on the line itself and guaranteed by the contractors who would also pay any interest that the line could not. That is to say Peto asked the Norfolk to issue £128,000 debenture stock for cash and lend the proceeds to his railway. Unsurprisingly the Norfolk directors demurred and postponed a decision. No such arrangement was ever entered into.

Things started to go seriously wrong in 1855. The joint committee running the combined railways were in favour of working the whole East Suffolk line when complete as part of a single eastern system. Robert Stephenson was commissioned to value the completed section to Halesworth. The East Suffolk was to estimate the cost to complete the new line and the Eastern Union was asked to do the same for the Ipswich/ Woodbridge section. In February Peto was a signatory to a report which estimated a cost of £194,686 for the line from Halesworth to Woodbridge, not far in excess of £8,000 per mile. But the Eastern Counties shareholders were becoming restive and that spring a shareholders' committee of investigation was appointed that spent three months in conducting a detailed review of large parts of their company's operations and accounting. The committee's work uncovered many scandalous matters that were detailed in a long report that devoted relatively little space to the East Suffolk line. Concerning that enterprise they simply concluded:

> We consider it our duty to direct your attention to the contemplated railway to be made from Halesworth to Woodbridge. The formation of this railway can only result in great injury to your property. It may take the cattle and fish traffic now passing over your lines; and should the proprietors seek alliance with your company it can only form another element of loss. We deeply regret that the projectors have so far forgotten their former advocacy of the existing lines of your company, as now to propose to make a line which is in direct opposition to it. Your committee recommend that the most strenuous opposition be given to this proposed line …

Although this was mild stuff in a report that contained the sentence, '… we come to the deliberate and unanimous opinion that the election of a chairman at a salary of £2,000 a year has acted most prejudicially to the interests of the company.' it is hardly surprising that when Waddington put a proposal to his shareholders at a special meeting in July 1855 that the Eastern Counties should work the new line, it was turned down. He resigned shortly after. On the same day as the Eastern Counties meeting a Norfolk shareholders' meeting commissioned an investigating committee to consider the interest and participation of the Norfolk in the line between Haddiscoe and Ipswich. But it may be that this was intended to be a joint committee from the three companies as two months later it was reported that the two Norfolk appointees had resigned since the Eastern Counties had not appointed any members and appeared to have rejected the whole proposition.

That autumn the East Suffolk directors decided to go it alone and a prospectus was issued on 1 September listing as directors eight Suffok gentlemen led by Lord Stradbroke and Sir Thomas Gooch but also Richard Till of the Norfolk, J. H. Gurney and H. T. Birkett of Norwich, Sir Edmund Lacon of Yarmouth, John Bagshaw, now MP for Harwich and J. C. Cobbold representing the Eastern Union. The proposition put to potential subscribers contained an undertaking by Peto personally to lease the entire line at six per cent per annum for fourteen years on a cost not to exceed £10,000 per mile, on the strength of which surely rash promise a sum of some £225,000 was raised. On 10 October Peto's letter of resignation, dated 22 September, was read to the Norfolk board. The text was not reproduced in the minutes but as he was now committed both to build and operate a railway in direct competition to theirs it was scarcely appropriate that he should remain their chairman.

Although a flattering motion of regret was passed at the board meeting stressing the entire approval and satisfaction of his colleagues of all that he had done since the railway was first projected and especially of his achievements in forming the alliance of the three companies on a fair and equitable basis, the remaining directors must have been relieved that they were no longer to be tied to the tail of such an erratic comet. In particular they had no financial stake now in the success or failure of the East Suffolk line. At the half-year shareholders' meeting in February 1856 Richard Till was in the chair but Peto attended and made a 'lucid statement of the circumstances under which he has felt bound to withdraw from the chair of the company'.

The Wells & Fakenham railway

Lord Leicester and the people of Wells had been anxious for a railway to connect their small, isolated but still prosperous port to the growing national system. In 1844 Leicester, lord of the manor of Wells and by far the largest landowner in Norfolk, and other landowners of the area, including Lord Hastings and Mr Lee Warner of Walsingham, had promoted the Wells/Thetford line (later cut down to the Wells/Dereham section) but this had been scotched in negotiations with the Norfolk, never reaching a parliamentary hearing. Once the Norfolk had completed its line to Dereham in 1846 it had planned to go forward to Fakenham, Wells and Blakeney but had built only as far as Fakenham before work was stopped when its operations were taken over by the Eastern Counties. However a substantial cutting had been made for nearly half a mile to the north of Fakenham station.

Wells then determined to go it alone. The line to Fakenham would be only nine and a half miles in length. The country, while far from level, did not present major engineering difficulties so that an estimate of no more than £10,000 per mile including rails and stations was considered reasonable. In November 1853 the Norfolk board minutes recorded that solicitors for Lord Leicester had offered on his behalf £30,000 towards a Wells line if the Norfolk would provide an equal amount. Notwithstanding that they had no free funds the Norfolk board agreed. As this was coincident with the new negotiations with the Eastern Counties, Peto had advised his board that it was undesirable that any of the allied lines should be officially connected with the Wells line while the joint operations Bill was before Parliament. Consequently he had 'arranged with the engineer to provide the capital which the Norfolk had promised'. But he, Major Tyndale (who died soon after and was replaced by Mr Wells) and Richard Till from the Norfolk board were to be on the provisional committee and the Norfolk would indemnify them. The Norfolk would work the line when made (and this notwithstanding that it worked nothing else at this time).

The new three-way agreement with the Eastern Union and Eastern Counties was formally approved by the Norfolk board on 14 February 1854. In that agreement the Wells project and the intention to work the line was acknowledged, though terms were not defined, and nothing was said about a capital subscription. A formal agreement with the Wells promoters was approved by the board on 23 February 1854 and sealed on 21 March. This latter agreement provided for the Norfolk to work the line (and after the first year to maintain it) for remuneration equal to forty-six per cent of the gross revenue that it generated. It also provided for sharing of receipts for traffic transferred from and to the Norfolk, committed both parties to promote the Bill, and gave the Norfolk an option to buy or lease the line at a price which if not agreed could be determined by arbitration. However, once again, no mention was made of a capital subscription.

At their half-year meeting in February 1854 the Norfolk proprietors had been advised of the proposals in general terms including the promise to work the line but again nothing was said about a share participation. At a special

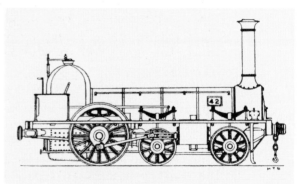

Norfolk Railway 4-2-0 No. 13 (E.C.R. No. 42) built 1846

meeting in June 1854 the Wells Bill (along with others) was put before the Norfolk proprietors and was approved. The Act was obtained in July authorising a company with a share capital of £70,000 and borrowing powers of £23,000. However subscribers had not been readily forthcoming while borrowing was not permissible until half the share capital had been paid up. Of the share capital £14,000 was to be raised in Wells itself, Lord Leicester subscribed £10,000 (not the earlier suggested £30,000) and £16,000 was promised elsewhere, principally from local landowners who were also willing to provide much of the land at a reasonable price. Thus the Norfolk was committed, morally if not contractually, to find the remaining £30,000.

In February 1855 the Norfolk board were advised that the Wells company wished to start work. George Berkeley was to be engineer and contractors (not Peto) were standing by. The company would like at least the deposit on the Norfolk's £30,000 capital subscription. The board referred the request to Peto and he, Till and Barber of their number were to see Waddington, presumably to confess all that might not already be known, and also perhaps to raise some money. The upshot of this is not recorded but by July nothing had been paid although the Wells company were now asking not only for the original deposit but also for a first call, total £6,150. The Norfolk board resolved to raise £24,350 from time to time to meet further calls as they arose. In July 1855 a Norfolk proprietors' meeting at last approved the company's share subscription.

At the Wells company's half year meeting in August 1855 Peto, as chairman now of this company too, reported that works had begun. He explained the delay in starting as due to the Norfolk having been unable to move in the matter until their arrangements with the Eastern Counties had been completed. 'As soon as those arrangements had been completed, the Norfolk proprietors had unanimously agreed to subscribe to the undertaking on their own account, irrespective of the Eastern Counties or Eastern Union.' (This might be thought, as an explanation of two year's limited progress, a rather too glib gloss over the process so far). He reported also the agreement to work the line. As to the future he was optimistic. The proprietors might expect a return of five or five and a half per cent. Of the 87 acres of land required 58 had already been purchased.

When in September Peto left the Norfolk board he remained on the board of the Wells company. He bequeathed to the Norfolk directors a disturbing problem in that there was no parliamentary permission for their subscription to the Wells company. One step taken that winter was to have lawyers prepare a Bill to go to the parliamentary session of 1856 to obtain the required authority. An Eastern Counties minute of that time nicely summarises the position:

> The Norfolk had lodged a Bill to regularise their subscription for 1500 £20 shares held by trustees on their behalf; this subscription had been made in December 1853 by directors without the company's authority; no mention of the Norfolk's subscription had appeared in the Wells Bill; no parliamentary application had been made concerning the shares in 1855; the shareholders' meeting of 15 July 1855 had been the first public mention of the subscription and the notice of the meeting did not specify that the subscription had already been made; the calls paid so far by the Norfolk thus lacked authority; and so the Eastern Counties intended to oppose the Norfolk's Bill,

which they did.

The Norfolk retained a leading parliamentary lawyer to press their case. Authority or not, the Wells line was progressing and must be paid for. In June 1856 the Norfolk borrowed £3,000 to pay calls and a further £1,000 for parliamentary expenses. Another £2,850 was required in July at which time Peto attended a Norfolk board meeting by invitation to discuss the commitments to Wells. By then the case before Parliament had been lost, as reported to shareholders in August, having been turned down by a special parliamentary committee with neither counsel nor directors heard and without it being possible to submit evidence. While the lawyers hoped to try again the following year the Norfolk so far had paid to Wells £18,150 in calls and now proposed to raise £30,000 to finance the whole investment by issue of 6,000 new five per cent Wells & Fakenham Railway preference shares to be offered to existing stockholders. They did in fact try this but were unable to raise more than £14,950, the balance of the investment remaining financed by borrowing.

In December they obtained the proprietors' approval to submit a further Bill in the 1857 session. The Wells company was now calling up further amounts due on shares and as usual the Norfolk were late with their subscription. As over half its capital was now paid up the Wells company was able to exercise its powers of borrowing by the issue of bonds. And now, with completion of the line in sight, the Eastern Counties began to take fright over the commitment, if indeed there was a commitment, to work the line. Further a new difficulty had arisen. The intention was to join the new line end on with the Norfolk's branch at Fakenham. The last bit of the route lay over land in the cutting already made by the Norfolk. Rails could be laid there by unofficial permission from the Norfolk people but the line could not be inspected nor opened to the public until the land underneath it was actually owned by the Wells company which also wished to have contractual rights to share the Fakenham station.

The position of the Eastern Counties directors as regards the Wells branch was that they would have preferred not to have anything to do with it. They doubted whether it could ever pay and feared that it would become no more than a millstone around the necks of the allied companies. Their permission was needed if the land was to be sold and they initially doubted if the Wells company had the right compulsorily to demand its purchase. When proved wrong on this latter point they continued to make every kind of difficulty, appointing representatives and then valuers to inspect the site and argue on every detail. A number of buildings had been erected on parts of the land in question and it appears that it had considerably greater value under the rules for compulsory purchase if it had been or could be used for operational purposes than if it could be classed as surplus land available for disposal.

The Norfolk had spent some £13,000 on the half mile of cutting, the station and the other buildings and initially the Eastern Counties insisted that no less should be recovered from the Wells company before the line could open. But here they were let down by their own chief engineer. He reported that most of the land to the north of the station was certainly surplus, the cutting and two bridges over it having been made solely to obtain material for use on embankments further south, and suggested a figure of £1,272 for its value on that basis, a reduction of over £5,000 compared to its value for operational purposes. The use of the station and remaining land might be settled by a temporary rental agreement. Even so the Eastern Counties insisted that the full £1,272 of the capital money must be paid before an operating agreement could be agreed finally and the Wells company, by now making its final calls on shares, was unable to find the money until late October.

Meanwhile the Norfolk had withdrawn their Bill put before Parliament in the spring of 1857 in the face of further opposition and remained without authority for their investment. Counsel advised that the shares, which were in the names of three directors individually, be put into their names collectively and that a deed of trust in favour of the company should be drawn up to which all three should subscribe confirming the shares as the property of the Norfolk Railway. The loss of the Bill was reported to shareholders at their half-year meeting in August at which time they were told also that the line was complete except for the junction at Fakenham, which awaited formal transfer of the land. It appears that the investment was never regularised before the Wells company was taken over by the Great Eastern in 1862. One Norfolk shareholder wrote both to the Norfolk and to the Eastern Counties protesting at any borrowing to finance the investment but his objections were simply ignored.

CHAPTER 11

Peto on shore,
at sea and abroad

PETO WAS HEAVILY INVOLVED with three further enterprises in the 1850s which had or came to have connections with each other and indirect connections with the Norfolk Railway.

The Victoria Dock Company

This private venture, promoted especially by G. P. Bidder on land that he had acquired near the river terminus of the short railway from Stratford to North Woolwich, built what was for its day the largest enclosed dock in the world. While the Norfolk Railway had no interest, direct or indirect, in this enterprise, it is necessary to explain something of its ownership and direction since several of those connected with the Norfolk or with the later marine enterprises were also involved. After obtaining its Act in 1850 Bidder also acted as engineer while Peto, Brassey & Betts were appointed as contractors. Peto, Betts and Richard Till and of course Bidder were on the initial board which was later augmented by others connected with dock and railway investment. Early investors included members of the Kennard family and R. W. Kennard, formerly a Norfolk director, was at one stage part owner, with Peto, Bidder, Till and others, of the closely associated Victoria Land Company. When the dock was completed it was leased to the partnership of Peto, Brassey & Best which was responsible for operations until it was finally purchased in 1864 by an amalgamation of the London and St Katherine Dock Companies.

The Royal Danish Railway

To explain fully the background to the building of the first Danish railways it is necessary to understand something of the political history of the period that was dominated for Denmark by the famous 'Schleswig-Holstein question', a matter of extraordinary complexity, only the barest outline of which need be given here. From the end of the Napoleonic Wars, in which Denmark had been on the losing side and as a result lost its control of Norway, the kingdom, ignoring its remote overseas possessions, consisted of the northern part of the Jutland peninsula south to the town of Kolding, the important islands of Fyn and Sjæland, on the latter of which stood Copenhagen, and numerous lesser islands. Except for Copenhagen the kingdom was largely agricultural and that was especially true of Jutland where large landowners raised mainly cattle and sheep and grew corn. Until 1848 the state was an absolute monarchy.

For centuries past the king of Denmark had been and at that time still was duke of the duchies of Schleswig (Danish Slesvig) and Holstein. Since 1815 Holstein had been part of the loose German Confederation, prosperous, and entirely German speaking. Schleswig, the southern part of the Jutland peninsula, was also relatively prosperous compared at least with the north, and was divided linguistically between Danish speakers, chiefly in the north, and German speakers, chiefly in the south. Altona in Holstein, close to the important free city of Hamburg, was the chief Danish port on the North Sea coast, though many miles from the open sea, far up the river Elbe. The North Sea coast itself, beset by extensive sandbanks, lacked good harbours but Tønning, at the mouth of the Eider river, and Ballum were viable while, in good weather only, ships could enter the Limfjord in the north via the narrow channel at Thyboron. The present port of Esbjerg was then no more than a fishing hamlet that shared its sheltered but sandy inlet with Hjerting, itself little more than a landing place without facilities. The sea passage around the Skaw at the north of the peninsula was long and notoriously dangerous. On the Baltic side harbours were frequent and good. Of those on the mainland Kiel in Holstein and Flensburg in Schleswig were the most developed.

The political problem was multifold. Denmark proper had no constitution but in the revolutionary atmosphere of the 1840s there was strong pressure on the king to assent to a democratic regime and parliamentary control. Holstein, fundamentally German in character, wished to remain so and, though loyal to its duke, under no circumstances wished to be

Tønning on the Eider

ruled by a constitution created to satisfy Danish interests. Schleswig was understandably divided but traditionally and (it was hotly disputed) constitutionally, could not be divided from Holstein. The king, Frederick VII, was childless, the last of the house of Oldenburg, and the successions, both to the Danish throne and to the duchies, were uncertain. When in 1848 the king yielded to pressure for a democratic constitution, and a constituent assembly gathered to draw one up, his action led to a revolt in the south, instigated by men who wanted a separate constitution for the duchies and the union of Schleswig and Holstein within the German Confederation. Their seizure of the fortress at Rendsburg, a town by the Eider river on the border between Holstein and Schleswig, sparked off a three year civil war in which for a while the rebels from the duchies were assisted by troops from a number of German states, principally Prussia.

The fiercely fought war may be said to have ended in a draw at the end of which the kingdom had obtained a new parliamentary constitution that did not extend to the duchies: these once again acknowledged the king as their duke but maintained their separate administrations. In the course of the peace negotiations an international conference of major interested counties, including Britain and Russia, had resulted in the choice of Prince Christian of Glucksborg as the successor to King Frederick both as king and as duke and had imposed an obligation on Denmark to draw up a new constitution that would apply equally to the whole country including the duchies, not differentiating between them. Over a period of twelve years successive attempts were made to do this, all ending in failure to please anybody. One reason for this lack of success was that the dominant party in the kingdom, resigned to the loss of Holstein, made considerable efforts to separate Schleswig from Holstein and bind it into Denmark proper. One means was seen as the building of railways.

As early as 1835 a commission had been set up to study the feasibility of railways in the duchies, from which resulted indirectly two privately financed lines in Holstein, that from Altona to Kiel and another from Neumunster, on the former line, north to Rendsburg, both open in 1844. By that time the commission was recommending railways throughout Denmark while town committees were being set up in Jutland to promote lines convenient to the locality. An important problem was the lack of much free capital but the major question was political. Was it desirable for a railway to be built throughout the length of Jutland and Schleswig or would it not be preferable to build a line or lines across the peninsula from east to west? The former would connect the agricultural districts via Rendsburg to Hamburg, already the major port for Danish cattle export, and was popular especially with the major landowners. But such a line, pointed out the Danish patriots and also the representatives of some of the towns, would further place the duchies and indeed the whole country into economic subservience to Germany. Thus, said one pamphlet, would the German bee suck the honey from the Jutland flowers. The alternative of east/west lines would enable exports to move more directly to England and also serve better to bind the peninsula districts to Copenhagen and the islands

On Sjælland a privately financed line over the mere twenty miles from Copenhagen to Roskilde, built by the English firm Fox, Henderson, was opened in 1847, but its further extension to Korsør on the western shore of the island was not complete for a further nine years. In 1846 a plan was put forward by the county of Viborg in central Jutland for a line south to Holstein to connect to another proposed by a major shareholder in the line north from Neumunster to Rendsburg; these would meet at the southern Schleswig border. This resulted in surveys and estimates in 1847 but also violent opposition from Danish nationalists. The proposals were for private finance but state guarantees, a method of finance impracticable at that time. In any event the whole matter was shelved with the outbreak of war in the following year.

Even before the war was quite over pamphlets on the subject were again appearing. Especially influential was one in 1850 by Frederik Klee and C. M. Paulsen advocating completion of the line across Sjæland, an east/west line over the island of Fyn and no less than three cross lines in Jutland and Schleswig, Flensburg to Husum, Fredericia to Hjerting and Århus to Hjærbæk. This pamphlet was translated into English in the hope of interesting English entrepreneurs and it was through Regnar Westenholz, Danish consul in London, that it first came to the notice of Peto. The war ended in early 1851 and almost immediately Peto with Robert Stephenson visited Denmark where he made contact with a number of Danish businessmen and with the government itself with a view to constructing a railway network.

Peto's ideas for Danish railways were ambitious including a line from south to north of Jutland, but at first he applied simply for a line from Tønning, via Husum to Flensburg. A report from *The Times* correspondent in Hamburg in May 1852 said that the Danish government was to agree to this since Peto (the report referred rather to The Lowestoft Steam Navigation Company) required no governmental assistance with finance. The concession would run for 100 years and the contractors would be exempt from any duty on materials imported for the purposes of construction. The company was looking to run steamships from Flensburg to Copenhagen, Stockholm and St Petersburgh while the line would improve postal communication between England and Germany.

In late August 1852 the concession was officially published, confirmed at 100 years (in fact in perpetuity with a guarantee against competition for 100 years) providing the line was built within three years. As Peto was to obtain all the finance he had been able to insist on a branch south from Flensburg via Schleswig to Rendsburg for connection there to the line from Neumunster on the Kiel/Altona route despite the Danish reluctance to enhance communications with Germany. The line was to be called

in Denmark the King Frederik VII's South Slesvig Railway, a name flattering to the king and politically significant since in fact Frederik was duke only in the area. It was to be a British company, officially named the Royal Danish Railway, with shares quoted on the London stock exchange. Construction began as soon as the concession was granted with the intention of opening by June 1854. Share capital was to be £540,000 in 27,000 shares of £20 each.

In fact it was not operational until early November 1854 when an article in the *Illustrated London News* described the ceremonial opening. The ubiquitous George Bidder was named as engineer, Robert Stephenson as his 'collaborator' and Peto, of course, as contractor. (In fact Peto was in partnership in this venture with Brassey and Betts as was to be the case in all his later Danish ventures.) Peto's party for the opening travelled to Tønning on the brand new ship *Cygnus* (property of the North of Europe Steam Navigation Company). There was a royal reception at Flensburg following which Peto entertained King Frederik aboard the *Cygnus* at Tønning. The numerous English guests included the stockbroker (and auditor) Joseph Lawrence, no doubt in recognition of his part in the raising of finance.

According to the *Illustrated London News* the total line with branches covered seventy-two miles. It was stated that the contractors had leased the line, which cost £540,000 including rolling stock and stations, for fourteen years at six per cent plus half profits. These figures were roughly confirmed by the report at the company's first annual meeting in the summer of 1855 by which time the capital spend was recorded as some

£557,000 (including capitalised interest, engineering and administration expenses totalling £42,000) with a further £25,900 held in cash and securities that would be payable to the contractors on completion. The main work outstanding related to the bridge over the Eider to connect to the line south from Rendsburg. The lease to the contractors had at last been completed; it was noted that whereas the lease at six per cent was for fourteen years the share of profits was to run only for ten at which point the lease could be terminated at the directors' option. Moreover there was a guarantee fund for the due fulfilment of the lease, a sum of £100,000 deposited by the contractors with trustees who had invested it in British and Canadian government stocks. In addition the contractors had deposited £25,000 with the Danish government.

A year later it was recorded that the bridge at Rendsburg was complete but that the net revenues for the first full year fell short of the rental that the contractors had paid to the company. The contractors as lessees had also to reimburse the company for its management expenses that to date had reached the rather surprising figure of £4,000, which included the running costs of a City office in King William Street. There were by then six British directors and five Danes including Westenholz and Dr Paulsen. Later that year a special meeting in Flensburg under the chairmanship of Westenholz resolved to raise a further £75,000 capital by means of debentures to pay for wharves, piers and other works at Flensburg and Tønning. By 1863 the accumulated capital spend was recorded as £656,000 which included all management expenses since formation.

Peto entertains the King of Denmark

It would seem that the Schleswig railway was a particularly blatant example of a contractor's line. Seventy-two miles for £600,000 is a cost of about £8,000 per mile, reasonable, even cheap at that time given that it included rails, stations, locomotives and rolling stock. (The Norfolk, excluding Lowestoft harbour, when finally complete, had come to over £20,000.) There can at the very best have been but £50,000 profit for the contractors. But then those same contractors had leased the line themselves at six per cent, an annual rental of some £36,000 payable for fourteen years, a total of £504,000. Even if the railway earned as much as five per cent return on capital after operating and maintenance costs, and not too many did, they would be out of pocket by £6,000 a year. Of course the rental would go into the company that had paid them to build the line but the company would need all of that to service its capital. Even if the contractors themselves owned all the shares they would presumably need the dividends to pay the interest on whatever loans they had raised to subscribe for them. Their best plan would have been to unload their shares in the company and still better their lease to someone else and that as soon as possible. Peto did not have it all his own way. The Danish administration would have far preferred a state owned line but could not insist since it had not the money to build one. But it did obtain an option to buy the line at the end of the fourteen year lease and inserted certain clauses in the law authorising the railway to ensure that adequate sums were transferred to reserve by the company so that the assets were not depleted.

The first train arrives at Flensburg

The North of Europe Steam Navigation Company

Lowestoft harbour was largely complete by 1851, by then under the management of the Eastern Counties Railway as with the rest of the Norfolk system. Although the accumulated capital cost had been somewhat reduced by the sale of certain plant, stores and equipment to the Eastern Counties, the fears of the Lowestoft shareholders in 1848 had been realised for expenditure on the harbour regularly exceeded its income. The Eastern Counties 1855 shareholders' investigatory committee said of it in one paragraph of its long report:

> We cannot understand why this harbour has been taken by the Eastern Counties. It can result only in taking trade from Yarmouth, and involving this company in vast expenses and loss: no favouritism, no preference shown to it, can ever make it of any value to you; its costs exceed its earnings ... it is and must remain a ruinous adjunct to the Eastern Counties; unless indeed the sea should wash up the sand to the destruction of the harbour – which your committee was informed on their visit of inspection to that place was most probable – thus relieving this company from any further loss.

It was true that harbour dues then and later were less than the costs of keeping the harbour open and in good repair but nevertheless this is the one paragraph in their long report that seems overly harsh. The object of a railway port was always the amount of traffic it could generate for the railway, not any bare profit that might be made from the harbour works themselves. Lowestoft was a better harbour than Yarmouth and one of the main reasons for its construction was to accommodate a fishing fleet with a base and the promise of fast transport inland. However even before the works were entirely complete the restless ambition of Peto was searching for further uses.

From early in the history of the Norfolk we have seen how ambitions grew to extend eastwards to the Continent. In 1846 there had been the experimental trip from Yarmouth to Rotterdam. The following year there had been the advertisement for the Great Yarmouth and Lowestoft Steam Packet Co with enquiries to be directed to the Superintendent of the Norfolk Railway. While there is no direct evidence pointing to a railway financial interest the mention of Lowestoft suggests that Peto himself was involved. In 1852 the company sold a shed on a wharf at Yarmouth and gave half the proceeds to William Johnson (earlier and briefly a director of the Yarmouth & Norwich) and his partners as some compensation for a loss they had apparently made in setting up a ferry service to Hamburg and Rotterdam. The first experimental voyage had been to Holland but although Lowestoft was not badly placed for communications with the Netherlands, Harwich in Eastern Union territory was in an even better position. Peto was engaged in building a railway in Norway from 1850

but the crossings thence from Hull or Grimsby were shorter than from Lowestoft. However the latter town was well placed for connections with Denmark and north Germany. By 1851 Peto with some other Norfolk shareholders had set up a firm known as The Northern Steam Packet Company under the management of Captain Andrews who had been Lowestoft harbourmaster since 1847. This firm initially acquired three steamships, *Prince*, *Enterprise* and *Lowestoft*.

How the ships were at first employed is unknown but at a meeting of the Norfolk Railway in late March 1851 Peto announced that one of them (*Prince*) was shortly to sail to Denmark where, as we have seen, the civil war had recently finished. The plan was to collect lean cattle and sheep in spring for fattening in England. It was hoped also to take on responsibility for carrying mail to Denmark which previously had gone via Hamburg. The first trip was adjudged a success and a weekly service was started in April to call at the tiny western Danish ports of Hjerting and Ballum and the rather larger Tønning. Whereas at the smaller ports cattle were brought aboard in slings, at Tønning they could be walked onto the ship from the quay. On arrival cattle could walk off at the Lowestoft quays where cattle yards were built alongside a spur of the railway. In later years the Danes preferred to fatten the animals themselves and regular voyages did not begin until after midsummer but continued until November. Either way there was to be traffic for the railway from Lowestoft (at preferential rates) and later for the Schleswig railway too.

The firm's original ships were not ideal vessels for animal transport and were soon replaced by others more suitable to obviate losses through overcrowding and injuries. The first of a series of these generally more substantial ships was the *Cumberland* (650 tons) which made her first voyage to Denmark in early May 1851 and over twenty similar runs that year. Meanwhile another vessel specially adapted for the cattle trade was under construction, the *City of Norwich* (700 tons) equipped with 250 stalls on her lower decks with tanks for drinking water while up to 500 sheep could be carried on an upper deck. Launched in June at Glasgow, on her first voyage from Lowestoft in August she crossed to Gluckstadt in Holstein in 24 hours carrying Peto and Robert Stephenson on their journey to negotiate the contract for the Schleswig railway. Thereafter she joined *Cumberland* on the run to and from Tønning. Another, older and somewhat smaller ship, *Royal Victoria* (492 tons) had been acquired in August to handle chiefly the Hjerting and Ballum voyages. All these ships were paddle steamers.

Details of actual voyages made have been obtained from a study of Lloyd's List which recorded all reported arrivals of vessels from abroad, more particularly British vessels, at ports around the world. From there it can be seen that the livestock traffic to Lowestoft ceased during the winter months as did much trade with northern Europe. Not only was the major part of the Baltic regularly iced but ice could also seriously affect or totally close the Elbe to Hamburg and sometimes even the Eider at Tønning. The firm's ships were either laid up or employed elsewhere; no trace of their movements during the winter of 1851/52 has been found. The first sailing of the 1852 season from Lowestoft to Denmark was at the end of March. That year the shipping firm offered free passage to Denmark for farmers and graziers wanting to buy Danish beasts. It was reported that Danish landowners were anxious to sell as poor winter feeding had left them with excess stock. For much of the remainder of 1852 the three vessels from 1851, joined in October by the *Jupiter* (500 tons), plied chiefly from Lowestoft to Denmark although in December the *City of Norwich* made at least one voyage to Oporto. Another, apparently Danish owned, was regularly bringing cattle from Danish ports to Lowestoft but otherwise only a few foreign sailing ships called there,

Unloading cattle
at Lowestoft

coming from the Baltic and probably bringing either timber or grain. However in bad weather Lowestoft was becoming increasingly used as a harbour of refuge and although this brought in little direct revenue there could be substantial work for the port in repairing damaged ships.

Lowestoft was not the only harbour along the east coast being developed in conjunction with a railway in the early 1850s. The long delayed Eastern Union branch from Manningtree to Harwich was not completed until 1854 but even before its arrival the Harwich corporation had constructed a new pier close to the proposed terminus of the line. Meanwhile a much more ambitious project at Grimsby had reached conclusion in May 1852 with the opening of the new Royal Dock. Here the Grimsby Docks Company, part of the rapidly expanding Manchester, Sheffield and Lincolnshire Railway group, had since 1848 been building a large dock entirely separate from a much smaller dock of 1801. The by now famous James Rendel, who had acted for the Admiralty in connection with the Reedham bridge, was engineer in chief. Unlike Lowestoft, where the engineers were able to build on and expand the earlier works, the Grimsby enterprise was thrust directly to seaward from the foreshore by the construction of a giant coffer dam to enclose the entire area within which the harbour walls and quays were built. With the entrance controlled by an enormous sea lock whose gates were operated by a hydraulic system requiring a 300 foot tower (still a seamark in 2006 though no longer in use) it is hardly surprising that the eventual cost of the development was over five times that at Lowestoft, a huge investment by a railway at a period when finance was hardly plentiful.

Peto had become a director of the Manchester, Sheffield & Lincolnshire Railway in 1850 and so it is not surprising that the board turned to him when the company was planning a passenger and cargo steamship service to Hamburg. George Dow, historian of the Great Central Railway which was the eventual title of the Manchester, Sheffield & Lincolnshire, records that the company guaranteed the steamship line a five per cent return on capital to set up the service. Certainly from a few days after the dock was open and through the month of June 1852 a twice weekly service from Grimsby to Hamburg was being operated by the Lowestoft ships *City of Norwich* and *Cumberland*. In July the *Cumberland* and in August the *City of Norwich* reverted to the Lowestoft/Tønning run being replaced by two three-year-old steamers, *Hamburg*, 600 tons and *Leipsic*, 550 tons, which until then had been operating between Hull and Hamburg for another company. Thereafter the frequency of the service dropped to once a week. From mid-July another steamer, the *Swanland*, began a weekly service from Grimsby to Rotterdam but this was originally a Hull steamer, not forming part of the Lowestoft fleet or seemingly owned by Peto interests.

The summer of 1852 saw a major development with the flotation of a new public company, the North of Europe Steam Navigation Company, with an authorised capital of £500,000, whose prospectus explained that it was to provide steam services between Harwich, Lowestoft and Grimsby in England and Continental ports from Christiana (Oslo) to Rotterdam, including both Tønning and Hamburg. The company's ships were to sail from Grimsby, Lowestoft and Harwich. Arrangements had been agreed with the various railroads serving those ports for connecting transport in England and the company would take over ships already in service. The vital underpinning of the enterprise was to be a system whereby shippers could, by a single through booking including all rail and shipping charges, arrange for their goods to travel from their origin to their final destination overseas.

Peto, named as deputy chairman in the prospectus, was undoubtedly the moving spirit behind the enterprise but the composition of the rest of the board is of significance. The chairman was the Earl of Yarborough, a major landowner in north Lincolnshire and chairman of the Manchester, Sheffield & Lincolnshire Railway. Another director was a Mr Geach,

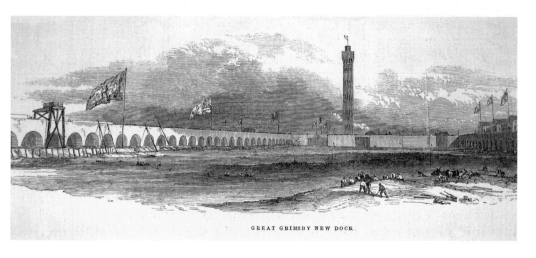

GREAT GRIMSBY NEW DOCK

also on that board. Then there were David Waddington and Lord Alfred Paget of the Eastern Counties. The former, who had been MP for Maldon for the previous five years had recently become one of the two MPs for Harwich. The Eastern Union was represented by J.C.Cobbold, now MP for Ipswich, while a further nominee was Robert John Bagshaw of Harwich itself, director of the Victoria Dock Company and son of John Bagshaw the other Harwich MP. There were also two directors of the Midland Railway, one from the Birmingham Junction who was also a director of the East & West India Dock Company, and two bankers. The board was completed by Richard Till of the Norfolk Railway and Victoria Dock Company, Captain Andrews (General Manager) and Regnar Westenholz, who had been so helpful in obtaining the Danish railway contract for Peto. With the sole exception of Andrews none of the directors could boast of any considerable experience in shipping.

The first meeting of the company was held in December 1852 where it was said, not entirely accurately, that all the shares had been applied for within a few days of the issue of the prospectus. No information is available at this time as to the identity of the principal shareholders but it can be assumed that the directors and particularly Peto and Yarborough were substantially involved. There is no suggestion that any of the railway companies themselves held shares. A first call of £2 10s 0d, had been made on the £20 shares in October and had been applied in part in buying and paying for the *Hamburg* and the *Leipsic*, at a cost of £31,500, which had presumably previously been on charter. A second call of similar amount was to be made, payable in February, and taken together with the surplus from the first, would be used to pay £55,979 for the four steamers previously owned by the Northern Steam Packet Company together with premises and other facilities at Lowestoft including a factory for the manufacture of machinery and ships equipment.

Prospects were said to be most encouraging. Trade to Hamburg was prospering and two more ships would soon be needed to trade from Grimsby. With the railway planned to cross Schleswig to Flensburg and another to extend from Copenhagen to the west of Sjælland, London to Copenhagen via Lowestoft and Flensburg could be reduced to 44 hours combining rail and the company's steamers. There were plans for direct sailings to both Christiana in Norway and Gothenburg in Sweden for which purpose two new screw steamers would be needed. A mail contract for five years with the Swedish government had been taken on although at very modest remuneration. There were great hopes for a service Harwich to Rotterdam and perhaps to Ostend, Antwerp and Dunkirk once the Harwich branch of the Eastern Union should be completed. It ought not to be necessary to raise more than half the nominal capital to achieve all this despite the need for further ships. The first annual meeting held in the following February, when mention was made of two 800 ton steamers under construction, merely confirmed all this.

Lowestoft regatta

Only one further ship was acquired by the new company in 1853, the *Tonning* of 988 tons built by the same Glasgow yard as the *City of Norwich*, which arrived at Lowestoft from her builders in September. Scrutiny of Lloyds List for the year shows that while the two Grimsby based ships continued a regular Grimsby/Hamburg trade, each averaging only about one voyage a month, the ships based at Lowestoft varied their destinations outside the cattle trading season with several voyages to the Netherlands, particularly to Harlingen in Friesland. Gothenburg in Sweden was another port of call. A Grimsby/Rotterdam service continued operated by ships which were probably chartered to the railway itself. Peto, whose yachting dated from at least as early as 1851, was now clearly in marine mode. At the 1853 Lowestoft regatta the *Ipswich Journal* called attention to his schooners, noted for their size and symmetry. One of these was the *Mayfly*, later acquired by Bidder. Nine years later Peto was the owner of a steam yacht capable of voyaging to the Baltic where it was said to have outclassed that owned by the king of Denmark.

At the next annual meeting in February 1854 excellent progress was reported. Capital raised from calls totalling ten pounds per share amounted to £202,625 of which only £112,479 had been effectively employed during 1853 but even so a profit of £7,493 had been achieved and a dividend for the year of four per cent was declared. As a measure of progress the revenue for the first half of the 1853 had been £19,787 but for the second half £52,701, (figures the less encouraging when it is realised that little trade at all was carried on by this company from January to March). All the railway companies were co-operating in the system of through bookings including the Great Northern in connection with the Grimsby/Hamburg route. The expense of insurance was great and now that the fleet was expanding a proportion of the risks would be self-insured. Traffic should be considerably increased when both the Harwich line and the Danish railway were completed. However in view of these prospects further ships would be needed and after all further calls on the shares would be required. Dow says that the Grimsby/Hamburg service was doubled from early 1854 after pressure on the shipping company by the Grimsby railway but there is little evidence from Lloyds List to back up this assertion which may be more representative of promises made than performance.

Ships were in fact being acquired at a somewhat startling rate throughout 1854. The main reason was the beginning of a new service first advertised in April, a regular service to Gothenburg from both Hull (at this time a far busier port than Grimsby and having superior rail connections) and London. There were four new ships acquired for the purpose, the *Gothenburg*, the *Oscar*, the *Scandinavia* and the *Courier*, all screw propelled rather than by paddles, and at least two of them newly built for the company at Scott Russell's famous yard on the Thames. One pair worked weekly to and from Gothenburg direct; the other stopped en route at Christiansand and Christiana (Oslo) in Norway. Lloyds List recorded shipping casualties; one spotted was an occasion when the *Gothenburg* ran down an anchored Swedish ship in Gothenburg itself and sank her. Other new ships were the *Prince of Wales*, the *Levant* and the screw ship *Candidate*. The latter two, along with the *City of Norwich* and the *Jupiter*, were advertised to run a weekly packet service London/Hamburg but it is doubtful how long this was kept up.

In the autumn of 1854 two new paddlewheelers *Aquila* and *Cygnus* were acquired to inaugurate a weekly service Harwich/Antwerp. As her first task however *Aquila* was used to convey Peto and a large party to and from Christiana at the opening of the new railway there. She then made her first run to Antwerp, leaving Harwich on 16 September. *Cygnus* arrived at Lowestoft from her builders on the Clyde on 2 October, her first (and only) service in 1854 being to take Peto and party to the ceremonial opening of the Schleswig railway. Earlier in the year the patrons of the Lowestoft regatta had been expanded to include not only Peto, Waddington and Paget but now also the Earl of Yarborough, Robert Stephenson, J.C.Cobbold, Francis Mills and Edward Ladd Betts.

In March 1854, with war with Russia in prospect, three company ships had taken sightseers to see a squadron of the fleet gathering for the Baltic sail past Lowestoft. The Russian war broke out only a few days later but even before that the *Tonning* had been chartered to move troops to Malta. That summer the deployment of the fleet in the Baltic and the transport of an army to the Black Sea created a major boom in shipping, especially as a steam powered navy operating abroad required innumerable ships to bring it coal and other supplies. A press report in August 1854 referred to just two company ships in government service, the *Tonning* in the Black Sea and the *City of Norwich* in the Baltic. However, while the service of the latter must have been brief as she is to be observed on many commercial voyages that summer, not only the *Tonning* but the *Prince of Wales* and the *Cumberland* are absent from Lloyds List for the whole of 1854 and in January 1855 are recorded at Constantinople, in there from Balaklava. Government charter may be an explanation too of the disappearance from British and northern ports for lengthy periods of several of the ships acquired in 1854. One of these, the *Powerful*, was still on government charter in 1856 while the *Prince of Wales* and the *Levant* are particularly mentioned in a press report concerning the transport of labourers and materials to the Crimea to build a railway from Balaklava harbour to the lines of seige.

Apart from the new services already referred to and the ships chartered to the government, the basic work of the company's ships in 1854 continued to be voyages to Denmark for livestock and to Hamburg for general trade. Judging by the number of voyages the Danish trade was at a low ebb that year whether because of a shortage of animals or a shortage of vessels available to carry them. Some ships normally employed to Tønning ran at times instead to Hamburg and Grimsby or Hull were sometimes used in lieu of Lowestoft. By the time of a half year meeting in August 1854 a fifth call of £2 10s 0d had been made on the company's shares, presumably to pay for the new ships, but a further call, previously forecast for February 1855, was not, it was said, to be made for the present. Revenue for the first half of 1854 amounted to £47,955 compared with £19,787 for the first half of the previous year. The company accounted annually to December and thus no accounts were presented but Peto, in the chair, said he hoped to explore some means whereby interim dividends could be declared in future. The report for the full year 1854 presented in February 1855 showed that revenue for the second half year had been £75,465 (1853 £52,701). A dividend of eight per cent was declared for the year.

SS Prince of Wales leaving for the Crimea

Something was going wrong with the relationship between the shipping company and the northern railway which applied unsuccessfully to Parliament in the 1855 session for powers to operate its own ships. Presumably this arose because the shipping company had not provided the increased Hamburg service desired and indeed in the latter part of 1855 even fewer journeys to Hamburg were being made. Nor can the decision to run the Scandinavian services from Hull have been palatable to the Grimsby management. It may be significant that Peto left the board of the railway company late in 1854 or early 1855. In the summer of the latter year that company promoted the Anglo-French Steamship Company in conjunction with the South Yorkshire Railway and French interests with the object of exporting Yorkshire coal to France using the Grimsby port. Yarborough was on the board of the new company which began operations in July 1856 using three steamers of its own.

For the first half of 1855 revenue of the North of Europe reported to the half year meeting was £103,449 compared with £47.955 for the equivalent period in 1854. The fleet had swollen to twenty vessels of which six were in government service. Calls on shares had by then risen to £15 but no more were planned. The chairman, the Earl of Yarborough, wished to retire, ostensibly due to ill health, but the shareholders begged him to stay. Perhaps the growing rift between the companies was the true reason but it is the case that during 1855 he was struck down with paralysis and never recovered his health before his death in 1862 although he remained chairman of his railway company.

With so many vessels, the names of some of which are not known and with those on government service rarely reported in Lloyds List, it is difficult to say exactly what they were all doing during 1855. The six ships on full time war service did not include the *City of Norwich*, although she took horses to Balaklava in March, for she was also employed on frequent commercial voyages. That year she abandoned Lowestoft as a base and was mainly employed in bringing Danish cattle direct to London where they were rested for a few days on the Rainham marshes before their final journey to Smithfield. The Antwerp service, started in late 1854 using *Cygnus* and *Aquila*, had incurred heavy losses. An attempt by the Eastern Counties to restart the route in May 1855 had quickly

The Earl of Yarborough

been abandoned due to further losses. One of the accusations of financial impropriety later made against Waddington related to this episode. It was suggested that while the railway had incurred a substantial loss on operations, the shipping company in which Waddington held shares had profited by supplying the two ships on charter.

Three ships were regularly operating a Hamburg/London service but also some cattle voyages. Four more, including a new ship *Propellor* were working the Gothenburg run. The *Leipsic* and the *Hamburg*, continued trading Grimsby/Hamburg but from mid-summer can also be observed using Hull as their terminus. Other North of Europe ships filled in gaps in the Grimsby/Hamburg schedule. At best only seventeen ships out of the claimed twenty can be identified. The company's report for 1855 presented in the spring of 1856 was referred to in *The Times* as having demonstrated a continuance of a remarkable degree of success. Dividends totalled an exceptional ten per cent. While government service had been remunerative the directors hoped for even better results now that the war had ended.

It is even harder than for 1855, given the apparent number of ships now owned, to work out from Lloyds List what they were doing in 1856. The Harwich /Antwerp service certainly did not operate that year although the Swedish service did. The *Aquila* and the *Cygnus* had been chartered to Peto's Tilbury Railway and were operating day trips to Margate. The Danish cattle trades were much as in 1855, partly to Lowestoft, partly to London, but the Grimsby/Hamburg trade had ceased from mid year with Hull being used ever more frequently by North of Europe ships from Scandinavia, from Germany and even from Denmark. With the Baltic at peace many British ships can be seen trading to Cronstadt, the port for St Petersburgh, but none bear names recognisable as the company's ships. A few steamers with British names trading east from Flensburg may have belonged to the company.

The half year meeting held in August 1856 brought a note of caution. True an interim dividend of four per cent was declared while it was said that the reopening of the Baltic following the war had brought a revival of trade there but the outlay to secure new traffic had been heavy and no further dividend increase was to be expected. Because five vessels were still on charter to the government another five were needed to secure trade. Captain Andrews waxed enthusiastic over the prospects of the company's vessels by-passing Cronstadt and working right up to St Petersburgh itself, something he maintained that other companies' ships were too deep to achieve. He acknowledged that the Grimsby/Hamburg service had been withdrawn after proving unprofitable. Finally, since the company was to be converted to a limited company, it was desirable to call up the remaining five pounds per share to purchase additional vessels.

After the report of the meeting in August 1856 there was no further relevant press item until in February 1857 the following portentous article appeared in *The Times*. Presumably based on an informed leak and after reciting a number of recent financial scandals it read in full:

An impression seems to be entertained that the North of Europe Steam Navigation Company is about to be added to the list of public undertakings the management of which has lately damaged the administrative reputation of our commercial men. For several years the directors have declared dividends ranging from eight to ten per cent, and at each meeting the most unqualified descriptions have been given of the extreme prosperity of the concern. There has been a total exemption from casualties and although the company benefited considerably from the employment of some of its vessels as transports during the war it was announced as recently as August last that its prospects had, if possible, become brighter than ever since the opening of the Baltic trade consequent upon the return of peace. The only drawback to these periodic representations has consisted in the making of fresh calls [on shares], but these were represented as simply necessary to provide vessels enough to prevent the great profits that were available from being seized by others. Nevertheless it was always found that the shares could not be retrieved from a discount, and that whenever the highly satisfactory statements at the various public meetings led to any recovery there were constant sellers to take advantage of it. It has now been announced that owing to the indisposition of the manager and the decease of the accountant the general meeting which should have been held this month must be postponed to the 25th of March and simultaneously there has been a further severe fall in the shares which has brought them to a discount of between 30 and 40%. The mere fact of the affairs of a public company being allowed to fall into a position in which the illness or death of any two of its officers can render an immediate statement of its affairs impracticable is in itself discreditable but the shareholders will probably be disposed to overlook that point if they can be satisfied that the representations hitherto made to them have been strictly correct. In that case it will be evident that those who are now parting with their shares are doing so in an idle panic. If, on the contrary, it should appear that the position of the company is not unquestionable, a serious account will have to be extracted from all concerned. The great respectability of the directors seems to preclude the possibility of there being anything seriously wrong and there will be every disposition to entertain that reliance even in the face of the unexplained symptoms now observable in the market for the shares.

It appears that after the article quoted above several shareholders had gone to see the directors and had been assured that all was well. However by the time of the delayed half year meeting held on 26 March it was clear that this was far from the case. Peto chaired the meeting and provided a statement of unremitting gloom. Soon after the previous meeting Captain Andrews had fallen sick during a visit to the Baltic and since then the disease from which he suffered 'had overthrown his intellect' so that he was no longer responsible for his acts. Because of this, and because of the death of the accountant, the staff working together with Mr Coleman, a professional accountant and auditor, were unable to get any accounts prepared until Tuesday of the week of the meeting and even then these were incomplete. However Mr Coleman was of the opinion that the loss for the preceding year was not less than £50,000 (and refused to assure the shareholders that it could not be more). Work was still proceeding. Peto offered no excuses, saying he had been as much deceived as any shareholder and had actually increased his shareholding from £20,000 to £60,000 on the strength of earlier optimistic reports. He revealed that there were fourteen vessels employed (of which eleven were chartered out), three under repair and ten unemployed. Coleman, questioned on how a half year dividend of 4% had come to be paid, said that he and the directors had been shown an statement of estimated earnings from transport service of £14,000 and from other sources of £10,000 and so all thought that a dividend absorbing £13,000 to £14,000 could safely be declared. Coleman was prepared to stake his reputation on the correctness of the 1855 accounts. The meeting was adjourned to allow a committee of shareholders to work with him and produce a full report.

The committee reported in June. They found that what was referred to as the 'money loss' was £60,199 but that, after charging depreciation of ships at an annual rate of five per cent, writing off formation expenses and the cost of goodwill purchased and making an allowance for bad debts and disputed claims, the total loss was £136,043. They noted that Coleman had expressed concern about accounting deficiencies as early as the previous October and that Andrew's remuneration was fixed in relation to dividends paid. There were now eighteen ships employed of which eight were chartered out and there were a further nine unemployed. The committee considered that with proper economy the company could be kept going and had found nothing to impugn the honesty or motives of the directors. *The Times*'s comment on the report was scathing as to the directors' lack of attention even though they were themselves major shareholders. 'Their position on the board was an honourable and profitable one and they accepted its advantages without giving anything in return.'

It subsequently transpired that the committee were far from unanimous in their opinions. The membership had been Charles Morrison, deputy chairman of the Victoria Dock Company, Mr Young, a shipowner, Mr Yates, the secretary of the Great Eastern Steamship Company, Mr Lawrence, the stockbroker who was also auditor of the Norfolk Railway, a Mr Godson and Mr Abel, a solicitor who acted originally as the committee chairman. At an extraordinary meeting held on 18 June to consider the report Mr Morrison stated that the government transport work would have been profitable enough had proper economy been exercised but the other branches were scarcely profitable at all. Despite that he thought that the company should continue to trade on its reduced capital: it would be difficult at the present time to sell the fleet. The size of the board should be reduced. He reported Andrews as still ill and the committee had been unable to question him. But Mr Godson rendered a long and tedious dissenting statement and raised endless questions. His chief complaints were that the committee had not even attempted to see Andrews and that they had declined to obtain a professional valuation of the ships. Other spoke more forcibly, demanding that the directors should refund the fees they had received. The entire board then resigned and three new directors were elected including Morrison.

Peto spoke on how he had been misled by Andrews but assumed himself the chief responsibility. His mistake arose from having entered into an undertaking the management of which he did not understand. He had seen the auditor in October after the latter had expressed concerns but had believed that any loss in the first half of 1856 would be compensated by profits in the second. (He did not explain why he had ever supposed there was a first half loss given the decision to pay a substantial dividend.) He greatly regretted the results but did not think it could be attributed wholly to neglect; he had been accustomed to see Andrews, whom he described as 'a very sanguine man' three times a week and had obtained regularly the particulars of the freight of each vessel and of the estimated expenditure. He and the other directors would indeed return their fees.

Subsequent to the meeting Mr Abel began a series of letters to the press and later twice circularised the shareholders. He had declined to sign the report and had resigned from the committee because he found that every one on it apart from Godson was a friend of Peto's. He lamented that Peto was the lessee of the Royal Danish Railway, the Victoria Dock Company and the Tilbury Railway, all of which had transactions with the steamship company which, not being at arm's length, may have contributed to the losses. Mr Godson's points were unfortunately not all valid but he was at least independent. Abel was certain that there were errors in the 1855 accounts, despite Mr Coleman's assurances to the contrary. As an example of an irregularity or conflict of interest he stated that in 1855 the company had bought a ship from Peto and his partners, had brought it home from the Baltic, had spent nearly £4,000 in repairing it and yet it had not since been employed. Above all he was suspicious of the complacency shown by Peto in October 1856 in brushing aside Coleman's concerns and again in February in assuring shareholders that there were no serious problems. Was this not so that the final two calls could be made and collected before any losses were revealed? Now the new board was to consist entirely of Peto's friends and colleagues, several being directors or otherwise connected with the Victoria Dock Company.

At the half year meeting in September Morrison as chairman regretted to report a further loss to June of £38,529 and warned that there was still more clearing up to be done. However the cattle trade was continuing satisfactorily. He deprecated what he said were regrettable letters to the press by some other members of the committee, which had included personal attacks. The best course for the future was to sell the ships and the Lowestoft factory as occasion arose while employing the remainder since it was better to obtain at least some revenue than to allow ships to rust in harbour. The acrimonious letters merely served to depreciate the value of the ships and to inhibit their sale. One shareholder said the new board should have no connection with Peto for the company 'had lost £19,000 in connection with the Danish railway'. Another attacked 'the system of trading with the west coast of Africa' which seems to have been an experimental series of voyages authorised by the new board. Mr Abel told how the old directors had been obliged to ask the committee to explain the company's state of affairs and had no idea that some ships had been mortgaged, let alone for how much. Robert Bagshaw, one of those former directors, said the Earl of Yarborough had resigned and sold his shares when the Grimsby trade and its associated railway arrangements had been brought to an end. Neither he nor any other of the directors had known of the losses and, apart from the earl, none of them had sold any shares.

Accounts as at 30 June 1857 presented to the meeting showed that of paid up capital of £440,000 a total of £187,000 had been lost leaving £253,000. This was represented by the depreciated value of ships and works at Lowestoft, £305,000, plus £5,000 stores from which had to be deducted £57,000 of net current liabilities, chiefly bills payable. There were outstanding claims against the company, it had been necessary to make provision against most debtors, there was very little cash and the company was insolvent unless ships could be sold. In response to a question concerning the value of the ships originally acquired Bagshaw said they had been valued by a Mr Dudgeon and by the well-known shipbuilder Scott Russell. He further admitted that when the last dividend had been declared the directors knew nothing whatever about the state of the company's affairs. A bitter discussion continued with angry remarks concerning the new directors as well as the old.

By the time of the next reported meeting in March 1858 matters had gone from bad to worse. The purpose of the meeting, that had been called by two shareholders, was to see if any scheme could be devised to form a new company out of the wreck of the old. *The Times* reported that

> The moving parties were persons who are believed to be disposed to screen the misconduct of the late directors and measures were therefore taken to keep the proceedings from publicity. It is under-stood however that, although a committee was nominally formed,

the plans suggested met with little real approval. The annual general meeting of the company will take place on Friday when no concealment can be practised, and when the public will have another opportunity of witnessing the extent of toleration which in the present state of commercial morality is invariably accorded in such cases.

In fact the meeting was adjourned with little business done, reconvening on 19 March when it was resolved to wind up. It had not been possible to set up a new company due to a lack of cash to pay off the creditors of the old. Current assets were stated at £22,000 but these were mainly claims on failed companies and disputed accounts whereas creditors amounted to some £52,000. It was impossible to sell ships except only the best and instead of the value of £305,000 given in September they were considered to be worth only £120,000. Mr Abel and others were seeking compensation from Peto who, while present at the meeting, did not speak.

A report prior to what may have been the final meeting in June 1858 said that the liquidation was proceeding. The former directors had declined to contribute but Peto had offered to buy three ships for £28,000 being £100 above the valuation put on them at the beginning of the year. Six others had been sold and fourteen remained. Following the sales there was about £14,000 net of realisable assets, most creditors having been paid. The remaining ships and other fixed assets were valued at £114,000 but most probably a considerable loss would be realised on sale. In fact at the subsequent meeting the figures referred to were even lower.

That meeting was an unhappy occasion. Peto and the other directors had declined any obligation, moral or legal, to take over assets and liabilities. They did not consider themselves responsible for the present position. If a new company was formed Peto would take an interest in it equal to what he had in the old one and would induce his friends to come in, but nobody could agree on a satisfactory scheme. A motion was put to condemn the old directors for the past payment of dividends at a time when a profit was forecast but when the dividend could be paid only out of a simultaneous call on shares. Also it was alleged that too much had been paid for the original ships having regard to subsequent valuations. The resolution was lost on a show of hands and a poll was demanded. The acrimonious meeting lasted all day at the end of which a liquidator was appointed. At one point Peto offered to rescind his purchase of three ships if within a month they could get a better offer. However he was prepared to defend himself at law against any accusations of bad faith.

The affair ended in farce and ill temper. The poll advertisement proved defective and was declared invalid by the scrutineers when the adjourned meeting reconvened. It was noted that not only had Peto and his friends voted against the motion of censure but even the supposedly insane Captain Andrews 'had method enough to send in his proxy'. After re-advertisement and a fresh poll the result was a resounding defeat for the censure motion. Peto and others with a third of the capital had been against and most other shareholders had abstained. There was further correspondence in the press for a week or two with Mr Abel complaining about procedural deficiencies and *The Times* criticising the shareholders as supine but thereafter nothing further was reported. Peto in his time was accused of many things but until his final misadventures in the 1860s this may have been his darkest hour. It is hard to believe that a man so generally able and in command of his affairs can have proved either so negligent or so incompetent in a business so close to his heart.

What was the real cause of the disaster? The Danish cattle trade did in fact continue as a private enterprise for a few years employing two or three ships but this seasonal trade was never likely to support the enlarged fleet. In any case there was little point in bringing fat cattle to Lowestoft if they were mainly required in London. Moreover the Eastern Counties had been forced to discontinue the concessional fares they had earlier charged for complete cattle trains. The majority of the ships were bought at high prices during a war which had caused a shipping boom and frenetic construction whereas the end of the war heralded a shipping slump with low freights and consequent low ship prices despite the renewal of Baltic trade. Following the bankruptcy in 1856 of the Royal British Bank, which had advanced money against ship mortgages, ships were being sold in that year and the next at sixty per cent or less of their value in 1854 and brokers gave evidence of a general fall in ship values of that degree. Moreover the majority of the North of Europe ships had been designed to carry mainly passengers and light freight employing inefficient high powered engines to attain maximum speeds over routes such as that to Hamburg whereas demand for long haul packet services was falling as continental railway services improved and short sea crossings were all that were required. The requirement in the later 1850s was for low horsepower, screw driven ships with maximum cargo capacity for heavy freight.

Lowestoft fish dock with harbour entrance beyond

CHAPTER 12

Terminus: 1855 to 1862

Five years of frustration: 1855 to 1860

After the departure of Peto from the board in 1855 the chairmanship, until the beginning of 1858 was taken over by Richard Till. There had been other changes on the board since 1851. Adam Duff retired in 1855, Major Tyndale died in the same year and Mr Anderson in 1856. Mr Barber, who had been particularly active in financial matters, resigned at the end of 1858. Directors continuing from earlier days were Horatio Bolingbroke, still the only Norfolk resident, Arthur Mills and J. S. Wells. The first new director was Sir James Anderson elected in 1855 but dying a year later. Other new directors were James Marke Wood of Prince's Park, Liverpool, elected 1856, after nomination by Liverpool shareholders, William Simpson and Lord Alfred Paget, both elected 1858 and in the same year the company's former engineer George Bidder who forthwith became chairman replacing Till. Bidder, who of course has appeared at every stage of this story, had for long been a great deal more than Robert Stephenson's junior. Although they had remained close friends and often appeared as a duo, yet Bidder had engaged independently in several enterprises, most notably as promoter and major shareholder in the Victoria Dock Company of which he remained a director. He was now a senior figure in the world of engineering, shortly to become president of the Institution of Civil Engineers, but experienced too in the world of finance. For the Norfolk he was a catch.

Leaving aside the complications of the Wells & Fakenham Railway, dealt with below, the board should have had an easy time in these years. The railway itself should have been run by the joint committee, and that would have left the company itself merely to act as a financial centre, receiving its share of the joint profits and using these to pay interest and dividends on its share and loan capital. Things did not work out in that way. Firstly there was an argument over the design and state of the Yarmouth/Norwich and Lowestoft lines where they crossed the Yare and Waveney marshes. Colonel Wynne, acting for the Board of Trade, had inspected the line and produced a damning report on the state of the several timber bridges which were suffering severely from rot. The Eastern Counties was having some replaced in brick and severe criticism was levelled at the Norfolk board for having passed over their railway in an unsafe state. The board commissioned Bidder, who after all had engineered the line, to produce a report explaining why timber had been used. This he did, at least to the board's satisfaction, which minuted that it 'justifies the directors in having placed implicit confidence in [Bidder] during the construction of the railway'. A critical article in the *Railway Times*, never a friend, suggested that Bidder's explanation of no alternative to timber at the time was fairly ridiculous and that the expedient of timber had probably been resorted to for speed and cheapness on a fixed price contract and so the Norfolk's line could not have been in a sound state when handed over to the Eastern Counties.

Next there was the related question of additional capital expenditure. While it had been assumed and perhaps agreed that additional expenditure on the Norfolk line would be authorised by the joint committee and paid for by the Eastern Counties which would charge interest on the accumulated cost to the combined revenue account, in the event the question of capital expenditure proved to be a running sore. Continuing expenditure on the existing line such as on the marshland bridges as well as on genuine improvements such as station enlargements, hardly likely of themselves to add to revenue, was constantly necessary. A goodly part of the original Norwich & Brandon line appears to have needed extensive reconstruction. The Eastern Counties, post Waddington, expected the Norfolk to pay. The Norfolk had no funds from which to do so and did not wish to borrow more.

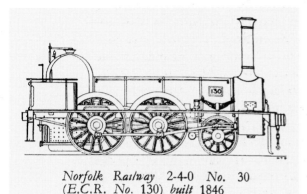

Norfolk Railway 2-4-0 No. 30 (E.C.R. No. 130) built 1846

By May 1857 the accumulated total of capital expenditure on the Norfolk line that the Eastern Counties had, they claimed, paid for amounted to over £70,000. Their shareholders committee in 1855 had severely criticised their own directors for allowing these sums to be added to their company's own capital account. However the legalities were unclear and a settlement was reached whereby only £50,000 would be paid by the Norfolk. The Norfolk directors agreed to raise further capital to discharge this but did not in fact do so and neither raised the capital nor discharged the debt; it would seem that the question became merged with other disputes between the parties. At much the same time the Norfolk board was querying capital expenditure at Harwich that the Eastern Counties had paid for and asking whether it should in fact not have been paid by the Eastern Union. Whichever company paid for capital sums, interest on the expenditure, providing it had been authorised by the joint committee, was charged to the joint revenue account before division of the profits.

Then the Norfolk felt obliged to take a position on every Bill lodged by its partners or by rivals and this entailed regular legal charges and parliamentary costs. Payment of these required financing. Many professional men were slow to put forward bills and claims relating to the period before joint operations continued to appear. The estate of a deceased solicitor in Thetford raised a claim for work allegedly done in 1845 in connection with the diversion of the line at Thetford. Perhaps this was chargeable to the contractors (i.e. Peto), perhaps to the company as successors to the Norwich & Brandon, perhaps to no one. Everything had to be investigated, old papers turned up, solicitors instructed to refute or negotiate. The company had been promised rooms at Shoreditch station for its office but these proved unsuitable and fresh premises had to be taken. The company secretary acted also for the Wells company but needed a bookkeeper and an assistant. Professional accountants had kept the books of both the Norfolk and the Lowestoft companies originally but their services were dispensed with after the Lowestoft books were merged with those of the Norfolk.

After 1855 The Norfolk still remained concerned, albeit indirectly, with the development of the East Suffolk line and the latter's campaign to force the Eastern Counties to work it. In 1855 two new railways, the Lowestoft & Beccles and the Yarmouth & Haddiscoe, were projected by local parties associated with the East Suffolk, including Edward Leathes and Sir Thomas Gooch, to connect to the latter railway's main line. The former railway looked for rights to connect to the Lowestoft line and to share its station. Arising from this the joint committee urged the Norfolk to double the track from Reedham to Yarmouth as a defensive measure. The Norfolk board resolved to oppose both new ventures but each obtained its Act the following year. Thus eventually Yarmouth achieved its Southtown station, so hotly argued for in the 1840s, and both ports were now on course to have a direct line to Ipswich and thence to London.

In 1857 the Norfolk board, though entirely on the sidelines, deplored the rival projects put forward by Peto and by the Eastern Counties. Peto, who with Brassey and Betts was lessee of the London, Tilbury & Southend railway threatened to build from Pitsea on that line to Colchester via Maldon and then, having obtained running powers over the Eastern Union line northwards, to run trains direct from Lowestoft into London's Fenchurch Street terminal via Ipswich, Colchester, Maldon and Pitsea. The Eastern Counties riposted with an almost identical alternative for a link Pitsea/Maldon/Colchester. The Norfolk board declined to sign the subscription agreement for the Eastern Counties' project until some attempt had been made for an amicable settlement with Peto. Both projects were abandoned once the Eastern Counties gave in that year and agreed after all to work the East Suffolk line. However for Peto it was a pyrrhic victory for the agreed charge was to be sixty per cent of receipts, fourteen percentage points or more above a normal rate.

In 1858 the East Suffolk merged with the recently completed Lowestoft to Beccles and Yarmouth to Haddiscoe, the Eastern Counties working the entire network. The East Suffolk was finally opened for its full length in June 1859. At the Norfolk shareholders' meeting in August 1859 the board expressed (as it turned out unjustified) optimism as to this eastern venture. However the costs of building all parts and branches of the East Suffolk, including the Ipswich/Woodbridge section of the Eastern Union and branches to Framlingham and Aldeburgh, soared until by final completion they totalled well over a million pounds. Peto as both lease-holder, contractor and, together with associates, principal shareholder had a tiger by the tail but the manoeuvres by which the finances of this railway were eventually unravelled and the terms of its acquisition by the Great Eastern Railway in 1862 are beyond the scope of this work.

Neither the Norfolk nor the Eastern Union was satisfied that the Eastern Counties were providing adequately for maintenance. In 1857 they engaged Peter Bruff, formerly the Eastern Union engineer, to act as an inspector on their behalf. Initially his reports confirmed their fears, but gradually delayed work was completed and by 1859 Bruff was reporting a more satisfactory state of affairs, at least as regards the main concern over bridge safety, but warned that fencing of the line to exclude livestock remained in a poor state. Bruff was also asked to act as an independent investigator into accidents on the network, the concern of the minority companies being whose fault the incidents were and whether the large sums being paid by the Eastern Counties as compensation to passengers for injury were properly chargeable to the joint operations. Another regular problem was that, as customary, the Eastern Counties delayed in passing over the shares of net revenue accruing to the other two companies so that the Norfolk, at least, was often behind in its payments of interest and dividends. There were regular arguments over legal costs; for example when Yarmouth Haven Commissioners sued the Norfolk over water leakage out of the rivers through Mutford Lock at Lowestoft substantial legal costs were incurred that the Norfolk insisted were the responsibility of the Eastern Counties. When the latter company did not reply to a letter asking for settlement the Norfolk secretary was instructed to begin proceedings against them.

After Waddington's resignation, the new Eastern Counties board was unhappy that the network should be managed by the joint committee where the Norfolk and Eastern Union representatives acting together had equal power to its own. Instead the Eastern Counties directors insisted on making all major decisions themselves, usurping the power of the joint committee. Understandably the Norfolk and Eastern Union boards were extremely unhappy about this and also over many of the charges to the joint revenue account made by the Eastern Union over and above those agreed in 1854. At first they protested, then tried to obstruct the workings of the joint committee and at last, acting in concert, brought an action in Chancery in late 1858 to force the Eastern Counties to adhere to what it was thought had been agreed originally.

The Wells & Fakenham line

The Norfolk had agreed in 1854 to operate the line for remuneration of forty-six per cent of revenue. The Eastern Counties maintained that they had no obligation to operate the Wells line at all, the agreement not being binding on either them or even on the Norfolk. However in response to pleas from a Wells deputation in September 1857 they relented to the extent that they offered to take on the responsibility for sixty-five per cent of revenue. Richard Till for the Wells countered with sixty per cent but with time running on and the line complete but not in operation, Wells eventually gave in and accepted the full sixty-five per cent on a temporary contract for one year. Even so the Eastern Counties would not act until the money agreed for the Fakenham land was paid over but when this was achieved in late October a group from the Eastern Counties examined the works and listed a number of minor changes they required before operations could begin. However before the work could be done a Board of Trade Inspector examined the line and on 27 November issued a certificate permitting operations on certain not too stringent conditions (not more than one engine in steam at any time on either of the two sections of the single line, Wells/Walsingham and Walsingham/Fakenham).

Faced with this the Eastern Counties waived for the moment their requirements for alterations and promised a special engine and carriages to be placed at the services of the Wells directors on opening day. The news was at Wells only by Friday the 29th of the month but it was decided to open on the following Monday. The town did its very best for the occasion. Despite the short warning a committee was formed, subscriptions raised and a holiday declared. So on the arrival of the first train from Fakenham on the Monday it passed through a triumphal, flower bedecked arch and was greeted by the thundering reports of fog-signals, a rattling *feu-de-joie* from the muskets of the coast guard, the clash of cymbals, braying of trumpets, unmeasured beating of drums and the cheers of nearly the entire population. While the train returned to Fakenham with an excursion party the dignitaries present, including the chairman of the Eastern Counties as well as the leading merchants and tradespeople of the town, were entertained to dinner by Lord Leicester at Holkham, where there were the usual speeches lauding the enterprise of those who had built the railway and hopeful predictions as to the town's future prosperity.

This was a promising moment for Wells as work was already in progress on the great west embankment that was to connect the town with the beach (and secure 500 acres of marshland for Lord Leicester).

Holidaymakers would now, it was hoped, flock to the town by the new railway while the same line would speed to London the herrings that a new fishery would bring to land. Mr Horatio Love, the Eastern Counties chairman since the departure of Waddington, perhaps encouraged by the wine, excelled himself in his speech to the extent that he must have prejudiced his company's position in later negotiations for, after his praise for the line and its backers, it would have done much harm to the reputation of his company had it at a later stage forced the local railway into bankruptcy. Certainly his reported enthusiasm for the prospects of the line in December 1857 did little for his negotiating position a year later when the temporary operating agreement came to an end.

Richard Till, director of both the Wells and Norfolk companies, came to the latter board in August 1858 with proposals for a ten year working agreement with remuneration of only forty-six per cent but at this stage the Norfolk directors could only refer him to the Eastern Counties board. Further he wanted the Norfolk to guarantee the bonds that the Wells company had issued but the Norfolk had no powers to do so. The Wells company stood upon their 1854 agreement with the Norfolk but lacked resources to attempt to enforce it. The Eastern Counties response was unhelpful. Their solicitor pointed out that the Wells company had no power under their Act to enter into the agreement in the first place and, while it was recited in the 1854 agreement between the Norfolk and the Eastern Counties that the Norfolk had agreed to work the Wells line, nothing was recorded as to the terms.

At this point the Norfolk shifted its ground. While the directors were uncertain of the strict legal position they felt bound to help the Wells company and hoped that the Eastern Counties would change its attitude; otherwise the Norfolk must somehow by itself manage to honour the agreement. At this the Eastern Counties directors, while unwilling to support the Norfolk under any agreement, found themselves willing to meet a deputation from the Norfolk and the Wells companies to see what could be done. This duly occurred on 23 November at which time the Wells proposal was for a ten year agreement with a fifty per cent charge for the first five years and forty-six per cent for the next five. By now Bidder was chairman of the Norfolk and as a member of the deputation showed that as a negotiator working from a weak position he had no peer. At this first meeting neither side moved. The Eastern Counties solicitor insisted on sixty-five per cent but did say that at least they would continue to work the line from the end of the month at a rate 'to be agreed'.

There was a further meeting a week later at which the Eastern Counties still refused to accept the Wells proposals but did show some willingness to compromise on the rate of remuneration. But Bidder refused to move at all and said that if no substantial concessions were made the Norfolk would endeavour to comply with the original agreement. He suggested that a big company such as the Eastern Counties owed something to small companies such as the Wells and would be wise to act so as to counter their unpopularity in the district. The Eastern Counties solicitor stood his ground but must have had a mixed message to convey to his board. Further his company's chief engineer gave as his opinion that a fifty per cent rate was adequate for most branch lines after a two year period of operation and that the actual costs on the Wells line were little greater after only one. So a revised offer was made of a three-year agreement with two years at fifty-five per cent and the last at fifty. One might have supposed that Wells would jump at that chance but Bidder's nerves were stronger. He demanded a ten year agreement or nothing … and after a long delay got it.

The following spring Peto left the Wells board and was replaced as chairman by Lord Leicester but another Norfolk representative was asked for and Bidder duly joined Bolingbroke and Till on the Wells board. The company was still in financial trouble and eventually it was agreed that the balance of purchase consideration for the land at Fakenham plus accrued interest should be financed by the Norfolk accepting a five year bond for £3,350 at four per cent interest. At this stage a further Bill was going through Parliament to authorise the extension of the line from its initial terminus at Wells to the quays at the waterside and presumably yet further finance was required.

The Wells line never achieved anything like the traffic that was once projected. As a holiday town it could not match Cromer or Sheringham and even though it attracted increasing numbers of visitors most came via King's Lynn and Heacham when a line was built from there in the 1860s. No herring fishery ever prospered at Wells and the harbour fell further and further into disuse once coal came to north Norfolk by rail from the Midlands rather than by sea from the North. However the line was not forgotten when all the East Anglian lines were merged to become the Great Eastern Railway in 1862. Under a provisional agreement of January 1862 it was provided that the Wells shareholders should get forty-five per cent of the cost of their shares paid in the form of four per cent preference stock in the Great Eastern (nothing would go to the Norfolk that would by then have ceased to exist). The Great Eastern would also assume responsibility for the Wells liabilities estimated at £3,000 and their debenture debt of £23,000.

The last two years: 1860 to 1862

Bidder proved to be a most effective chairman, for instance receiving the special thanks of the board in June 1860 when he persuaded the Rock Life Office to advance a five year loan at four and a half per cent in order to repay £60,000 of the company's bonds then falling due. Perhaps the Rock's approval of this loan was eased because Bidder had for many years been a director of the Rock (as was Peto). But it was his success in dealing with the other two allied companies that he came ultimately to deserve the thanks of all his shareholders.

The revenue of the combined lines from 1858 to 1860 had shown but little increase and the Norfolk were understandably disappointed by the results that Bidder explained as hampered by 'a system of management which deprives passengers and traders of their due facilities'. Worrying, too was the inadequate rate of renewal of the permanent way. But even while the Chancery suit dragged on a greater spirit of co-operation between the companies was gradually developing. Under the terms of the 1854 settlement the three companies were obliged to put forward by the end of 1861 proposals for a full three-way merger (which must also take in the Newmarket and East Anglian lines). At the beginning of 1860 the Eastern Counties put forward a new scheme of amalgamation and although this was rejected by the other two companies as not being in accordance with the 1854 agreement (the Eastern Counties were to have a majority of the direction and the separate existence of the three companies would continue) it suggested some degree of progress.

There began, too, to be more progress on moving matters forward through the joint committee while regular discussions took place outside the main committee between the Norfolk and Eastern Union representatives to co-ordinate their positions. When the Eastern Counties put forward a long slate of new proposals to Parliament in 1861, mainly in Essex and south Suffolk,

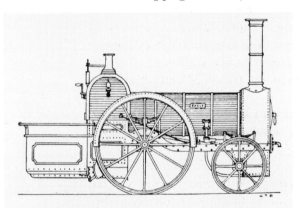

Norfolk Railway 2-2-0T "Eagle" built 1849

Bidder and Cobbold did all they could to have the majority withdrawn or cancelled fearing that the capital cost could not be justified by any expectations of increased revenue. One line, however, they supported. In 1859 there had been a proposal for a line south from Bury via Clare, Dunmow and Ongar to join the Blackwall Railway at Barking. Had that gone forward the Eastern Counties would have promoted a line from their terminus at Loughton via Epping to Ongar. Although the former proposal was withdrawn the latter went forward, promoted not by the Eastern Counties but by a company described to the Norfolk shareholders as 'an independent company friendly to the associated companies'. Now in 1860 a new version of the Bury line south via Dunmow and Ongar was being put forward that Bidder and Cobbold thought promising as a possible means of escape from the Eastern Counties or at least a bargaining counter. This new line was thrown out by a parliamentary committee in early 1861 but Bidder in particular was anxious that it be revived, to be built perhaps by a joint company to be owned by the Norfolk and the Eastern Union, with any dissenting shareholders being bought out.

With a deadline looming, activity in preparing a merger Bill that would satisfy all parties became intense during 1861. In a series of meetings Bidder and Mr Maynard, the Eastern Counties solicitor, drafted heads of agreement which might form the basis of a tripartite merger which were circulated to all the three boards and agreed to by each. Although these heads of agreement did not represent the final terms agreed they did serve to release the hiatus that had persisted for so many years. The joint committee ceased to be at loggerheads and elected a chairman (Mr Love, Eastern Counties chairman). Deputations from the Committee, plus such other directors as were willing, were to go to the major towns of the region and ask there what was wanted of the merged company. Initially the towns chosen were Colchester, Harwich, Ipswich, Lowestoft, Yarmouth and Norwich, to be followed by Cambridge, Bury, Lynn and Peterborough. In marked contrast to the recent past the Committee began to discuss fares, timetables and customer relations. They agreed, too, all outstanding capital expenditure proposals including all the proposed new lines for which purpose the Eastern Counties issued £600,000 of new shares to be offered to the shareholders of all the allied companies. The Chancery suit was settled by the Eastern Counties admitting a number of points on the accounts and reimbursing each of the other two companies £14,000 on revenue account. It was as though a fairy had removed some spell previously inhibiting action.

Looking forward to the merged company Bidder was keen that the Epping line to Ongar should be built. When the promoters, via the Eastern Counties, asked for financial assistance in July 1861 to make their parliamentary deposit, Bidder promptly offered the loan of £13,000 of Norfolk bonds. This was going too far for his co-director Simpson who, rather than be party to any such transaction, refused to hand over the bonds of which he had custody and resigned from the board. No Norfolk director, unless perhaps Peto himself, had previously ever resigned on a point of principle, at least not so far as can be gleaned from the minutes, though there might have been several opportunities. Director James Wood wrote protesting at the transaction that he said would be illegal and an unauthorised dealing but did not resign. By June 1862 a total of £40,000 had been loaned to the Ongar company (but only £4,000 via Norfolk bonds) and Bidder had arranged with Brassey to build the line on a cost plus basis being paid as to £40,000 in cash and the balance by debentures to be guaranteed by the Eastern Counties which company would be the major shareholder. Why he was so enthusiastic for this line is a mystery. It was not one of the Great Eastern's major successes.

Another Bidder enthusiasm was a direct line to be constructed from Doncaster to March in Cambridgeshire, passing through no major towns, to be devoted exclusively to slow trains carrying nothing but coal. From

March to London they would pass over Eastern Counties lines, bringing substantial revenue to the joint operations. That they might severely interfere with passenger traffic was not a matter dealt with in the minutes. At any rate the Norfolk directors were favourably inclined and the joint committee too, at least for a while. Bidder's Victoria Dock Company was to advance money toward the preliminary expenses. No more is heard of this scheme until after the Great Eastern merger when it, or later variants, was pushed hard by Bidder and some other directors ultimately leading to their resignation when a committee of investigation judged the company's financial state too poor to risk further involvement. A similar scheme for a direct line north from the Cambridge area via Lincolnshire to the Yorkshire coalfields had been the basis of the first Northern & Eastern plans in 1835 while Hudson's plans for the Eastern Counties in the 1840s centred on similar schemes. Finally, but not until 1879, the Great Eastern achieved a connection to Doncaster via March and Lincoln by constructing a new line jointly with the Great Northern Railway.

The formal Bill for the amalgamation was laid before Parliament in January 1862. A new company, the Great Eastern Railway, was to be formed that would acquire not only the three allied companies but also the East Anglian Railways and the Newmarket & Chesterford companies already being worked by the joint enterprise. The new company would issue equivalent preference shares or debentures to replace the guaranteed, preference and debenture stocks of the merging companies and would issue ordinary stock and some new preference shares to ordinary share-holders of the three allied companies to preserve the ratio of 5:1:1 as laid down in 1854. Bidder had put forward precise suggestions for the financial terms in letters subsequently published and these were broadly accepted (See Appendix 6). The Wells company was also to be brought in as explained above while at a late stage it was found necessary also to buy out the East Suffolk shareholders.

The Lowestoft shareholders were to continue to receive their guaranteed dividends (but did not until 1879 exchange their shares for equivalent preference shares in the Great Eastern Railway). There was an additional complication in that the Eastern Union ordinary stock was divided into two classes and in order to satisfy both and to obtain unanimous consent additional Great Eastern stock had to be made available for them over and above their basic one-seventh share; this extra was volunteered by the Norfolk to break what might otherwise have proved a deadlock. Nevertheless Bidder's calculations had done well for the Norfolk share-holders as was acknowledged at their last meeting when it was resolved to present him with one thousand guineas. Perhaps just as satisfactory to him was that he was one of the two Norfolk directors who obtained a seat on the board of the Great Eastern. Horatio Bolingbroke declined the second seat feeling that over twenty years as a railway director was more than enough and the place was taken by J. S. Wells.

Map A5   East Anglia, Lines at the creation of the Great Eastern Railway, 1862

Shows the East Anglian network at the time of the merger of all lines into the newly formed Great Eastern Railway.

All lines building at the start of 1847 have been completed (and part of the Newmarket & Chesterford already dismantled). Further lines built have been the Norfolk's branch northward from Dereham to Fakenham (1849), then continued by the Wells & Fakenham to the coast (1857), the link from Bury to Newmarket (1858), the Harwich branch from Manningtree (1854) and the entire East Suffolk system from Yarmouth Southtown to Ipswich with branches Beccles/Lowestoft, to Leiston and to Framlingham (1859). A line had at long last been begun along the Waveney Valley from Tivetshall eastward but by 1862 had reached no further than Bungay. Finally a line being built by a private consortium of local people was in progress from Lynn to Hunstanton but was incomplete at the time of the GER merger.

As on the previous maps lines and proposals westward of Cambridge and King's Lynn are not shown except for the Peterborough/Ely branch of the Eastern Counties, and the branches north and west to Wisbech. Lines and proposals southward of Suffolk are shown only so far as they were or might have been relevant to developments in Norfolk and Suffolk. The line from London east to Southend via Pitsea, which had figured in the politics and negotiations leading to the operation of the East Suffolk by the Eastern Counties was not taken over by the Great Eastern and is not shown. The boxed area is shown in more detail in Map B on Page 221.

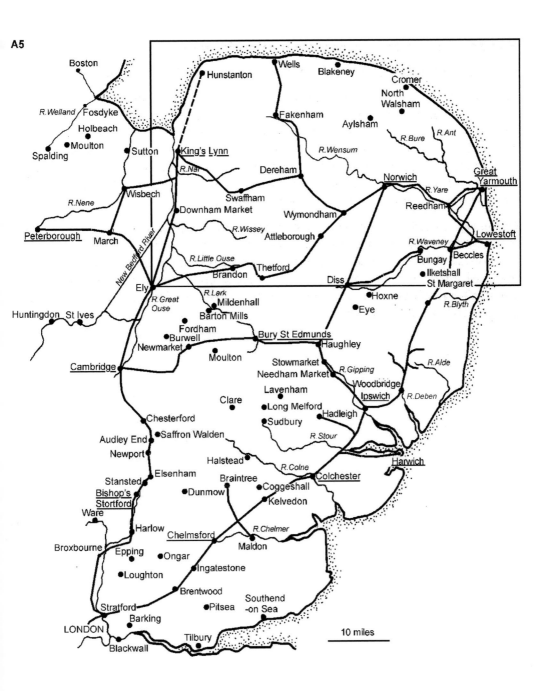

Epilogue 1 – The Great Eastern Railway

The successful amalgamation of all the East Anglian railways into the Great Eastern Railway may have solved all the immediate problems resulting from previous rivalry but the resulting company was heavily burdened with debt and preferential share capital in much the same fashion but on a larger scale than any of its predecessors. So serious was the problem that for a while the company was actually placed in receivership. There were further lines to be built in Norfolk, notably a line from Norwich via North Walsham to Cromer and another from Lynn to Hunstanton. Both and some lesser lines were in the event built by independent companies, avoiding any need for the Great Eastern itself to raise yet more capital although it operated all the new lines when complete. None were actually acquired by the Great Eastern until near the end of the century. By that time the railway, through a series of reforms and improvements, and especially through cultivation of holiday traffic to the seaside and to the Broads, had gradually reached a state of reliability and comfort so as to live down the cruel jibe that East Anglia was cut off on three sides by the sea and on the fourth by the Great Eastern Railway.

Within the Great Eastern, which merged into the London and North Eastern Railway in 1923, and within its successors to the present day the greater part of the Norfolk Railway has continued in being. The northern branch beyond Dereham including the Wells & Fakenham line, is now unused and largely dismantled, although a narrow gauge holiday railway runs between Wells and Walsingham. The section from Wymondham to Dereham is used only at weekends by trains run by a preservation society. The Yarmouth terminus is once again at Vauxhall and no trains cross the Bure or run on the south pier. Underused since the catastrophic contraction of the fishing industry Lowestoft harbour is nevertheless still active. It was the Eastern Union line that was electrified and by which Norwich travellers go to London but the remaining Norfolk lines are busy with local traffic and recently a through service to Cambridge was reinstated.

Epilogue 2 – The Royal Danish Railway

Although after the demise of the North of Europe Steam Navigation Company the Danish railway ceased to be of even indirect concern to the Norfolk Railway it may be of interest to consider its ultimate fate. The years between 1851 and 1864 were occupied in Danish politics by an interminable argument within Denmark with foreign powers concerning the drafting and implementation of a new constitution for a united state incorporating the duchies that would be satisfactory to all interests. Eventually the Danish government lost patience and in late 1863 proposed a constitution that would incorporate Schleswig fully into Denmark proper but would leave the other duchies alone, an understandable but dangerous course of action. Just as that measure had passed through the parliament and before it could receive royal assent, the old king died. Prince Christian, ascending the throne as Christian IX, hesitated three days and then signed the new constitution. By doing so, and thus by breaking the peace treaty that had concluded the previous war, he precipitated the country into a new war with Prussia and Austria, these states purporting to uphold the rights of an alternative claimant to the dukedoms who proclaimed his intention of taking all the duchies into the German Confederation.

The combined might of Prussia and Austria rather quickly overwhelmed the Danish forces. Initially attempting to defend the southern Schleswig frontier along the Eider and Schlei rivers and the line of the ancient Dannevirke earthwork, they were soon outmanoeuvred and shut up in their fortified lines at Dybbol north of Flensburg and opposite the town of Sønderborg on the island of Als while enemy troops ranged over the

Flensburg from its fjord

whole of Jutland. Then after a month of intensive bombardment the Prussians launched an assault on the Dybbol position that could not withstand the attack. After suffering heavy casualties the Danes retreated onto the island, while an international conference attempted to broker a peace. Ignoring the hopeless weakness of their negotiating position the Danes held out stubbornly for retaining all Schleswig when the Prussians were prepared to split the duchy in two. At length the peace brokers gave up. The Prussians renewed the war and successfully launched an amphibious attack on Als, destroying or capturing all the Danish army that could not escape by sea. At this Denmark called it a day. At the final peace negotiations the whole of Schleswig passed to Prussia and Austria who very soon conveniently proved that the claim to sovereignty by their ducal candidate was after all invalid. After the Prussian victory over Austria just four years later the entire region became part of Prussia.

From 1859, after long arguments within Denmark over routes and financing, Peto, Brassey & Best were building over 300 miles of further Danish lines including a connected series from Flensburg to the north of the Jutland peninsula and another across the island of Fyn. But although the contractors were also the operators of these lines, some of which were open by the outbreak of the war, unlike the southern Schleswig line, all except those in northern Schleswig were destined to be state owned when the system was complete. Meanwhile in the summer of 1863 Peto had managed to negotiate with the company operating the Kiel/Altona railway a provisional working agreement whereby that line, the Neumunster/Rendsburg line and the Royal Danish itself would be worked as one and the Kiel/Altona company would extend its route from Altona into Hamburg itself and so effect a junction with lines leading south into central Germany. Before the end of that year Peto, Brassey & Best had actually bought the Neumunster/Rendsburg line.

The war in 1864 had less effect on the Danish railway system than might have been expected. On the Danish side the line across Sjælland proved invaluable in transferring troops from Copenhagen to the front line by a combination of railway and ship. The south Schleswig railway was placed at the disposal of the Danish military but a proposed branch along and behind the line of the Dannevirke was incomplete and could not be used. The majority of the Danish forces retreating from the Dannevirke in the severe winter of 1864 marched on a route parallel with the railway from Tønning to Flensburg without boarding a train. Nevertheless the English manager of all the Danish lines, Mr Louth, reported in February 1864 that he had worked seven heavy trains to the front line to assist the retreat to the entire satisfaction of the Danish authorities and had subsequently managed to remove all the rolling stock to Flensburg. When the Danish commander had required him then to destroy a bridge he had had all the rails and girders removed and stored in the river below so avoiding damage to the basic structure.

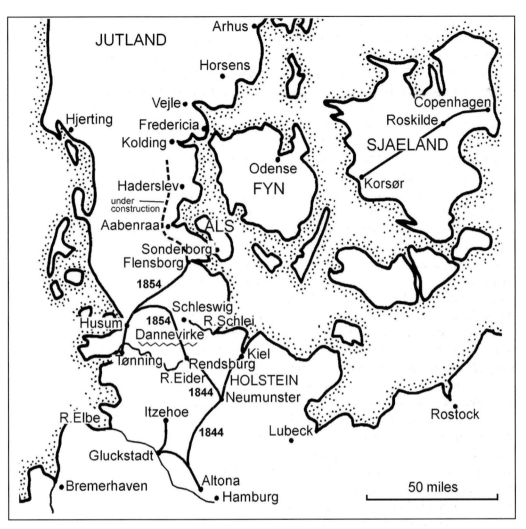

JUTLAND
Arhus
Horsens
Vejle
Hjerting
Fredericia
Kolding
Haderslev
under construction
Aabenraa
ALS
Sonderborg
Flensborg
1854
Husum
Schleswig
1854
R.Schlei
Dannevirke
Tønning
Rendsburg
R.Eider
Kiel
1844
Neumunster
HOLSTEIN
Itzehoe
1844
Lubeck
R.Elbe
Gluckstadt
Bremerhaven
Altona
Hamburg

Odense
FYN
SJAELAND
Copenhagen
Roskilde
Korsør

Rostock

50 miles

Railways in Schleswig Holstein, 1864

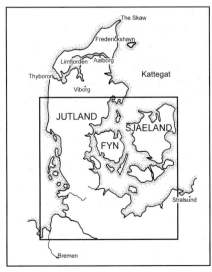

The Skaw
Frederickshavn
Limfjorden
Aalborg
Thyboron
Kattegat
Viborg
JUTLAND
SJAELAND
FYN
Stralsund
Bremen

When the enemy arrived in Flensburg the Prussian commander Field Marshall von Wrangel ordered the restoration of the line and Louth obeyed after consultation with Danish officials. But when he was further required to hand over the operation of the railway to the army he protested and it was agreed that the railway would be worked for the invaders but at normal rates and that the company would be paid for repairing war damage. In the event the revenue of the railway was greater in the year of the war and its immediate aftermath than it had ever been before. The Prussian troops made no attempt to hinder the continuing construction of the line north from Flensburg and when the general in command of the troops in northern Jutland overran the lines under construction and ordered the destruction of certain bridges he was recalled home to explain why he had blown up a bridge still within its guarantee period and thus still the property of the neutral English contractors. However, although the latter were eventually compensated and the bridge rebuilt, Denmark had lost the war and it was Denmark that had to pay.

A brief press report in early January 1865 stated that it was understood that the Royal Danish line was to be purchased by the Prussian government. The shares by then were being quoted at about fifteen per cent under par whereas shortly before the war the discount had been nearer thirty per cent. From early September 1865 the Royal Danish shares ceased to be quoted in London. Immediately prior they had been quoted at near par so it would seem the shareholders were expecting full value in a liquidation. Sources conflict as to exactly what happened next. Possibly the partnership of Peto, Brassey & Best bought out the other shareholders in the Royal Danish at this stage. Certainly a threat by the partnership to extend the line from Neumunster toward Berlin, bypassing Altona and Hamburg, put pressure on the Kiel/Altona company. This threat may have been no more than a maneuvre designed to ease the pressure on the partnership which was in dire need of cash to complete its lines in Denmark. In any event the upshot was that the Kiel/Altona company felt obliged to buy the lines south of Rendsburg.

From 1870 all the lines in that area of Germany were bought and thereafter operated by a new company, the Schleswigsche Eisenbahn AG with headquarters in Altona, the money to purchase the various interests being provided by the Frankfurt bankers Erlanger & Sons. All the lines were in turn taken over by the Prussian state railway in the 1880s. Those north of Flensburg reverted to Danish ownership in 1920 when northern Schleswig once again became Danish following a plebiscite in the aftermath of the Great War. Just when and at what rate the British shareholders in the Royal Danish company were repaid is lost in the complexities of the winding up of Peto's affairs.

Epilogue 3 – Sir Samuel Morton Peto

By all accounts a conscientious contractor respected by his workforce, a devout Baptist with the persuasive tongue of a lay preacher, it was nevertheless through his skill and nerve as a financier, his reputation of success, his extraordinary ability to borrow more and more, that he achieved what he did. But Peto, honoured as Sir Morton Peto, baronet, for services in organising the construction of a railway to the front during the Crimean War, overstretched his resources, suffered severe losses in several ventures (not least the North of Europe Steam Navigation Company and the East Suffolk Railway) ultimately resorted to desperate financial measures in support of the London, Chatham & Dover Railway, and crashed in the panic of 1866 when his principal backers, bankers Overend Gurney, suspended payment causing the partnership of Peto & Betts to suspend payment in turn. Thomas Brassey succeeded at enormous personal cost in saving and continuing the partnership of Peto, Brassey & Betts but in 1867 Peto himself, Betts and another partner Crampton were made personally bankrupt, Peto then living abroad for several years. Although Peto was later discharged from bankruptcy the whole complex financial position created by the several failures took some thirty years, well beyond his death in 1889, to be cleared up. What is certain however is that, although his financial dealings in the mid-1860s were reckless, even criminal by later standards, he hardly deserves to be compared, as has been done, with the crooked financier Melmotte in Trollope's *The Way We Live Now*. He built real railways, many still in use today.

Norwich, with railways to 1862

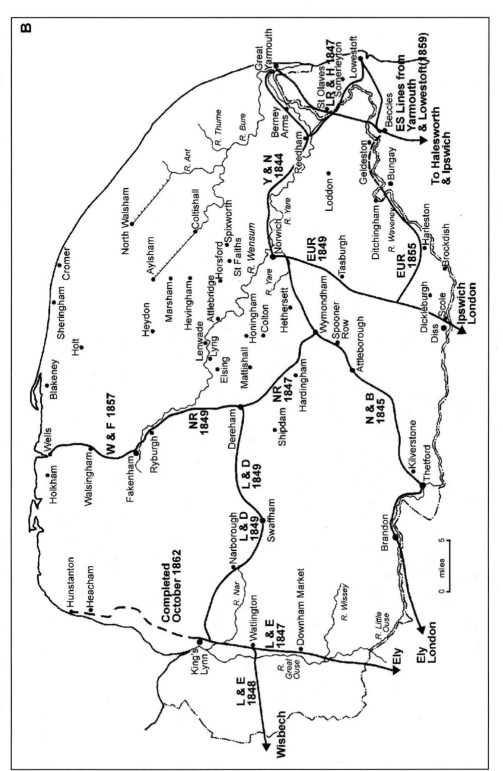

B

Railways in Norfolk at the creation of the Great Eastern Railway, 1862

NOTE ON SOURCES

Primary records

There are no surviving records of the predecessor companies themselves and the first internal document available is the directors' minute book of the Norfolk Railway itself which is complete from the company's formation. The earlier history is therefore taken up to that point largely from press reports, principally from the two competing Norfolk newspapers, the Whig *Norwich Mercury* and the Conservative *Norfolk Chronicle*. One or other of these papers has been perused throughout the period from 1836 to 1848, selectively for the earlier years and comprehensively from 1842 onward. Despite their vicious differences in matters of local and national politics, the reports in the two papers on railway matters are usefully complementary while the advertisements and prospectuses placed by actual and proposed railway companies are customarily although not invariably identical. For later years, during which local interest in railways became somewhat less intense, it has proved more rewarding to look up reports of company meetings, the dates of which are roughly predictable, in *The Times* which throughout the forties and fifties carried a regular section on railway news. For all periods the *Railway Times*, perhaps the most thorough of the several railway magazines which sprang up at that time, though strongly prejudiced in favour of shareholders and against railway directors (and especially Peto), gives the most complete reports of meetings and the accounts presented at meetings to members. The *Ipswich Journal* carried much information on Lowestoft shipping which has been usefully summarised in extracts available at the Lowestoft Record Office.

The Acts incorporating any railway actually authorised are available in the House of Lords library as are the preceding Bills with plans and estimates, the committee reports on those Bills and the transcripts of evidence supplied in support and in opposition. Until 1845 these Acts are voluminous specifying every detail governing company administration. That for the Yarmouth and Norwich Railway, for example, runs to over 100 pages yet supplies little now of interest beyond the names of some subscribers and those of the initial directors. The Norwich and Brandon Act is similar. From 1845 every railway Act had to incorporate the standard text of three consolidating Acts dealing with company and railway administration so that the Acts of individual railways were much shortened. That of the Lowestoft company is only twelve pages and had it not been for some special requirements concerning the harbour and navigation would have been shorter yet. The most circumstantial detail is contained in the transcripts of evidence but the volume of this is formidable and tends to be repetitive while the standard of the notetaking varies and in some cases it is clear that important testimony has either been omitted, misheard or, as to place names, confusingly misspelt.

The directors' minutes of the Norfolk railway from its formation in 1845 to its merger into the Great Eastern in 1862 are contained in the Public Record Office under references RAIL 519/3 and 519/4. The members' minute books, including the half yearly accounts, from 1852 to 1862 are under references RAIL 519/1 and 519/2. RAIL 519/6 contains correspondence and other papers chiefly relating to the final year of the company's independent existence. The members' and directors' minute books of the Lowestoft company from its formation are under references RAIL 441/1 and 441/2 and, most valuable, the company's accounting journal and general ledger from formation until the accounting records were incorporated into the books of the Norfolk in 1852 are available under reference RAIL 441/3 and 441/4. RAIL 1116/11 contains the first accounts of the Great Eastern Railway and also the final accounts of some of its constituent companies.

Both before and after 1845 it is usually impossible to determine who were the initial subscribers beyond any actually named in an Act let alone the size of their subscriptions. An exception is the Lowestoft company where the surviving accounting journal actually lists deposits under shareholder names. However for 1845 alone some heroic clerks in the Board of Trade prepared for Parliament a massive summary of every subscription to every railway contract put forward that year (about 200) sorted alphabetically by subscriber recording for each his occupation and address as given in the subscription agreements filed with the Private Bills office. [PP 1845 xl (317,625)] Because this document (actually two, dividing individual subscriptions of £2,000 and over from those smaller) runs to over 650 pages, each with approximately 70 subscriptions, examination has been restricted to extracting details of subscribers to East Anglian railways with Norfolk or Suffolk addresses plus a substantial sample of the remainder (all over £2,000 and approximately one in every thirty five of the rest).

Partly because of the uncertainties of sampling but chiefly it would seem because most subscription lists were not by any means full when the Bill was filed it has not proved possible (again except for Lowestoft) to build up a full list of subscribers even for 1845 East Anglian railways but in every case, extrapolating from samples, a good idea is available of the source of the majority of the capital subscribed in that year. For 1846, with even more Bills coming forward, it would appear that the clerks or their masters quailed at the magnitude of the task and confined their efforts to subscriptions of £2,000 and over. [PP 1846 xxxviii (473)] Thus the list is shorter but still with some three hundred pages and, dealing with even more railway projects, not well suited to extracting the comparatively rare East Anglian entry. Instead of a formal sampling plan the lists have been examined solely by looking up the names of all shareholders and directors who featured prominently in the 1845 lists plus all exceptionally large subscriptions to any railway.

All of the original lines that comprised the Norfolk and Lowestoft companies still exist except for the line north from Dereham. Invaluable information on the routes of railways which were proposed and surveyed but never built can be found amongst the deposited plans preserved originally by the local authority and now in the Norfolk Record Office under the general reference C/Scf1. The routes of those actually built but now closed can of course be found on older Ordnance Survey maps and often on the ground. Much information concerning the rivers and bridges can be found in the Norfolk Record Office under reference Y/PH3, minutes of Yarmouth Harbour Commission together with a number of plans and drawings of bridges and bridge approaches.

Most useful for financial information including capital structures and the text of important reports and agreements is *Bradshaw's Railway Shareholders Guide*. The editions for 1849, 1851 and 1856 have been consulted.

Secondary sources

Henry Grote Lewin, *The Railway Mania and its Aftermath, 1845–1852* (Newton Abbot, facsimile republication 1968) gives a chronological account of the successive annual proposals before Parliament and the fate of each but, covering as it does the entire country, can provide little detail. Richard S. Lambert, *The Railway King 1800–1871*, (London, 1934) provides a racy biography of Hudson in whose erratic career the Eastern Counties played only a relatively small part and the Norfolk even less. In 1988 A. J. Peacock devoted much of his two volume work, *George Hudson, 1800–1871, the Railway King* (York, 1988/9) to rubbishing much of Lambert's work and providing a far more detailed examination of his financial operations and manipulations including those concerning the Eastern Counties Railway. More recently A. J. Arnold and S. McCartney have gone over the oft-trodden ground in more measured fashion in *George Hudson, the rise and fall of the Railway King* (London, 2004). G. P. Bidder is the subject of a privately published work by E. F. Clarke, *George Parker Bidder, The Calculating Boy* (KSL Publications, Bedford, 1983) which, though concerned particularly with his mathematical abilities, gives in addition to a summary of his engineering works, much information concerning his origins, background and later career.

Gordon Biddle, *The Railway Surveyors* (London, 1990) is excellent in describing in detail the tedious steps which had to be taken to promote, survey and obtain parliamentary permission for a new railway. Harold Pollins, 'Aspects of Railway Accounting before 1868' in M.C. Read (ed.) *Railways in the Victorian Economy* (Newton Abbot, 1969) is useful background as is Henry Parvis, *Government and the Railways in Nineteenth Century Britain* (London, 1964). David Brooke, *William Mackenzie, International Railway Builder* (The Newcomen Society, 2004), while dealing almost entirely with persons and railways unconnected with East Anglia, provides unique information concerning the methods of control and accounting employed by contractors in the 1840s. Jack Simmons, *The Victorian Railway* (London, 1995) gives a comprehensive overview of the social effects of the nineteenth century railways in Britain.

Turning to works specifically dealing with East Anglia, Cecil J. Allen, *The Great Eastern Railway* (London, 3rd edn 1961) is the standard work but can deal only in outline with the early history of the several lines which were amalgamated into the Great Eastern in 1862. D.I. Gordon, *A Regional History of the Railways of Great Britain* Vol.V (Newton Abbott, 1968) is encyclopaedic but has little space for the earliest period. Hugh Moffat, *East Anglia's First Railways* (Lavenham, 1987) by contrast is an excellent study, detailed and with fine maps and illustrations. However despite the title the book is primarily about the Eastern Union Railway and deals with Eastern Counties and the Norfolk mainly as those companies related to the Ipswich based railway. No book previously written has concentrated on the Norfolk company alone but George Dow, *The First Railway in Norfolk* published by the London and North Eastern Railway in 1944 gave a clear account in the year of its centenary of the building and opening of the Yarmouth & Norwich.

The story of the North of Europe Steam Navigation Company is told partly from perusal of Lloyds Register of Shipping and Lloyds Lists from the years of its operations but principally from the company's original prospectus and subsequent reports of its meetings contained in *The Times*. That of the Royal Danish Railway comes, apart from an article in the *Illustrated London News* of 11 November 1854, largely from modern Danish works, specifically Steen Ousager, *Guldsnore På Jernbane* (Odense, 1991), Niels Jensen, *Sonderjyske Jernbaner* (København, 1975) and Asger Christiansen, *Fra Hvide Mølle til Scandia* (Roskilde, 1986) but also from one random copy of its accounts contained in PRO 1116, from occasional reports in *The Times* and, for its final fate, from a German publication, *Die Eisenbahn in Flensburg 1854–1979* (Eisenbahn-Kurier Verlag GmbH, Freiburg im Breisgau, 1979).

Peto cries out for a satisfactory biography. That by the Reverend Dr Edward C. Brooks, *Sir Samuel Morton Peto Bt.* (Bury Clerical Society, 1996) is an uneven mine of information and digression from which it is difficult to discover what Peto was engaged in at any particular time and especially difficult to disentangle any financial information. Perhaps that information is simply not available but the article by P. L. Cottrell on Peto in the *Dictionary of Business Biography* (London, 1985) gives a useful summary, dealing especially with his final debacle and bankruptcy in 1866 arising from his dealings with the London, Chatham & Dover Railway.

Illustrations

The cover picture and its reproduction on page 156 is from a Rock engraving of 1855 supplied by courtesy of Suffolk Record Office. The illustrations on pp. 187 and 201 are reproductions of engravings by Henry Charles Trery from 1852 also supplied by Suffolk Record Office. The illustrations on pp. 126, 127 and 152 are supplied by courtesy of Picture Norfolk, a department of Norfolk Libraries and Museums. The Lowestoft Harbour plan has been taken from deposited plan C/Scf1/254 held in the Norfolk Record Office.

Other illustrations have been taken from the following sources:

London & North Eastern Railway booklet *The First Railway in Norfolk*, 1944	pp. 70, 166, 171, 174, 203, 209
Norwich Mercury 1842–45	pp. 35, 36, 37, 46, 47, 48, 58, 64, 65, 66, 67, 72, 107
Illustrated London News 1845–54	pp. 6, 14, 69, 97, 98, 102, 108, 111, 130, 137, 151, 163, 179, 182, 183, 184, 186, 188, 189, 191, 193, 194, 215,
Asger Christiansen, *Fra Hvide Mølle til Scandia* (Roskilde, 1986)	pp. 5, 159

APPENDIX I

Projected lines to East Anglia from the west: 1846

Table C referenced in Chapter 5

Railway	*Line*	*Comments*
East Coast Railway Share capital £1,100,000	Boston to Lynn via Holbeach and Sutton. Branch Holbeach to Spalding. Possible further branch to Wisbech. Connections at Boston and Spalding to proposed Cambridge & Lincoln	Line Boston to Grimsby originally proposed but later withdrawn. Committee originally included several influential Lynn names, also later withdrawn although a Lynn town meeting in November endorsed this as the best option. Engineers Sir John Rennie (consultant) and Hamilton Fulton (acting).
Boston, Stamford & Birmingham Share capital £1,000,000	Main line via Welland Valley joining Midland Railway near Harborough. Branches from Boston to Spalding and Market Deeping and from Spalding to Lynn	Numerous posited junctions throughout Midlands. Associated with Midland Railway. Originally advertised committee had midlands or northwestern addresses only. Latterly obtained some Lynn support.
Rugby & Huntingdon Share capital £1,000,000	As title via Harborough and making use of Leicester & Bedford tracks through Kettering	Whereas Huntingdon is outside area of this study, the Rugby & Huntingdon was mentioned by the putative Ely & Bury (see Chapter 5 Table B) as a likely connection.
Lynn & Ely extensions	Possible extensions from Wisbech branch to Spalding and to March	These were approved by Parliament in 1846 but never built. The Wisbech/March link was built by the Eastern Counties.
Ely & Huntingdon (Associated with Lynn & Ely)	Extensions from Huntingdon to Bedford and to Biggleswade	Only a small portion of the Ely & Huntingdon itself was ever built and none of these extensions.
Norwich & Exeter & Andover Junction	Obscure. Boasted that by it Yarmouth would be connected to Falmouth!	This can hardly have been serious and no capital requirement, engineers or even committee was named.
Wisbech, Peterborough & Birmingham Share capital £300,000 for eastern section only	From Lynn close south of Wisbech to Peterborough (and thence on existing tracks of Blisworth & Peterborough and London & Birmingham)	Junction at Lynn with Lynn & Ely. Engineer Thomas Rumball. Two Yarmouth and one Norwich name on long list of provisional committee. Heavy emphasis in advertisement on virtues of port of Wisbech.

Railway	Line	Comments
Lynn, Wisbech, Peterborough, Midland Counties & Birmingham Junction Share capital £325,000 for eastern section only	Line in fens as title. No indication of plans west of Peterborough. Formal advertisement referred to a new road bridge at Lynn and the construction there of docks.	Committee included no East Anglian residents. At a meeting at Lynn it was concluded that this line was uncalled for and undeserving the support of the town.
Great Grimsby, Louth, Horncastle, Lincoln & Midland Junction Share capital £800,000	Grimsby to Lincoln with junction at latter with Lincoln & Nottingham Railway	No connection with East Anglia but included because of proximity and of three Yarmouth men on committee also on Waveney Valley line. Engineers Robert Stephenson and Frederick Swanwick.
Wolverhampton, Walsall, Stamford, Peterborough & Norwich Share capital £2,500,000	In east via Wisbech, Swaffham and Dereham	Advertisement asserted that line would not compete with those of others. Probably connected with plans filed in Norfolk for lines Swaffham, Narborough & Watlington or alternatively Downham to Swaffham via Stradsett and Fincham. Committee included three Norwich and three Yarmouth residents.
Peterborough & Nottingham Share capital £550,000	Via Stamford and Melton Mowbray	Engineers Sir John and George Rennie. Advertisement stresses benefits to East Anglia but no East Anglian committee members.
Midlands & Eastern Counties Share capital £1,500,000	Cambridge to Worcester via Northampton	Advertised that arrangements had been concluded with Eastern Counties and Ipswich & Bury and two directors of each to join board. Aim is to extend over others' lines from Cambridge to Harwich.
Harwich Docks, Birmingham & Central England Share capital £1,400,000	This was somehow to join Harwich to Blisworth on the London & Birmingham	Advertisement ignored completely the various lines which must be crossed to achieve its aim. No East Anglian residents on committee. Plans filed showed the construction of vast docks between Harwich and Parkeston.
Leicester, Melton Mowbray & Spalding Share capital £500,000	'To commence at the Spalding station of the Norwich, Dereham, Lynn & Holbeach railways' and from there proceed west to join the Midland Railway	Committee included two directors of Grand Union [See p.78] and two of Peterborough & Nottingham.

Major subscribers to Norfolk Railway related issues in 1845 and 1846

	Norfolk director? *	Y & N extension 1845 £	N & B branches 1845 £	Diss & Colchester 1845 £	Lowestoft 1845 £	Subscribed to all railways 1845 £	Norfolk extensions 1846 £	North of Norfolk 1846 £	Subscribed to all railways 1846 £	Address
Samuel Anderson	Y				6,000	6,000			191,500	London
John Bagshaw				2,000		87,000		12,375	83,775	London
Alfred K.Barber	Y					?	9,100		16,800	Upper Clapton
Stephen N.Barber	(Auditor)					?	51,300		53,450	London
E.L.Betts	Y			4,000		16,500	17,860		68,420	London
George P.Bidder	Y		500		2,000	2,500	2,240		9,840	London
Henry T.Birkett					3,140	?	4,000		9,000	Norwich
Horatio Bolingbroke	Y		300			2,300		2,000	2,000	Norwich
W.L.Chute			2,000		1,000	2,000	7,240		9,740	The Vine, Hants
W.F.Cooke				8,000		?	4,520		11,520	Kent
Adam Duff	Y	5,000	500	1,000	6,060	31,890	102,260	24,650	136,610	Blackheath
George Carr Glynn			2,000	3,000	1,500	151,520	5,500		47,720	London
Thomas Grissell			12,500	40,000	8,000	73,000	44,980		51,220	Lambeth

	Norfolk director? *	Y & N extension 1845 £	N & B branches 1845 £	Diss & Colchester 1845 £	Lowestoft 1845 £	Subscribed to all railways 1845 £	Norfolk extensions 1846 £	North of Norfolk 1846 £	Subscribed to all railways 1846 £	Address
J.J.Hamilton				6,000		12,500	10,160		?	Devon
R.W.Kennard	Y	5,000	500	1,000	4,000	75,375	3,100		87,100	Theobalds, Herts
Sir Edmund Lacon	Y		1,000			1,000			nil	Ormesby, Norfolk
J.E.Lacon						?	4,320		4,320	Ormesby, Norfolk
E.F.Maitland	Y					?	2,740		7,740	Henley
George Merrett				6,000		6,000	3,000		3,000	Norwich
Francis Mills			12,500	40,000	8,000	670,300			5,000	London
Henry Newbery	Y								102,480	Manchester
Alexander Nisbett				10,000		25,000	15,000		?	Sussex
S.M.Peto	Y	5,000	12,500	40,000	10,000	113,675	70,600		108,100	Somerleighton
George Stephenson	Y	5,000	1,160		2,520	28,380		11,300	17,300	Chesterfield
Robert Stephenson					2,000	5,750			2,000	London
Richard Till	Y				620	?	2,000		233,500	London
Charles W.Tyndale	Y	5,000	500	2,000	7,000	590,530	5,040	12,275	203,135	Brompton
Charles Wardell	Y	5,000	500	2,000	6,360	76,610	2,620		71,220	London

* refers to a directorship at any time in the company's history

Note: Subscribers received scrip in acknowledgement of deposits paid and such scrip was negotiable and often sold. There is thus no assurance that any given subscriber eventually received shares to the value applied for even if the railway project received parliamentary approval.

APPENDIX 3

Norfolk Railway capital outlay

	31-Dec 1847	31-Dec 1852	31-Dec 1854	31-Dec 1857	31-Dec 1861
Railways, including land	1,281,785	1,408,915	1,514,412[C]	1,519,864	1,518,220
Locomotives and rolling stock	156,031	A			
Other	186,334				
Parliamentary & law		130,793	144,768	151,332	151,447
Capitalised interest		102,646	120,784	121,682	121,677
Salaries & advertisements		13,625	13,625	13,625	13,625
Miscellaneous		24,687	25,554	24,911	24,911
	1,624,150	1,680,666	1,819,143	1,831,414	1,829,880
Lowestoft company					
Railway		119,154	119,154	119,154	119,154
Harbour		195,015	200,460	196,738	196,738
Harbour rental redemption		25,000	25,000	25,000	25,000
Miscellaneous		12,242	12,242	12,242	12,242
	262,738	351,411[A]	356,856	353,134	353,134
Investment in Fakenham & Wells				30,000	30,000
New works after 1854				8,200	9,619
Claims on and open accounts with Eastern Counties		138,202[B]			
Cash and other net assets	19,537	40,294	33,981	1,162	1,532
	£1,906,425	£2,210,573	£2,209,980	£2,223,910	£2,224,165

Norfolk Railway capital

	31-Dec 1847	31-Dec 1852	31-Dec 1854	31-Dec 1857	31-Dec 1861
Share capital					
Ordinary stock	866,250	866,250	866,250	1,002,190	1,002,190
Shares of February 1847	43,595	137,855	135,940		
Extension shares	337,785	441,980	441,980	441,980	441,980
Lowestoft shares	194,593	240,000	240,000	240,000	240,000
5% preference shares				14,420	14,690
Calls in arrears	−838	−15,240			
Forfeited shares			−8,529	−5,725	−5,740
Net share capital	1,441,385	1,670,845	1,675,641	1,692,865	1,693,120
Loan capital					
Mortgage loans	420,950	302,545	114,800	83,645	79,510
Other borrowings	44,090	55,804			
4% Debenture stock		181,379	419,539	447,400	451,535
Total borrowings	465,040	539,728	534,339	531,045	531,045
	£1,906,425	£2,210,573	£2,209,980	£2,223,910	£2,224,165

Notes

A Prior to 31 December 1852 all rolling stock and other plant and equipment including plant and stores at Lowestoft had been transferred to the Eastern Counties Railway at valuation.

B Includes £21,860 being the cost of the assets referred to in Note A less the valuation at transfer. In fact this is the depreciation suffered during use prior to transfer, a loss which the company initially declined to acknowledge.

C By 31 December 1854 all outstanding claims on and from the Eastern Counties Railway had been settled, largely adversely to the Norfolk which treated the losses arising as a result as an additional cost of its lines.

Norfolk Railway, capital structure December 1861

Last balance sheet prior to merger into the Great Eastern Railway

	Authorised £	Issued £
Yarmouth & Norwich shares		
7,500 of £20 each, original Act	150,000	150,000
1,875 of £20 each, overruns and connection to Norwich & Brandon	37,500	37,500
For extension into Norwich	40,000	–
Norwich & Brandon shares		
19,000 of £20 each, original Act	380,000	380,000
22,000 of £10 each, Thetford diversion and Dereham branch	220,000	220,000
Norfolk Railway shares		
39,375 of £2 each for loan redemption	78,750	78,750
Original conversion to ordinary stock	906,250	866,250
Norfolk Railway shares created for loan redemption February 1847: 9,850 shares of £20 of which only 9,063 subscribed for and only £15 called	197,000	135,940
Final total ordinary stock	£1,103,250	1,002,190
Guaranteed extension shares		
£20 shares, guaranteed 5% dividend		
15,000 shares created 1846 Fakenham and Wells	300,000	300,000
20,000 shares created 1847 Waveney Valley. 18,490 shares subscribed for: only £2 deposit paid	400,000	36,980
6,000 shares created 1847 North of Norfolk. (Original deposit repaid by issue of 600 5 ½% shares)	120,000	–
14,500 shares authorised but never created	290,000	–
£20 shares, guaranteed 5½% dividend		
21,000 shares created 1847 Yarmouth extensions etc.	105,000	105,000
Total extension shares	£1,215,000	441,980
carried forward	–	1,444,170

	Authorised £	Issued £
brought forward	–	1,444,170
Lowestoft Railway & Harbour Company shares guaranteed by Norfolk Railway		
4% shares issued 1845		120,000
6% shares issued 1847		120,000
Norfolk Railway 5% preference shares to fund investment in Wells & Fakenham Railway. 6,000 shares of £5 each authorised 1856: 2,938 subscribed for		14,690
		1,698,860
Forfeited shares held by company		5,740
Net share capital ranking for dividends		1,693,120
Loan capital		
Mortgage loans		79,510
Norfolk Railway 4% Perpetual Debenture Stock £506,700 authorised 1852 and issued subsequently as required to redeem loans		451,535
Total share capital and borrowings		£2,224,165

Norfolk Railway profit and loss accounts, 1854 to 1861

	1854	1855	1856	1857	1858	1859	1860	1861
	£000	£000	£000	£000	£000	£000	£000	£000
Revenue of the combined system	1,189	1265	1341	1356	1350	1369	1391	1418
Working expense allowance to Eastern Counties at 46%	547	582	617	624	621	630	640	652
Net operating revenue	642	683	724	732	729	739	751	766
Deduct:								
East Anglian lines surplus	25	26	27	30	27	27	27	28
Compensation to injured passengers	11	5	8	7	4	16	11	4
Interest charges on Newmarket Railway	13	19	20	23	23	23	23	23
Interest on new works after 1853 inc Harwich & Woodbridge branches	5	21	20	25	23	31	34	34
Great Northern Railway for shared use of Hitchin station etc.	17	17	17	17	17	17	17	17
Divisible surplus	571	595	632	630	635	625	639	660

| | 1854 | 1855 | 1856 | 1857 | 1858 | 1859 | 1860 | 1861 |
	£'000	£'000	£'000	£'000	£'000	£'000	£'000	£'000
1/7th to Norfolk Railway	82	85	90	90	91	89	91	94
Interest received	1	1	1	2	1	1	1	1
Settlement of Chancery action								16
Mortgage interest	4	3	3	4	4	4	3	3
Dividends & interest on guaranteed stocks	52	52	52	53	53	53	53	53
Directors' fees, office and legal expenses	2	1	1	1	2	2	2	2
Profit available to Norfolk ordinary stockholders	25	30	35	34	33	31	34	53
Annual rate of dividend actually paid on £1,002,190 ordinary stock	2.25%	3.00%	3.25%	3.50%	3.25%	3.00%	3.25%	5.00%

Merger terms to produce
The Great Eastern Railway

	Eastern Counties £	Norfolk Railway £	Eastern Union £
A] Bidder's argument of 6 November 1861			
Existing equity	5,851,170	996,690	1,056,355
To preserve 5:1:1 ratio merged equity should be shared	5,851,170	1,170,234	1,170,234
Annual prior charges	289,540	56,882	70,570
If prior charges in 5:1:1 ratio would be	289,540	57,908	57,908
Difference		1,026	−12,662
Difference capitalised at 40 years purchase		41,040	−506,480
Equity at 5:1:1 adjusted for prior charge excess/ deficiency	5,851,170	1,211,274	663,754
But because EUR was hardly likely to agree to this Bidder suggested on 7 November, ordinary stock ...	5,851,170	1,000,000	850,000
plus additional preference shares at 3.5%		200,000	
B] When the merger Bill was published the proposition had become, ordinary stock ...	5,854,015	1,170,803	1,170,803
plus 5% preference shares	826,520	296,080	
C] EUR still raised objections, needing more stock to pay their B shareholders at par (the A shareholders getting considerably more). To reach agreement the Norfolk conceded a further £34,197 to the EUR to give ...	5,854,015	1,136,606	1,205,000
plus preference shares now at 4.5% only	826,520	296,080	

Comparisons

		Eastern Counties		Norfolk Railway		Eastern Union	
		£	Ratio	£	Ratio	£	Ratio
Total received by shareholders, inc preference and guaranteed shareholders							
GER pays ordinary dividend at 2%	A	406,563	5	83,882	1.032	87,570	1.077
	C	443,814	5	92,938	1.047	94,670	1.067
GER pays ordinary dividend at 4%	A	523,587	5	103,882	0.992	104,570	0.999
	C	560,894	5	115,670	1.031	118,770	1.059
GER pays ordinary dividend at 6%	A	640,610	5	125,882	0.983	121,570	0.949
	C	677,974	5	138,402	1.021	142,870	1.054
Total received by former ordinary shareholders							
GER pays ordinary dividend at 2%	A	117,023	5	27,000	1.154	17,000	0.726
	C	154,274	5	36,056	1.169	24,100	0.781
GER pays ordinary dividend at 4%	A	234,047	5	47,000	1.004	34,000	0.726
	C	271,354	5	58,788	1.083	48,200	0.888
GER pays ordinary dividend at 6%	A	351,070	5	69,000	0.983	51,000	0.726
	C	388,434	5	81,520	1.049	72,300	0.931

Index

Part 1: Persons, includes all persons mentioned in the text more than once

Part 2: Railways in East Anglia, including projected railways

The Royal Danish Railway and other railways in Denmark and north Germany are dealt with in Chapter 11, pages 178–84 and 215–18.